they are; they experience a disruption in their sense of personal continuity. In an effort to repair this disruption and to stabilize a viable sense of identity, they activate a series of behaviors designed to restore their familiar home world. In addition, they may seek out a member of the native culture with whom they share certain characteristics. In extreme cases, the anthropologist's sense of identity will completely collapse, which leads to active efforts to reconstruct a new identity, first through appropriation of the native culture ("going native"), and later through identification with the work and the discipline of anthropology itself.

If anthropologists remain insensitive to or unconscious of these psychological maneuvers, their data may become hopelessly skewed and distorted. But conscious, creative, and methodologically significant use of these psychological factors can produce a more complex and humanly rich account of a culture than is otherwise possible.

John L. Wengle is an anthropologist who serves as a research analyst with the United States Government.

]

Ethnographers
in the Field

John L. Wengle

Ethnographers in the Field

The Psychology of Research

The University of Alabama Press
Tuscaloosa and London

Library of Congress Cataloging-in-Publication Data

Wengle, John L., 1956–
    Ethnographers in the field.

    Bibliography: p.
    Includes index.
        1. Anthropology—Field work—Psychological aspects.
I. Title.
GN33.W46   1988   301'.0723   87-19218
ISBN 0-8173-0389-8 (alk. paper)

British Library Cataloguing-in-Publication Data is available.

Grateful acknowledgment is made to the following individuals and publishers for permission to reprint from their works:
A Diary in the Strict Sense of the Term. Bronislaw Malinowski. 1967. New York: Harcourt, Brace, and World. Reprinted by permission of Valetta Malinowski and John Hawkins & Associates, Inc. *An Asian Anthropologist in the South.* Choong Soon Kim. 1977. Knoxville: University of Tennessee Press. Used by permission. *Crossing Cultural Boundaries: The Anthropological Experience.* Solon T. Kimball and James B. Watson, eds. San Francisco: Chandler Publishing. Used by permission. "Into the Heart of Sisala Experience." Bruce Grindal. 1983. Manuscript. Used by permission. *Never in Anger: Portrait of an Eskimo Family.* Jean Briggs. 1970. Cambridge, Mass.: Harvard University Press. Used by permission. *Reflections of a Woman Anthropologist: No Hiding Place.* Manda Cesara. 1982. New York and London: Academic Press. Used by permission. *Return to Laughter.* Elanor S. Bowen. 1954. New York: Harper and Brothers. Reprinted by permission of Laura Bohannon. *They Studied Man.* Abram Kardiner and Edward Preble. 1961. New York: Thomas Y. Crowell. Reprinted by permission of Harper & Row.

To My Parents and Family

To Berta

To Ryan (for all the unknown help)

Contents

Preface

This book is an exploration of anthropological fieldwork. It is not, however, of the kiss-and-tell genre that has become so popular recently, nor does it belong to the "how anthropologists know what they know" class of books; epistemological concerns are discussed throughout the book, but they do not dominate the text. Rather, my primary purpose is to understand and then to elucidate certain psychological ramifications of an initial and traditional fieldwork experience among professional anthropologists. I have attempted, mostly through interviews, to determine the psychological changes that typically affect the advanced graduate student who has undertaken fieldwork to gather the material necessary to complete a dissertation and, at the same time, training in anthropology. In using the adjective *traditional*, I simply mean that the student did not study his or her own culture or people, but rather studied a foreign culture, and did so alone. My hope is that this book will better enable us to understand the psychology of fieldwork and therefore to gain a comprehensive knowledge about the nature of anthropological endeavor.

The book is divided into four parts. In Part I, "Understanding Fieldwork," I present the basic idea that underlies and animates my thinking about fieldwork, namely, that the process of fieldwork subjects the anthropologist to an attack against his or her sense of self and that, in turn, the anthropologist defends against this attack through the activation of certain behaviors designed to maintain and bolster the threatened self-representation. As will be apparent from this brief description, I tend to concentrate almost exclusively on the dark and unflattering aspects of fieldwork. I chose this perspective—it would be more correct to say that the perspective chose me—primarily because whatever else fieldwork is, it is *always*, to some degree, identity-dystonic. Also, of course, I chose this perspective because it speaks more directly to my own experiences than the at least one hundred other ways of conceptualizing the problem. I am not writing a textbook; I am not after the definitive, encyclopedic, here-all-questions-cease study of fieldwork. Fieldwork is fun; it is an emotionally gratifying, completely human experience. It is a venture in self-analysis and self-clarification. It is joyous. It is a host of genuinely positive experiences. But it is also dark and an existential limit situation, and it is this latter aspect that I wish to nail down and expose to light. Volume 2 of this work, currently in preparation, will discuss in greater depth the ego-gratifying aspects of the field experience.

Part II is devoted to a discussion of "plain old everyday fieldwork." By this terminology, I do not mean to imply that the case studies—really vignettes—I consider in this section are less genuine, less interesting, less unique than those considered elsewhere in the book. Rather, I am looking at fieldwork experiences resulting in less extensive or catastrophic identity fragmentation than in the cases discussed in Part III. Three of the four vignettes presented in this section are drawn from interviews with graduate students and one with a senior colleague.

Part III, "Fieldwork as a Study in Extremes," consists of three case studies of anthropologists, for each of whom fieldwork was a shattering rite of death and rebirth, that is, a searing and traumatic attack against his or her sense of identity. Two of these studies (Manda Cesara and Bronislaw Malinowski) are based on published accounts of fieldwork experiences and one (Sue) is based on an interview I conducted with a graduate student.

Before turning to the last section, let me offer a comment or two about my interviews with informants. First, I do not consider them interviews in the very professional and unfortunately pompous sense of the word. They were conversations with people about their fieldwork experiences. They were relatively unstructured, although I did occasionally ask certain specific questions (see the Appendix), relatively friendly, and fairly long conversations. I found it useful and productive to schedule one long conversation (up to six hours in one case) followed by one or two shorter talks to tie up any loose ends. Most of the people I spoke with had severe constraints on their free time and preferred this format. In all cases but one, I talked with graduate students who had been back from the field less than two years; the one exception, reported in Chapter 4, was an individual who did his initial fieldwork about fifteen years ago. The range of geographical areas and topical interests represented by my informants was very great. In addition, I selected my informants from major universities, each with a long-established and very well-respected department of anthropology. I cannot judge whether the individuals I spoke with were typical. I am not sure what "typical" would mean in this case. Certainly the people I spoke with were very serious about their work and about contributing to anthropology. That was enough for me. Also, as will soon be apparent, my sample emphasizes, although is not exclusively confined to, the experiences of female, Western anthropologists who undertook their fieldwork alone, without benefit of family or research teams. The significance of one of these factors—sex—is briefly considered in the epilogue. I hope others will be spurred on to investigate whether the psychological factors uncovered here also operate for non-Western anthropologists and for anthropologists who enter the field with their spouses, families, or both, as members of research teams, or in other capacities. There is a lot of work left to be done.

The decision as to what information to elicit from my informants was very difficult. The range of potentially relevant material is enormous. Pertti Pelto and Gretel Pelto (1973), for example, devised a questionnaire designed to assess the relationship between psychological stress during fieldwork and the geographical location of the field site, presence or absence of a spouse, extent and type (that is, quantitative, intermediate, qualitative) of training in field techniques and methodology, prior experience of psychotherapy, living arrangements and food supply in the field, and other factors. In addition, one might consider sociocultural factors such as gender, ethnic-religious classification, and social class. Hortense Powdermaker (1966) has given us a particularly vivid description of the problems she encountered as a middle-class Jewish woman trying to do research among the elite moguls in Hollywood. Probably the best that one can do in this situation is to admit that, at some level, psychological variables intersect with sociocultural ones ultimately to shape the anthropologist's experiences during fieldwork. In this study, I concentrate on more purely psychological factors and tend to elicit information concerned specifically with the anthropologist's sense of identity during fieldwork.

I have presented the interview material in some depth and detail for two reasons. One, in its complexity and human richness, its poignancy and humor, the material is fascinating. Two, despite my belief in the correctness of my basic approach, I realize that there are as many different ways to interpret the meaning and significance of a particular behavior as there are schools of thought. I hope that the material I have presented will encourage others to find meanings in it different from mine.

A final point about my interviews is that they were just that; in no case did I actually observe a fieldworker in action (direct observation of an ethnographer poses formidable methodological and ethical problems). This "failure" almost inevitably gives rise to a particularly vexing question, namely, what is the relation between the ordeal of fieldwork as it is experienced by the anthropologist and the ordeal of fieldwork as it is later reconstructed and recounted? At the very least, it is probably reasonable to expect a fair bit of secondary elaboration in the remembrance of field experiences. Aside from a few general comments about this secondary elaboration (for example, the likely presence of certain defensive reactions, rationalizations, and the like), its actual nature and the direction it takes will depend on the interplay of a number of complex psychological and sociocultural factors (for example, specific personality variables, nature of the audience, situational constraints, the amount of time elapsed since returning from the field, and so on).

Part IV of this book is devoted to summarizing the main lines of my argument and exploring a few of its implications.

Some information on the terminology used is in order. I have tried to write without jargon and, particularly with regard to my interview and case studies, as evocatively as was feasible without losing precision. I have tried to retain the sense of experience and to remain phenomenologically true to my informants' descriptions. I use several terms to describe the graduate student in the field: student-initiate, student anthropologist, would-be anthropologist, initiate-anthropologist, and others. These terms should be read as interchangeable. I also alternate between talking about an individual's sense of self and sense of identity. Although some would object to this mingling of self and identity, I believe that from the theoretical perspective afforded by psychoanalytic phenomenology, there is no difference in meaning between these terms. I use them interchangeably; both refer to the same constellation of experience; both have a "social" and a "depth" dimension. Perhaps most important, I have preferred to write in the singular; I am, in brief, no fan of crowds. This tendency, however, gives rise to the problem of masculine versus feminine pronouns and more generally to that of sexist language. In this book, masculine and feminine pronouns are used interchangeably, although the former occurs more frequently. Unless explicitly noted, either form is used generically to cover all human beings. I hope this compromise will prove satisfactory to all concerned.

To acknowledge all those responsible for this book would be difficult, if not impossible. I have not made a conscious effort to point out the similarities and differences between my thought and that of others who have dealt with the psychology of fieldwork. I do not find such an exercise useful. Mostly what I have tried to do here is to open a case, to work out a few ideas, and to be provocative enough to stimulate further inquiry.

Readers of the work of Mircea Eliade and Ernest Becker will recognize the debt I owe to these men. Less obvious, because I did not come across his work until long after this book was completed, is the debt I owe to Vincent Crapanzano. His brief article "On the Writing of Ethnography" anticipates, although in a highly abbreviated form and in a somewhat different psychological idiom, much of what I have to say here. Robin Fox, Bonnie McCay, Susan Gal, and Miles Richardson kindly and critically read earlier versions of the manuscript and made many useful suggestions. George Atwood, with his remarkable clinical sensitivity and knowledge of self-psychology, was instrumental in determining the shape of Chapters 4 to 6. The individuals who allowed me to interview them about their field experiences were open and honest. The anonymous reviewers of The University of Alabama Press were particularly constructive in their comments, a reaction I found refreshing and, unfortunately, unusual. Judith Knight, the chief editor of The University of Alabama Press, was always understanding and made the often psychologically trying experience of putting a book manuscript together a little more fun. Trudie Calvert, copy editor, also provided valuable assistance in the preparation of this manuscript.

A last word. Many readers of this volume may wonder why I do not comment on my own field experience. Why don't I talk about my own sexual cravings, food preferences, diary entries, and the like during fieldwork? The reason is not because I did not experience these things but because an earlier version of this book was my fieldwork. The nearest I have been to a jungle was a new exhibit at the Bronx Zoo; the only fishing village I have been in was on Cape Cod. I am aware, acutely aware—perhaps overly aware—of the delicate position this puts me in. Always there can be the standard reproach: "Who is he to tell me about fieldwork when he's never done it?" Much could be said about this issue, and many fancy arguments could be made both for and against. Let me say simply that I have tried hard to listen carefully and empathetically to my informants and to those who have written about their field experiences. And I have tried to use my own experience as a stranger in a strange land, more limited than the field anthropologist, yes, but still as one who can taste the emotional resonance of the word *home,* as a foundation upon which to enter the anthropologist's world. Fieldwork is a deeply emotional experience for those who undertake it; let these people judge whether I have been successful.

This book is a footprint, not a monument.

Prologue

What I am after here is an attempt at recollection, an attempt to detail those largely personal events that led one man to see in fieldwork a problem worth understanding. It is a central tenet of psychobiography that, on one level, an academic, scholar, thinker, any person, investigates and takes a particular approach to a topic not because of "gaps in the literature" and other more or less rational reasons, but rather because of a series of unusual events, a great teacher, a quirk of fate (getting lost in a library, for example) that dovetails and resonates with that person's own past subjective history. In its most extreme form, one might argue that nobody does anything interesting for primarily rational reasons.

So, I am after personal reconstruction—light, personal reconstruction. There is a time and a place for heavy direct psychobiography: the therapist's couch always and very occasionally—rarely—in a book. Heavy personal confessions that get written down all too easily turn pompous, self-serving, and disingenuous.

Much of what I have to say here, at least over the next couple of pages, will sound remarkably naive and unsophisticated. This is simply because, as an undergraduate major in anthropology, I was remarkably naive and unsophisticated. I did not know what the hell anthropology was, what fieldwork was, and as to the connection between the two, I frankly didn't care much. Not then anyway. Besides, as has been remarked somewhere, sometimes some rather pretty ideas are developed from the most naive and wrongheaded of starting points.

The first courses that students take in anthropology are designed, as all introductory courses are, to inform them of the nature of the discipline. In the case of anthropology, I learned quickly that it is hard to overestimate the importance of fieldwork. Margaret Mead (1965:1), for example, went so far as to say that "anthropology is fieldwork." Although this is somewhat of an overstatement, Mead was and is undoubtedly correct in defining the essence of sociocultural anthropology as consisting of fieldwork. By fieldwork, Mead simply means that to understand the life ways of a group of people, anthropologists have traditionally lived with them for a long enough period of time to be able to internalize, to some extent, their ways of perceiving the world. Anthropologists participate in the cultural life of their people yet also maintain enough distance from it to record its features more or less objectively. Probably most young prefieldwork anthropologists think of little more than this procedure when they talk about fieldwork. Certainly for a time this was all I had thought of in connection with fieldwork. Two events conspired to alter my thinking, however.

The first experience occurred during my junior year in college, in response to a discussion that I had instigated with a senior colleague concerning Claude Lévi-Strauss's important work *Tristes Tropiques.* After having discussed several points of primarily philosophical import, I commented that Lévi-Strauss had obviously been deeply touched by his fieldwork experience. Suddenly, what had been a mutually stimulating dialogue turned into a vituperative polemic. I was curtly informed that I had committed an anthropological faux pas. Lévi-Strauss had never done fieldwork, and for that reason alone he was not to be considered a "real" anthropologist.

The second experience that led me to recognize the extent of the psychological ramifications of fieldwork was somewhat different, although provoked once again by my careless disregard for the importance of fieldwork. I had been discussing with my adviser the implications of Ernest Becker's work for the future development of social theory. Although most encouraging, he pointed out that I should begin to develop a project testable in a field situation. I pointed out that there was no reason to do so because I had no intention of going into the field. In fact, I said that I thought the emphasis on fieldwork had turned into a cult within anthropology. After a brief silence, I found myself once again being harangued. There is no reason for me to go into detail here. Suffice it to say that I was told one absolutely had to do fieldwork, if for no other reason than as an "experience."

I was deeply impressed by these two experiences. Intellectually, I realized for the first time the link between fieldwork and "being" an anthropologist. And yet, more than any particular intellectual point, it was the tone of these arguments that impressed me most profoundly. That is, these two people had become fiercely emotional and defensive about the subject of fieldwork.

A postfield professional anthropologist may find these two events neither interesting nor strange and may even think my mentioning them stupid, if not disingenuous. Nevertheless, it is an anthropological truism to assert that those cultural features of a particular society that are the most deeply ingrained are the least likely to be explicated and questioned by the native members themselves. It is this tendency, among others, that renders the Socratic maxim "know thyself" so problematic for the individual or group. Anthropologists have traditionally avoided this problem by studying foreign cultures, cultures in which they are strangers. As one who has never felt particularly "at home" as an anthropologist—undoubtedly for psychobiographic reasons—I find myself in precisely this same position, a stranger, vis-à-vis other anthropologists. It is from this position of marginality that I can function as a participant-observer of other participant-observers, in this case, anthropologists. And it was from this vantage point that I found these strong emotional outbursts about fieldwork so very interesting. I had read enough of psychoanalytic theory to realize how important a diagnostic feature strong emotional responses can be.

But diagnostic of what?

It was these two simple, similar, yet hardly breathtaking experiences that catalyzed my interest in the problematic nature of fieldwork. I carried these experiences in my memory for a long time, and it was on their account that I turned to the literature on fieldwork. Here I will need to bracket the personal nature of this inquiry and adopt a more analytic tone and stance.

Despite—or perhaps because—fieldwork is the "culture focus" of anthropology, only a few studies have sought to clarify the nature of the psychological import of fieldwork (for example, Devereux 1967; Freilich 1970; Hill 1974; Jones 1973; Meintel 1973; Nash 1963; Obeyesekere 1981; Winthrop 1969). Although the reasons for this relative neglect are multifarious and demand a full-length study in their own right, one of the more interesting assessments of this "problem" argues that much self-analysis from within anthropology has been impeded by the "mystique" surrounding the discipline (Braroe and Hicks 1967; Freilich 1970). The "mystique" of anthropology refers to the largely subterranean and generally unspoken ideas and attitudes, the background assumptions held by anthropologists about their profession. The predominant flavor of

xvii

much of the anthropological mystique is romantic. Anthropologists are forever lonely, forever homeless, intrepid adventurers off in search of a simpler, more pristine past world. The mystique has it that fieldwork is "deeply untellable," profoundly moving, but incapable of being described except perhaps through intuitive means. The experience of fieldwork is the sound of one hand clapping; it is a ream of blank paper.

Over the past decade or so, however, anthropologists have shown an increasing interest in reporting, even if not systematically analyzing, the trials and tribulations of the field experience. Dennison Nash and Ronald Winthrop (1972) attribute this "emergence of self-consciousness in ethnography" to several factors, the most important including the embarrassing results that were produced when two or more anthropologists studied the same culture (for example, Redfield/Lewis, Mead/Freeman as a recent example; by embarrassing I mean that the account offered by each anthropologist differed greatly from that of the other); the increasing personal involvement of anthropologists in the lives of their people, that is, the development of "action" anthropology; and the vociferous assertions of independence by non-Western peoples, including particularly their right to read, judge, and comment on "their" anthropologist's study. Whatever the ultimate cause for this increase in self-reflexive interests may be—for surely any general explanation would need to consider the increase in self-reflexive interests apparent in the other (human) sciences today—anthropologists are currently more open and willing to discuss their field experiences publicly than ever before. Indeed, monographs and articles on the field experience are appearing with ever greater regularity as time passes. Many of these accounts are sensitive portrayals of the intellectual and personal upheaval experienced by the anthropologist as he attempted to establish dialogue and develop rapport with "his" people. The emphasis throughout many of these works is on fieldwork as a psychologically affecting experience.

It is impossible to construct an ideal type or even a typical model of an anthropologist's experience, in concrete detail, during fieldwork. And yet one characteristic does seem to stand out in all the accounts of fieldwork that I am familiar with.[1] I am referring to the associated problems of disorientation, worry, depression, fatigue, loneliness, stress, and the like. For ease of presentation, I will refer to these characteristics under the general heading of anxiety. By using this term, I am trying to draw attention to the thought of men such as Paul Tillich (1952), Rollo May (1977), and Georg W. F. Hegel, all of whom view anxiety as arising in connection with "fear for one's entire being." Rosalie Wax (1960:175–76), in an account of her fieldwork experiences, illustrates this point precisely: "The anxiety which this student suffered in trying to defend the self of which she approved was so agonizing that she was unable to describe it adequately in her document."

Now this revelation *is* interesting. For Wax is arguing, at least implicitly, that the stress, fatigue, depression, anxiety, and so on experienced by the fieldworker are the result of matters relating directly to the status of the self, and more particularly to disintegrative inroads made against the structure of the self. Perhaps this idea may help to explain the reactions I inadvertently elicited from my two senior colleagues. It is well known that narcissistic rage, the reaction to self-dystonic interaction, is often cloaked in bitter invective or more simply in an exaggeratedly overblown response of any coloring. And perhaps, from this perspective, one might even find some truth in the romantic ethos, in the mystique surrounding anthropology and anthropologists. One need only posit an intimate connection between fieldwork and the self of the anthropologist, a very reasonable assumption, for the pieces to begin to fall into place.

The final piece of the puzzle that I shall mention here, for this is only an introduction, concerns the self-doubts about the significance of their life and work that certain (many) anthropologists experience during their fieldwork. This tendency was first drawn to my attention when I stumbled over Malinowski's comment (1967:167) that he viewed "the life of the natives as utterly devoid of interest or importance, something as remote from [him] as the life of a dog." It was powerfully, if more humorously, confirmed by Lévi-Strauss's statement (1977:428) of the significance of his own "fieldwork" experience: "As he practices his profession, the anthropologist is consumed by doubts: has he really abandoned his native setting, his friends, and his way of life, spent such considerable amounts of money and energy, and endangered his health, for the sole purpose of making his presence acceptable to a score or two of miserable creatures doomed to early extinction, whose chief occupations meanwhile are delousing themselves and sleeping."[2] I have heard this doubt echoed again and again, less eloquently but no less poignantly, by my anthropologist informants.

Whence the origin of this self-doubt? What is its significance? In an immediate and superficial sense, there is much about fieldwork that would encourage such feelings: the natives are not interested in the anthropologist's project, the data has not been coming in fast and furious, the strangeness of it all is too overwhelming to be handled properly, the professors back home write, from the comfort of their armchairs, and encourage—"suggest"—that the student "look at" a few more things, "consider" this possibility—another loose end and where they all come together, if they do, nobody knows. Yes, there is much in fieldwork that would encourage self-doubt. But this listing of specific depressive aspects of fieldwork threatens to send us off on a wild and fruitless chase. I think all we need understand right now is the tautologously obvious: one experiences self-doubt when one doubts the viability and vitality of one's self. Self-doubt indicates, to paraphrase Sigmund Freud very loosely, that one's sense of self is haywire, that one has gone a little nuts, become a little sick. And so we return full circle and find the same theme again, that fieldwork is always, to some degree, identity-dystonic.

The foregoing considerations, ranging from the emotionally laden defensive outbursts about fieldwork to the self-doubts about the meaning of their life and work experienced by certain (many) anthropologists during their fieldwork, have led me to the point that I now believe a major, if largely unexplored, aspect of fieldwork must lie in its self-psychological import for the individual. The remainder of this book, or at least a large part of it, will be devoted to specifying the nature of this "self-psychological import." There is also, however, a second aspect of this book that deserves mention here.

As intrinsically interesting as the psychology of fieldwork may be—as I hope to demonstrate shortly—it becomes even more interesting, and more important and vital, when one realizes the potential contributions that it can offer to anthropological methodology, to understanding the act of "anthropologizing" itself. It is to this goal principally that the majority of studies of the psychology of fieldwork have tended. The psychological orientation of Pelto and Pelto (1973; 1978) had as its guiding theme, for example, the attempt to formulate a more rigorous and trustworthy field methodology. And Ganneth Obeyesekere (1981) has focused specifically on how the anthropologist can use his own feelings and desires aroused during fieldwork, in a creative and methodologically significant sense, to further his understanding of any given culture. Of all the studies on the psychology of fieldwork, however, one stands out as preeminent in its contributions to methodology, that by George Devereux (1967). Devereux's now classic account is a systematic attempt to

PROLOGUE

ferret out the many sources of bias and distortion that exist because of the anomalous position, considered both structurally and psychologically, of the anthropologist vis-à-vis the indigenous population. He discusses a host of possible psychological factors, many of which stem from his fundamentally Freudian orientation (for example, castration anxiety, transference and countertransference, unconscious identification with proffered roles as a source of gratification [externalization of the ego ideal]), that can affect and ultimately determine the anthropologist's view of any given culture. Devereux's work, which will be taken up in part in Chapter 7, is a reminder of the intimate connection that exists between the psychology of fieldwork and anthropological methodology.

To complement these authors' impressive arguments about the importance of a psychology of fieldwork (including that of the anthropologist) to anthropological epistemology, one need only consider the results that occurred when two ethnographers studied the same cultural group. As I have already mentioned in my discussion of the work of Nash and Winthrop, these results were embarrassing to anthropologists and especially so to those who saw their discipline as a "science." The problem was that no two ethnographers seemed to be able to agree on what their people were really like. John Dollard and Hortense Powdermaker, for example, disagreed in their characterizations of America's Deep South. Margaret Mead and Reo Fortune, similarly, offered different interpretations of Arapesh culture (Nash and Winthrop 1972:530). As disquieting as these disagreements might appear, they pale in significance when compared to the Redfield/Lewis controversy, "a landmark in American anthropology" (Agar 1980:7). Briefly, in 1951, Oscar Lewis restudied the Mexican village of Tepoztlan where Robert Redfield had conducted fieldwork in 1930. Redfield, with his "folk" leanings, had portrayed a friendly and harmonious peasant village, whereas Lewis, with a darker eye, saw a village beset by turmoil, envy, and hostility. These two accounts differed on nearly every matter; small details, broad interpretations, impressions of world view, all were portrayed differently. The most recent of these controversies is, of course, the currently famous Mead/Freeman debate. Similar to the much earlier Redfield/Lewis debate, this discussion revolves around the "true" nature of Samoan culture, in which life was either idyllic, with little storm and stress, or nasty, brutish, and violent, depending on who one happens to believe.

From my perspective here, the key issue in any of these debates is not who is right and who is wrong, but rather that the debates exist at all. Although it is reasonable to assume that there are many factors that condition the nature of the differing interpretations of each investigator, surely one that must be considered is the personality of the investigator and its effect on his interpretation of field data. Thus the existence of these controversies forces us to recognize that the psychology of fieldwork, in its broadest sense, can have serious epistemological implications for anthropology. One who investigates the psychology of fieldwork is, then, virtually compelled at least to offer some suggestion as to its methodological implications.

And so this book is primarily about the self-psychological import of fieldwork, about what fieldwork psychologically does to the anthropologist. But for that reason, it can also offer a methodological comment or two. To fulfill this double responsibility, I will stop occasionally, here and there—albeit briefly—to interject a whisper about how anthropologists know what they know—about anthropological epistemology.

Ethnographers in the Field

Part I
Understanding Fieldwork

1

On Death and Fieldwork

There came to him an image of man's whole life upon the earth. It seemed to him that all man's life was like a tiny spurt of flame that blazed out briefly in an illimitable and terrifying darkness, and that all man's grandeur, tragic dignity, his heroic glory, came from the brevity and smallness of this flame. He knew his life was little and would be extinguished, and that only darkness was immense and everlasting. And he knew that he would die with defiance on his lips, and that the shout of his denial would ring with the last pulsing of his heart into the maw of all-engulfing night.
    —Thomas Wolfe, *You Can't Go Home Again*

A small, heavily laden aluminum boat moves sluggishly up a river in the jungles of South America. Its occupants are two: a bush missionary and a young graduate student about to embark on his first stint of anthropological fieldwork. The heat and humidity are oppressive. Worse yet, the dry season has begun, and hordes of venomous gnats have descended on the travelers in an orgy of bloodlust. Arriving at last, the young man prepares to meet his subjects, a small group of Indians with whom he will live for at least a year and about whom he hopes to write a doctoral dissertation. Pushing his way through a small clearing in the jungle, our initiate-anthropologist meets his people for the first time. The greeting is other than he had fantasized; face to face and eye to eye, he is confronted by a dozen well-muscled, naked, filthy, hideous savages. Great gobs of green mucus hang from their nostrils. And they are, of course, curious. With slimy, mucus-laden hands, they examine our student over and over again. Satisfied that he is harmless—perhaps even saddened a little by it, for they were spoiling for a fight—they leave him alone to ponder his situation. He is completely alone in a stinking rat hole in the jungle, living among a people with whom he cannot communicate, a people who at this moment revolt him. And he cannot leave, for his entire career, his prestige ranking within the discipline of anthropology, his professors' respect—and much else—depend on his maintaining a stiff upper lip, on organizing this chaos into a Ph.D. thesis. Our young student has arrived home. He will live here for the next thirteen months.

A young woman, interested in the relationship between ritual and social identity, decides to conduct fieldwork on a small island in the Caribbean. For the first two months of her stay, she is made to feel entirely unwelcome. People make fun of her dress, jeer at her manners, and occasionally warn her to leave. "Yankee, go home," appears to her to be the prevailing sentiment among her people. Then relations thaw, and she begins to feel accepted. She is getting good data, making friends, and feeling more at ease. Coming home one night from a small get-together, she is brutally raped. She withdraws from her world, grows more isolated, and starts drinking heavily. She begins to hallucinate, hearing violin music at odd times of the day and night, music that reminds her of old movies and gives rise to a sense of ending, of completion. She chooses not to leave her field area, however. Her committee members, she tells me, always considered her flippant and insouciant and lacking in professional commitment. She is determined to score "identity points" by working through her trauma and completing her fieldwork and dissertation. Two years later, the young anthropologist is looking for a job, her dissertation completed and her identity points made. But problems still lurk under the surface, and her trauma is not over.

These two brief vignettes describe, or at least hint at, the many and varied experiences that anthropologists undergo while doing fieldwork. The first, and justly famous, vignette is taken from the work of Napoleon Chagnon (1968); the second, relatively unknown, is taken from my work with an informant. Together they propose the problem of this study, namely, what does fieldwork do, psychologically, to the anthropologist?

When anthropologists have thought about fieldwork as a topic in need of explanation, they appear to recognize it, either implicitly or explicitly, as a rite of passage (Abbott 1982; Alland 1975). According to Arnold Van Gennep (1960:10), a rite of passage accompanies every change of place, state, social position, and age of an individual or group. Every rite of passage, when analyzed structurally, can be broken down into three subphases: separation, transition, and reintegration. The stage of separation (in the case of anthropology, passing the qualifying exam) is characterized by symbolic gestures, observances, and so forth that indicate to the wider society that a

4

particular individual or group has become detached from its previous status. The transitional or liminal phase (fieldwork proper) is a nebulous period, characterized by an absence of the traits that either existed in the past or will exist in the future. Reintegration (completion of the dissertation) marks the end of the status passage. A new status has been achieved, and consequently the individual or group is enmeshed in a new structural position with new rights and duties. These rites are most conspicuous at the times of critical transitions in life (birth, puberty, marriage, and death).

In drawing on this idea of fieldwork as a rite of passage, I want to concentrate my attention on the liminal period because this stage appears to correspond to the time the anthropologist is actually in the field (Wengle 1983). To characterize this stage, I will be drawing on the work of Mircea Eliade (1958) and Victor Turner (1967; 1969).

The initiate, upon entering the liminal stage, becomes structurally invisible, because he is no longer classifiable by his past status, nor is he yet able to be classified by his future status. In relation to his past status, the individual is considered a corpse, to his future status, an infant. Negatively speaking, this is a condition of ambiguity, paradox, and contradiction. In short, the condition is profoundly unstructured. The symbolic representations of this stage are, as Eliade (1958) brilliantly demonstrates, markedly pointed toward notions of death and rebirth. Recent theoretical work (McManus 1979) also suggests the breakdown of cognitive schematic frameworks, in the Piagetian sense, during this stage. Positively viewed, the individual's freedom from structural restraint gives rise to critical analyses, reflection, and novel thought. Ideas that had once been accepted unthinkingly are now thrown open to inspection. And of the utmost importance, it is during this stage that the initiate is "taught" the ritual and esoteric knowledge ("sacra") that will make him a true member of his society. The "sacra" serve as "the symbolic template of the whole system of beliefs and values in a given culture, its archetypal paradigm and ultimate measure"; they "stamp into the neophytes the basic assumptions of their culture" (Turner 1967:108).

In drawing a parallel between fieldwork and rites of passage, anthropologists have tended to concentrate their attention almost exclusively on the structural nature of the status transformations marked by these rites. The "new rights and duties" have received a disproportionate share of the total analytic effort. As a consequence of this emphasis, the underlying problem of such status transformations, that of corresponding psychological changes, has been left relatively neglected. As Regina Holloman (1974) has pointed out, very few field studies of rites of passage have been concerned with the systematic examination of the psychological changes that occur within individual participants.

In an effort to consider fieldwork as part of a psychologically affecting rite of passage, I suggest that three points contained within Turner's description of the liminal phase deserve special emphasis. First, it should be relatively apparent that fieldwork, conceived of as the essence of modern social/cultural anthropological training, can be construed as the sacra of that discipline.[1] Fieldwork has traditionally maintained the uniqueness and served to emphasize the separateness of anthropology from the other human sciences; that is, fieldwork served as the "boundary-maintenance" device separating anthropology from its compatriot sciences. This equation linking fieldwork with the sacra of anthropology does not imply, of course, that fieldwork is beyond the pale of criticism; anthropologists have often voiced one or another methodological caveat about fieldwork as a basic source of knowledge. But surely, no anthropologist has ever maintained, at least publicly, that fieldwork is not fundamental to the discipline. No anthropologist has ever uttered, at the start of his career, "fieldwork be dashed, to the library I belong." Second, the liminal stage of a rite of passage entails a symbolic death for the individual, by which I mean that the individual experiences an attack against his own sense of self/identity (see Lifton 1956). Third, the sacra somehow "stamp into" the initiates the basic assumptions of their culture, molding them into full members of their culture.

Might it not be possible to consider these three points as all of a piece, as all interrelated? I believe that such a consideration strikes at the heart of the fieldwork question.

Beginning with the third and last point mentioned above, I find, just as Anthony F. C. Wallace (1968:50) did before me, certain similarities between the nature of the stamping-in process in a typical rite of passage and the very old and well-known procedures that are subsumed under the heading of thought transformation. Roger Burton and John Whiting (1961:90), for example, in discussing the liminal period of a rite of passage, state: "The hazing, sleeplessness, tests of manhood . . . together with promise of high status—that of being a man if the tests are successfully passed—are indeed similar to the brainwashing techniques employed by the Communists."

Enough is known about the techniques of thought transformation to allow for a simplified presentation of the techniques employed. Typically, an individual is removed or isolated from his normal surrounding environment and placed under extreme physical and mental pressure. Eventually, this pressure destroys the individual's sense of personal inner continuity and plunges him into emotional collapse; the individual is symbolically dead. At this point, the individual experiences a process of "ritual opening" (Holloman 1974:273)— the individual is stripped of his ego defenses, resulting in a heightened sense of vulnerability and suggestibility. Following this "opening," the individual is provided with a new meaning framework in which he can embed his experiences and derive some sense of their significance (Lifton 1956; Sargant 1959; Wallace 1956). Robert J. Lifton, in his study of Chinese thought reform (1956:190), emphasizes the importance of the group as the provider of this larger meaning framework: the initiate "experiences the 'togetherness' of intimate group living, suffering, and 'reform'; the rewards of self-surrender—of merging with an all-powerful force and sharing its strength." Lifton has further pointed out that, for the individual, thought reform is an "agonizing drama of death and rebirth" (ibid.:188).

To understand fully the dynamics of this process of rebirth (self/identity transformation), it is necessary to determine the depth psychological significance of the individual's loss of his sense of self, that is of his symbolic death. Before this question can be broached adequately, however, it is necessary to clarify what I mean by "sense of self/identity" and why I feel that during fieldwork, the initiate-anthropologist experiences an attack against it.

For my purposes here, an individual's sense of self/identity has two significant faces, an inner and an outer one. The individual needs to feel himself an autonomous and independent entity, and yet at the same time also needs to feel himself dependent, a part of something larger, more powerful, and more enduring than himself; one's sense of self is notoriously Janus-faced, composed of both "ego" and "we-go" needs. In both these aspects of his experiencing, the individual strives to maintain a sense of continuity, coherence, and integrity (G. Klein, 1976:178–79). An individual's ability to maintain this sense of stable identity depends, in turn, on a number of interrelated factors. For one, Edith Jacobson (in Spiegel 1959:106) has argued that the stability of an individual's sense of identity depends directly on the "innumerable identifications" he has established with the familiar, personal and impersonal, concrete and abstract, animate and inanimate objects of his past and present exis-

7

tence. When these many identifications are threatened, as for example when an individual's social or physical environment changes rapidly, his sense of identity will be threatened. For another, and this point is actually an extension of Jacobson's, the individual's sense of identity depends very significantly on the responses and reactions that he produces in and receives back from other people surrounding him (Berger and Luckmann 1967; Erikson 1980; Kohut 1977; Lichtenstein 1977; Mead 1934). The total gamut of sensory cues that are reflected or mirrored back from the other help to stabilize the individual's sense of identity; without a relatedness to another human being, one's sense of identity collapses.[2] This is not meant to imply, however, that *any* other human being will be sufficient for, or provide, the necessary quality of relatedness to enable the individual to maintain his sense of identity. Not every person can function as a "significant other." Phyllis Greenacre (1958:618), in a careful analysis of this problem, concluded that an individual needs an other who is relatively "similar" to interact with if each is to retain his respective sense of identity. In support of this conclusion, she has pointed out that often, in an effort to forestall identity fragmentation, missionaries travel in groups to foreign countries, even when there is no other logical reason to do so. In a more recent analysis, Gary Thrane (1979:330) reached an identical conclusion: "It is only in the eyes of our own like, of our own ilk, that we can find a mirror." These conclusions can be readily understood; for one to maintain identity, the other who is vastly different, who shares with the individual only similar physical characteristics and is limited therefore to relatively nonempathic interaction with him, cannot be of much value as an identity-syntonic mirror. The sense of self/identity is then purely intrapsychic, although its development and maintenance depend on a tangled web of sociological and psychological factors. His sense of identity serves as the framework of meaning and value for the individual; without a firmly anchored sense of identity, the individual cannot assure the significance and meaning of his life (Lichtenberg 1975; Spiegel 1959).

There is every reason to believe, based on the description just provided, that the initiate-anthropologist experiences an attack against his sense of identity during fieldwork. Often the student is literally thrown into the field, having been told nothing, or next to nothing, of what to expect. One of my informants expressed this point precisely: "Oh, sure we asked for advice. We said tell us about fieldwork, give us some suggestions. And it was something that, as I recall, the department just had a very hard time dealing with. They didn't want to offer something on issues that come up in the field. They agreed to meet with us a few times at lunch and whenever we pressed them on important issues, on what the hell the field was like, they couldn't deal with us at all. A waste of time." There is no formal psychological preparation for fieldwork per se; gone are the days—which never existed except in the minds of a few mavericks— when it was understood that fieldworkers could benefit from a taste of psychoanalysis. The so-called "field manuals" that exist for the student are little more than vast recipe books, good on meth- odological concerns but nearly silent on matters of psychological adjustment. The student is also under tremendous pressure to justi- fy his existence in the field—to the natives, to himself, and to the funding agencies and faculty judging his performance. His reputa- tion and career are dependent, in some (probably large) measure, on his performance in the field. In all likelihood, the fieldworker is far less than fluent in the natives' language, and certainly he is ignorant about his place and behavioral responsibilities. Related to this latter point, the student loses the mirroring function of his significant oth- ers, that is, he loses his sense of self-esteem and self-worth reflected back from others. Considered more globally, the student's entire world, as mirror, has changed radically. This entire constellation of characteristics produces a psychological climate that is hardly con- ducive to maintaining a sense of selfsameness and continuity in time and a feeling of embeddedness in the wider environment. As Ruth Landes (1970:123) states in speaking of her fieldwork experi- ence: "One's concept of self disintegrates because the accustomed responses have disappeared."

This phenomenon of identity loss and the reasons for it have been indirectly realized by anthropologists through their descriptions of "culture shock." Kalvero Oberg, the anthropologist most responsi- ble for that term, describes the "disease" as one

> precipitated by the anxiety that results from losing all our familiar signs and symbols of social intercourse. These signs or cues include the thousand and one ways in which we orient ourselves to the situations of daily life: when to shake hands and what to say when we meet people, when and how to give tips, how to give orders to servants, how to make purchases. . . . Now these cues which may be words, gestures, facial expressions, customs, or norms are acquired by all of us in the course of growing up and are as much a part of our culture as the language we speak or the beliefs we accept. All of us depend for peace of mind and our efficiency on hundreds of these cues, most of which we do not carry on the level of conscious awareness. [In Foster 1973:191–92]

9

In other and shorter words, and in the terminology of this essay, culture shock is precipitated by losing the innumerable identifications the individual has established with his home world. Culture shock is precipitated when the individual loses the mirroring function of his life-world, his physical and social environment. Culture shock is the threat the individual feels in relation to his sense of identity when plunged into unfamiliar circumstances.

The question, some pages back, that produced this discussion on identity concerned the psychological significance of the individual's loss of his sense of identity. It is fair to say that most self/identity theorists, and here I would include anthropologists, sociologists, philosophers, and psychologists, consider the maintenance of a stable sense of identity to be extremely important to the human being. Among anthropologists, A. F. C. Wallace (1968:48) speaks of the "desperate fear," the "desperate emotional crisis" (1966:139), and the "struggle" (Wallace and Fogelson 1965:383) accompanying loss of the sense of identity and the attempt to reformulate it. And Yehudi Cohen (1964:15), in describing a sense of identity as a boundary, argues that "when a human being loses his boundaries, he will become psychotic or die." L. S. Cottrell (1978), an interactionist psychologist, argues that the individual will go to extraordinary lengths to maintain his sense of identity, even, when warranted, giving up his life to sustain it. Among psychoanalysts, Heinz Kohut (1977) has characterized the individual's affective experiencing of identity (self) loss as one of "disintegration anxiety," whereas W. R. D. Fairbairn (1952), Harry Guntrip (1968), and Thomas Ogden (1983) all talk, to varying degrees, about "annihilation anxiety." Hans Lichtenstein (1977:243) equates the necessity for identity maintenance with self-preservation. And finally, James McCarthy (1980) devotes an entire stimulating book to demonstrating that the loss of the sense of identity is psychologically for the individual an imagery of death. The majority of evidence, then, leans toward the view that, for the individual, the loss of his sense of identity is a symbolic death.

In considering the human experience of death, and for the human animal symbols are all too real, so that symbolic death at some level equals real death,[3] traditional psychoanalytic theory is not enough. As Irwin Hoffman (1979) suggests, psychoanalysts have not paid nearly enough attention to the problems involved in an individual's adaptation to his own mortality. Although certain hints can be found in Freud's writings concerning such a perspective (Nachman 1981), these are never developed adequately. Certain offshoots of psychoanalysis have, however, found a central place in their theories for the experience of death as a primary phenomenon. I am referring here to the work of Otto Rank (1931; 1941), especially as given currency in the writings of Becker (1973; 1975) and Lifton (1971; 1976).

According to these thinkers, the fundamental motivational force underlying much of human behavior is the fear of death and the consequent striving for symbolic immortality. In Becker's words, "Man from the very beginning could not live with the prospect of death. . . . Man erected cultural symbols which do not age or decay to quiet his fear of the ultimate end—and of more immediate concern, to provide the promise of indefinite duration" (1975:3). In the face of his own inevitable mortality, man pales and attempts a psycho-symbolic transcendence of death through identification with "cultural symbols denoting renewal" (Grof and Halifax 1977:193). Lifton (1971) argues that there are five specific, although not mutually exclusive, modes for achieving symbolic immortality: the biological (family, state), theological (afterlife), creative (Freud will never die), natural (organic cycle), and experiential (psychic loss of self). An exploitive identification within the bounds of one or more of these modes allows the individual to obtain a modicum of security, the assurance of the expansive meaning of his life—symbolic immortality—in an ever-changing world.

In further developing this line of thought, Lifton has argued that an innate imagery of death is present throughout the human life span (1976:19). This imagery, although continually evolving, begins by being organized around three nuclear oppositions: connection/ separation, movement/stasis, and integration/disintegration. The content of each pair of oppositions ranges along a continuum originating in the physical and ending in the psycho-symbolic. Hence, considering the positive pole of each opposition, connection refers, at first, to what John Bowlby (1973) calls "attachment behavior" to the mother, and later, to a feeling of embeddedness within larger historical currents, ideas, groups, and so forth; movement refers, at first, simply to physical action, then later to symbolic development, progress, change, and psychological individuation; integration refers, at first, to physical intactness, and then later to the adequateness of an individual's inner world of forms and images to encompass his actions and self-world relationships. The negative pole of each opposition refers, of course, to the opposite quality of experience from that just discussed. By noting that these oppositions, or more precisely, their negative poles of separation, stasis, and disintegration are activated in the liminal stage, Lifton demonstrates that each rebirth that occurs at every major life change, as marked by a

11

rite of passage, rekindles the individual's death anxiety that is inevitably associated with such imagery (1976:41). It is possible to restate this position in more traditional terminology by noting that from the "ego's viewpoint" a "breach in the apparent coherence of our mental logical process would seem to be a sort of death" (Bateson 1979:126). Although neither Lifton nor Gregory Bateson specifically says so, both are referring to the disintegration of an individual's sense of self/identity. A breach in our sense of understanding and continuity—feelings of separation from larger historical currents, of psychological regression and stagnation, of an incapacity to order our self-world relationships—are all commonplace symptoms of the loss of the sense of identity (see Hallowell 1955). It is, then, the threatened loss of his sense of identity during the liminal phase of a rite of passage that forces the individual to confront the terror of his own death.

Every rite of passage, and in particular every liminal phase of the rite, exposes the initiate to his innate anxiety about death in the form of separation, stasis, and disintegration, that is, in the loss of his sense of identity. On the basis of the previous analyses of Lifton and Becker, one would expect the initiate to pursue one or another mode of assuring symbolic immortality, to find the "cultural symbols denoting renewal." Such being the case, a question remains to be asked: Where are the cultural symbols denoting renewal for the not-quite-yet certified anthropologist? In what do such symbols of renewal consist? The same question can be asked in different terminology: Where is the anchorage in which the initiate-anthropologist will embed his new sense of identity?

Such symbols are certainly not to be found, at least not permanently, in the foreign culture in which the initiate is immersed, although often they are first sought there. These symbols simply cannot offer the necessary emotive power the would-be anthropologist needs to transcend his death fear. They are, after all, very recent acquisitions of the anthropologist's understanding. At best, such symbols are still foreign and therefore superficial. They lack the power, the massive reality that comes with depth.

In my view, the answer as to where these symbols of renewal are to be found has already been answered by the anthropologist Hazel Weidman (1970:241) in her discussion of how she withstood the rigors of fieldwork: "It meant becoming an anthropologist—and anthropology . . . for me, provided the kind of meaning and significance that religion does for others." And what is the significance of religion? "The human individual knows that he must die, but has

12

thoughts larger than his fate. . . . Religion is an effort to be included in some domain larger and more permanent than mere existence" (Feibleman in Dobzhansky 1969:36). I mean to argue here that anthropology can take on the functions of a religion and serve as a symbol of renewal for its death-tainted initiates.[4] Or, in the alternate terminology of this essay, anthropology comes to serve as the focal symbol, the anchorage point, around which the student-initiate will reformulate and recrystallize his sense of existential identity: "Becoming an anthropologist represented the culmination of many years of synthesizing and integrating cognitive and emotional elements into a unified psychological system that allowed me as a person to relate most meaningfully to others while being at ease with myself. In essence, anthropology helped me to establish an identity" (Weidman 1970:241).

This last thought, that anthropology itself serves as an "identity peg" (Goffman 1956) for the individual points to an additional consideration relevant to the question: How or through what does the student-initiate identify with the symbol of anthropology? As I argued earlier, an individual's sense of identity is notoriously Janus-faced. On one hand, an individual needs to feel himself a part of or embedded within some larger, more enduring whole; in my complementary terminology,[5] the individual achieves his symbolic immortality through, and at the level of, the group. On the other hand, an individual needs to feel autonomous, separate, unique unto himself, that is, he needs to feel a sense of personal symbolic immortality. In my emphasis on anthropology as a symbol of renewal I have been arguing for only one-half of the answer, that concerning group symbolic immortality and the sense of embeddedness. From what, then, does the student-initiate derive a sense of his own personal symbolic immortality, his own uniqueness as an anthropologist? It seems to me that the individual secures this particular aspect of his new identity through self-identification with the creative work arising out of the field experience.[6] By depositing his "immortal self" within his work, the individual guarantees his autonomy while, at the same time, belonging to a larger, more enduring group, in this case, the discipline of anthropology. (For a description of this process from a somewhat different psychological perspective, see Wallace 1956; 1966 on "mazeway resynthesis.")

Certain aspects of this last point need to be clarified before I can proceed. Upon returning from the field, the student-initiate does not yet have a firm sense of his new anthropological identity. He is not hey presto an anthropologist; the establishment of a sense of identity is a process. Critical to this process is the mirroring the student-initiate receives once he returns from the field. Just as a lack of mirroring from significant others eroded his sense of identity in the field, so a certain minimum of positive mirroring will be necessary to stabilize the student-initiate's sense of himself as an anthropologist. This mirroring can originate from various sources: the student's dissertation committee, other students, other specialists in his field (either through personal contact or, for example, through the acceptance of a paper for publication). If the student experiences reasonably consistent and positive mirroring, his self-identification with his work and therefore with anthropology will grow stronger and more secure. The capstone of this process comes with the completion and successful defense of the Ph.D. dissertation. Many of these points are illustrated in elegant fashion by one of my informants. In response to a question concerning her feelings about leaving the field, my informant responded:

> My biggest concern was that I failed as a fieldworker. That I didn't really understand the people. A sense that there was so much I didn't know, and yet I couldn't ask any more questions. . . . I left feeling I had done a poor job in the field. I wasn't fully digesting anything; I wasn't writing enough stuff up. I should have done more analysis in the field. . . . I wasn't coming home triumphant. . . . There was still so much to do.
>
> Q.: Do you feel yourself to be more of an anthropologist now than before you went to the field?
>
> A.: I certainly do. *I certainly do.* I don't feel like a student now. I'm writing up my research. It doesn't have anything to do with the university structure and with Ph.D.'s and what goes on there. *It's my stuff.* I'm an anthropologist now. I don't have to wait for the Ph.D., for an academic job, to be one. That's immaterial. I am one now. And the fieldwork, that's why.
>
> Q.: What happened between the ending of your fieldwork and the present to alter your feelings of failure?
>
> A.: Well, one thing that has been really nice is the reaction I'm getting from specialists in the area where I worked. I went down to talk with a few of them last week and they were impressed with my findings. They wanted to know how I had been able to get the kinds of information I had. Nobody else has been able to get in the ceremonies that I had. They said, this is so good, how did you get this material? That made me more confident in my work, made me feel very good.

I do not think these statements need fancy explication. The doubt about her sense of identity as an anthropologist, the positive mirroring that stabilized and solidified that identity, and the identification with her work and with anthropology are all illustrated in her thoughts. A second example, shorter but equally direct, was reported by another informant:

> No. I feel myself less of an anthropologist, actually. I haven't been thinking in anthropological terms for quite a while now. You don't do that in the field. It wouldn't be appropriate for interacting with people. . . . And I haven't written any scholarly articles or published anything since I went to the field. I don't feel very much like an anthropologist, at this point. That feeling of being an anthropologist stopped somewhere after I returned to the field a second time. I don't feel it now. I don't know what it means to feel like an anthropologist now. One thing was that I had no professional support mechanisms. Nobody was saying, "W., you're a professional anthropologist." It's only quite recently, it's only been in the United States that people talked as if I was supposed to be an anthropologist. Your perception of self is really based on how others perceive you, isn't it? So, I'm now being perceived as an anthropologist, and, it's funny, I'm starting to feel like one.

When this process of positive mirroring fails to take place, the student-initiate will have a more difficult time organizing his sense of identity around the symbol of anthropology. Another of my informants illustrates this point precisely. This individual had returned from the field for a two-week vacation. Her comments on her return are telling:

> I remember when I came back for two weeks in January, the department was having a party. And I tried to talk to several people about, several faculty members about what I was experiencing, in terms of a loss of self-confidence, basically. Loss of self-esteem. I'm, I mean I always thought of myself as a very competent human being. At my age I've learned how to deal with things. . . . I would emphasize my surprise again at the failure of anybody here to be willing to talk with me about my experience. When I . . . tried to talk about what it was like, there was no response. . . . I think that a lot of people are afraid to acknowledge their weaknesses. They try to isolate their emotions and pretend they don't exist. . . . An unwillingness to appear vulnerable . . . to students. . . . That was one thing. And they seemed unwilling to acknowledge, I mean I just didn't say let's talk about feeling insecure, having little self-esteem or confidence. I was more subtle than that. But still they acted like they didn't understand. I felt like an idiot. Was I doing something wrong in the field? I began to question

15

my sense of values. Did I really want to be an anthropologist? I didn't know anymore.

The lack of positive mirroring—the failure in empathy of her self-objects—produced in this individual much self-doubt and questioning of her sense of identity as an anthropologist.

One comment made by the first informant cited here merits special elucidation, particularly in the present context. I am referring to the statement "I don't have to wait for the Ph.D., for an academic job, to be one [an anthropologist]. That's immaterial." The sentiments contained in this thought are echoed clearly in the following passage from a different informant: "I think that regardless of what my fieldwork comes to in academic terms, I've already decided that that really doesn't matter. Because I had the experience to make friends, and enter into a kind of relationship with people that I never had before, and that's of the greatest value to me. I have these friends, and this family I have now, my family, that's extremely important, powerful for me, more important than the academic issues, the intellectual concerns, than occupations."

Without gainsaying the importance of the fieldwork experience in the making of an anthropological identity—it is, after all, fieldwork that sets the stage, that cultivates the need for a new sense of identity—it is possible to see in the emphasis on the experience of fieldwork, and therefore the deemphasis on the importance of academics and occupations, a defense against a dimly felt sense of attack against the newly crystallized identity as an anthropologist. Raoul Schmiedeck (1979) has demonstrated that of all the possible constellations of bonds that serve to help maintain an individual's sense of identity, none is more important during young adulthood than those relating to one's occupation. Because the occupational forecast for newly hatched anthropologists is dim, I regard the student-initiate's emphasis on the experiential aspect of fieldwork as an attempt to maintain continuity with that one aspect of his experienced sense of identity as an anthropologist that cannot ever be denied him.[7] From this perspective, it is interesting that the only two of my informants who did not emphasize the experiential aspects of fieldwork were individuals who either had no worries about securing an academic position or experienced the field as remarkably identity-syntonic. I will say more on this point later.

Inevitably, a question arises at this point in my analysis that goes something like this: The fieldwork experience that you are thinking of is surely most unusual and probably rather extreme. Given what we know, do the majority of student-anthropologists really experience their fieldwork as a sort of symbolic death? Or are you talking about a few oddballs, discussion of whom would throw little or no light on the "typical" anthropologist's experience of fieldwork? In a word, do all fieldworkers experience the full range of psychological changes that you discussed above? And if not, why not?

This question has always proved particularly vexing to me, and I have vacillated a great deal in my feelings toward it. In my earlier work (1983; 1984), for example—work in which I was blinded by what I then thought of as the beauty of an uncorrupted model—I was content to answer yes, all fieldworkers and all aspects of relevant reality do indeed follow the dictates of my model. Innocents abound! Truth is ugly, however, and hence although I still believe that any and every fieldworker undergoes, *at some level and to some degree,* the experiences I have described, two factors now appear to me to be central in determining the depth and intensity of psychological change experienced by the anthropologist.

The first of these factors concerns the relative degree of overlap or discrepancy between the cognitive maps of the anthropologist and his people. The greater the overlap, the more suitable will be the mirroring the anthropologist receives from the indigenous population, the less will his sense of identity fragment, and vice versa (see Oberg 1972:84). Actually determining the degree of overlap or discrepancy between cognitive maps, however, is not simple or self-evident. A priori, it might be expected that the young, white American anthropologist who chooses to do fieldwork among a highland New Guinea tribe will experience a greater cognitive clash than if he had chosen to study a small French farming community. Certainly there does seem to be a greater difference in cognitive maps between an American and a New Guinea highlander than between an American and a French farmer. Were all other things equal, this discrepancy would produce a greater cognitive clash in relations between the first named pair. But, alas, all other things are not equal, or at least not necessarily so. The point that I am leading into here has been beautifully expressed by one of my informants: "I think it's easier if you're in a place that's very different. You don't expect any similarity. But if you're in a place like I was, you think, oh it's just like the United States. And the differences can be very subtle and catch you completely unaware. They look like they dress alike but it's not quite alike. So when you dress, they think you look funny or just badly dressed."

A similar point was made by another informant who had worked

17

in a European community: "It wasn't the easy way out for me [fieldwork in Europe]. If I had gone to a culture where I could have remained emotionally intact and still gotten good data, because it was such an alien culture, I wouldn't have had the kind of intimate relationships I had . . . I wouldn't have had what I'm calling the disintegration and the rebuilding."

It may be easier to reconcile the dissonance produced by the psychological clash of very different cultures than by ones that appear similar. Depending on his particular personality structure, the student-initiate may attempt, and find it easier, to wall off or isolate the more obviously different native than a more similar brethren. Elanor S. Bowen (1954:212–14) illustrates this tendency in her use of the term *savage*. Reacting to a joke about a blind man, her response is precise: " 'Quite.' My voice was as cold as my heart, and, as always seemed to happen here when I was deeply upset, I spoke English. 'Quite.' Typical peasant humor, but I am not a peasant and you are a bunch of savages." Denigrating the other (especially in one's native language[8]) is a remarkably efficient way of isolating oneself from disturbing influences that emanate from interaction with that other. Although it is remarkably efficient, this process does have limited usefulness. Even for one whose preferred or habitual mode of defense is splendid isolation, contact with the world of objects is ultimately necessary for sanity and survival; even the most deeply regressed schizophrenic reaches out to the world in some way (Fairbairn 1952; Searles 1979). And aside from these general human considerations, certainly for the anthropologist the range of usefulness of an isolatory defense is very limited. After all, to acquire the data he needs, he must interact, live, and probably feel with his people. In such a situation, the usefulness of isolation is probably limited to certain specific and short-lived instances when the student-initiate feels a deep need to defend his sense of self against disintegrative inroads.

I have raised these points in relation to cognitive clashing simply to point out that one must be very careful before concluding, without qualification, that, for example, working in a French farming community is always more pleasant, less shocking, and less likely to produce significant psychological change than working in the highlands of New Guinea or the rain forests of South America. The question of cognitive clashing must be investigated in relation to each fieldworker's particular personality dynamics as they relate to the studied culture.

A second factor that bears directly on the degree of psychological change experienced by the anthropologist during fieldwork concerns the state of the individual's self as he enters the field. If the structuralization of the self has been interrupted (developmental arrest) or otherwise disturbed and the stability, boundaries, and affective coloring of the self-representation are insecure and dark, there will be a predisposition toward feelings of self-fragmentation and self-loss (G. Klein 1976; Stolorow 1975). Such individuals lack the ability, in times of stress, to regress in the service of their own egos. They lack the sustenance provided by the emotional wealth that accompanies securely integrated and positively toned internalized (self) object relations (Kohut 1971; 1977).

When these two considerations—the relative difference in cognitive maps and the state of the student-anthropologist's self as he enters the field—are paired together, it is apparent that the fieldwork experience may produce psychological changes ranging along a continuum from the minor and superficial to the major and profound. If the student, who might be considered a "genital character"—the psychoanalytic ideal personality type—experiences little cognitive clashing, minor psychological change can be expected; if a student with marked vulnerabilities in his self-representation experiences much cognitive clashing, the fieldwork venture will be a shattering rite of death and rebirth. The middle range of the continuum will be, as middle ranges always are, soft and gray, with varying degrees of significant psychological change for the individuals falling there. Although the majority of student-initiates will probably fall in this middle range, the bias of my work falls unquestionably toward those who had a more psychologically affecting experience. I am particularly interested in those individuals who experienced fieldwork as a shattering rite of initiation. Even though these cases are more intrinsically psychologically interesting, it is also my belief that often the soft and fuzzy normal can be seen clearly only in relation to the hard and clean extreme. In analyzing an extreme instance of a phenomenon, both the events that need explaining and their conditioning antecedents stand forth much more clearly from the jumble of background factors than in middle-range cases. Once one has identified the characteristic features in the extreme case, it is then possible to turn and isolate these otherwise obscured features in the more normal case. This basic principle underlies much of the theory of "deviance" research in sociology as well as, and this is actually more relevant to my work here, the method of case study analysis in psychoanalytic psychology.

2

Fighting Back
Identity Maintenance in the Field

In its widest possible sense, however, a man's Self is the sum total of all that he can call his, not only his body and his psychic powers, but his clothes and his house, his wife and children, his ancestors and friends, his reputation and works, his lands and horses, and yacht and bank account. All these things give him the same emotions. If they wax and prosper, he feels triumphant; if they dwindle and die away, he feels cast down.
—William James, *The Principles of Psychology*

Let us try to imagine the feelings of a young student-anthropologist during the first few months of his initial fieldwork experience. The chances are very good, judging from all the available personal accounts of fieldwork, that our student is feeling less than euphoric and more than likely is depressed. If asked, he would probably maintain that his mood was justified: the natives are lazy, they won't cooperate, and worse yet, they refuse or are unable to understand the enormous importance of his work; they treat him like an idiot, or at best, like a person who is a little queer (imagine a grown-up, a twenty-six-year-old person, who cannot speak properly or do the simplest tasks correctly); the weather, the terrain, the importance of time— everything that our student knew so well and took for granted—is different.

Considered somewhat more abstractly, and from the vantage point of an outside and uninvolved investigator, the depression our student is feeling is at least partially rooted in the difficulties associated with maintaining a stable sense of self/identity while in the field. Most notably, in separating from his home world, the student-anthropologist has lost the innumerable identifications forged with that home world and the mirroring functions of his significant others (self-objects). In a word, he has lost two of the most potent means available for maintaining his sense of identity. What is our student to do then? Must he remain depressed and give up the sense of identity that he has struggled for twenty-six years to solidify? Is he to take this assault on his sense of identity sitting down, so to speak, and without a fight?

One of the few things about human beings that can be said with some degree of surety is that they will fight like hell and use every means at their disposal to maintain their senses of identity. When defending their senses of identity, people are nothing if not inventive, flexible, determined animals. Our anthropological fieldworker, then, may have lost the two most potent means of identity maintenance, but they need not remain irretrievably lost. If the anthropologist has lost the innumerable identifications with his home world, he must try to recover them; if he has lost the mirroring function of his significant others, he must try and recover it. The various behaviors used by the anthropologist in these interrelated quests form what I call defensive/reparative behaviors; they are defensive in trying to prevent identity fragmentation and reparative in mending damage already incurred.

Probably the simplest and most direct way for the anthropologist to regain a sense of the innumerable identifications with the home world that he has lost is through generating some link or continuity with that world. And people being what they are, inventive and flexible animals, this link may take one of many forms. Considered globally, this link may be established through the simple, albeit powerful, yearning "for the comfort of accustomed things" (Casagrande 1960:xii). To borrow Anthony Forge's (1967:223) description of this condition, during fieldwork the anthropologist develops a longing for his "civilization," both in terms of "Beethoven, beer, and bread" and as a place "where one has a place, where one is known." This link may be established through the recall of past memories, whether in dreams, in déjà-vu experiences, or simply in plain old everyday fantasies (see Hallowell 1955:94). Letters to and from the field, novel reading, or cravings for familiar foods and sex partners may serve to establish this link. Anything that offers the possibility of establishing a sense of symbolic continuity with the home world may be seized upon by the fieldworker as a means of identity maintenance.

It is interesting to observe in the light of this discussion that the typical symptoms of "culture shock"[1] are, or can be interpreted as, defensive/reparative attempts to maintain one's sense of identity. Typical symptoms of culture shock include the delay and at times

21

outright refusal to learn the language of the host country, village, and so on (one's native language is a powerful identity marker); an absent-minded, faraway stare (looking homeward); a desire for the company of people of one's own nationality (positive mirroring and remembrance of things past); and that "terrible longing to be back home, to be able to have a good cup of coffee and a piece of apple pie, to walk into that corner drugstore, to visit one's relatives, and in general, to talk to people who really make sense" (Oberg in Foster 1973:191).

There are a number of outstanding examples of this attempt to establish symbolic continuity with the home world in personal accounts of fieldwork. Although certain of these will be presented in greater depth in Parts II and III of this book, it is important to examine at least a few of them here. The majority of these examples need little additional commentary to reveal their significance.

Perhaps the two most explicit examples of this attempt to maintain continuity in one's sense of self are to be found in Bowen's (1954) account of her fieldwork in Africa:

> I needed a change, and not just a change of weather. After all, I had been in the bush since late July, almost four months. And it was still seven weeks to Christmas. . . . I ruffled the pages of my diary impatiently. I was perfectly alright, I told myself. It was merely a matter of hanging on to my resolution never again to forget who and what I was: an anthropologist and an American, an heir to civilization. The English were quite right. One had to dress for dinner. *One needed a symbol, some external sign,* to assist daily remembrance of what one was. It did not occur to me that the need for such artificial aids was alien to me and a sign that I was no longer myself. Instead, to help me over the next seven weeks, I called the cook and gave detailed orders for a Thanksgiving dinner. At the same time I told Sunday to lay out evening clothes, set the table with my best, and put out all the liquor in a fine array. I was no longer trying to learn how to survive in my new environment; I was concerned with sealing myself off from it. (222, 225; emphasis added)

> The fate they [natives] abhorred was a necessity to me. . . . Being alone and quiet was essential to some of my paperwork. But above all else, it was only in the privacy of my hut that I could be my real self. Publicly, I lived in the midst of a noisy and alien life. If I wanted conversation in my own language, I had to hold it with myself. If I wanted familiar music, I had to sing it to myself. If I wanted counsel from my own people, I had to turn to my books. I could escape my cultural

isolation only by being alone for a while every day with my books and my thoughts. *It was the one means of hanging on to myself,* of regaining my balance, of keeping my purpose in being out here before me, and of retaining my own values. (162; emphasis added)

Cornelius Osgood (1953) and Jean Briggs (1970a; 1970b) provide impressive evidence that food can maintain, or help to maintain, one's link to the home world. First, Osgood describes his experiences in the Canadian arctic: "Among my supplies for the winter I had transported five cans of preserved fruit . . . but my attitude toward these symbols of civilization had developed into almost worship, and the idea of consuming them I viewed as a sacramental rite. . . . On my birthday, I opened the third of my cans of fruit for lunch having shared two in former celebrations" (37, 193). Although Osgood does not mention the nature of these earlier celebrations, it is impossible to ignore the significance of the one he does mention. An individual's birthday is a powerful identity marker, and what better way to celebrate it than with a can of preserved identity (fruit)? Briggs described similar experiences among the Eskimo:

> The value that my . . . food supplies had for me . . . was primarily symbolic. . . . Fish were usually plentiful, and I was rarely hungry; nevertheless I craved the solace of oatmeal, dates, boiled rice . . . and much of the time my secret thoughts crept guiltily around one problem: how best to create opportunities for gorging myself on these familiar foods without having to share them with the visitors. It is hard for anyone who has not experienced isolation from his familiar world to conceive the vital importance of maintaining symbolic ties with that world and the sense of deprivation that results from their absence. One can be driven to lengths that seem ludicrous once one is safely back on home ground. Unpacking on my return, I was amazed to find eight sesame seeds that I had hoarded, carefully wrapped in tinfoil, for an emergency: a time of emotional starvation. Food provided many comforts beyond the fundamental satisfaction of a full stomach. (1970a:228–29)

> The evening was a time of recuperation—a time to read Jane Austen, to indulge in secret feasts of half-frozen dates and chocolate, and simply to think . . . uninterrupted. Books, food, and thoughts all provided a much needed link with the world I had left behind. (1970b:23)

The following example is particularly interesting in that it concerns the experiences of a non-Western, more particularly a Korean, anthropologist on a field trip among two American Indian groups:

23

The cultural similarities between the Cherokees and rural Korean peasants struck me. Eerie feelings of déjà-vu crept over me when I spotted a woman carrying a child on her back and a dipper made from a gourd hanging on a wall. For a few moments, I was back in a Korean peasant village, a law student conducting a survey. . . . And, also, as I saw Joan's mother, she brought back memories of my grandmother whom I had forgotten while I have been living here in America. In some ways, I feel as if I am in my native village attending the meeting of the village elders. I feel I should speak Korean, illusion though it is, and you would understand the language. (Kim 1977:69, 114)

Diaries and letters to and from the field are apt to be excellent sources in aiding the maintenance of one's sense of identity. One of the more important functions of diaries is to translate otherwise chaotic events into some order that makes sense to the individual in terms of his own lived past. As Rosemary Firth puts it in talking of her diary: "It became for me a sort of lifeline, or checking point to measure changes in myself. . . . Mine was used as an emotional outlet for an individual subjected to disorientating changes in his personal and social world" (1972:15). I will be discussing diaries and letters in great depth in the pages ahead (especially in relation to Malinowski's field experiences), so these few comments must suffice for now.

It is also possible for an anthropologist's dreams to serve as identity-maintenance devices. Laura Nader (1970), for example, reports that while in the field she noticed an extraordinary increase in the number of dreams she was able to remember. The majority of these dreams focused on her early childhood and teenage years in her natal culture. Barbara G. Anderson (1971) points out that this latter phenomenon is typical among anthropologists in the field. Surely, one function of this dreaming of past memories is identity maintenance; it is as if the dreams were saying, on one level, "Do not lose yourself completely. You are still the same person you were as a little girl. There is continuity, despite your feelings to the contrary."

In addition to reinforcing past memories, dreams can serve the cause of identity maintenance by blurring the distinction between the anthropologist's home world and his current field area. On this point, Frederica DeLaguna (1977) is brief but effective. Describing the sounds that emanate from an iceberg-filled bay in Greenland, she states: "During the day I do not notice the noise very much, but at night I am astonished to hear how loud it is. It does not seem to be a strange noise, for when I am half asleep I seem to hear the familiar

24

noises of home: a train shunting, traffic going down the road, the subway roaring past" (123).

The last point that I wish to consider here, before turning to a second class of defensive/reparative behaviors, is the problem of sexuality for the fieldworker. Obviously, this is a touchy subject and little has been written about it. The overwhelming impression one gets from the few references to this topic (for example, Hsu 1979:518; Stocking 1968:193), as well as from personal anecdotes—the best source of data—is that the vast majority of anthropologists remain celibate while in the field. There are a host of standard anthropological rationalizations available to help one understand this behavior, or lack thereof, but certainly one of the more neglected—identity maintenance—must be given a hearing. An anthropologist's self-imposed celibacy can help him preserve his sense of identity by forcing him to direct his probably acute sexual needs and fantasies outside of the field environment and back to his home culture. By doing this, the anthropologist creates a "strong and ever present link" with his home culture and so solidifies his sense of identity (Forge 1967:224). The celibate anthropologist is, if nothing else, secure in his sense of identity.

Dressing up in good clothes, celebrating holidays, keeping a diary, writing and receiving letters, dreaming of past memories, avoiding sexual relations with natives, and craving familiar foods are but a few examples of the many and various means used by a fieldworker to maintain or reestablish continuity with those innumerable identifications with his home world that compose a major part of his sense of identity. However effective these maneuvers may be, they must inevitably be considered secondary to another class of defensive/reparative behaviors, those associated with the mirroring content provided by another human being. A person's sense of identity is, at bottom, instilled and maintained through those reflections mirrored onto him by his significant others (Kohut 1977; Lichtenstein 1977; G. H. Mead 1934). Thrane (1979) and Greenacre (1958) have further emphasized that not all people are equally suitable to serve as identity-syntonic mirrors; for an individual to be a successful mirror, he needs to be more or less similar, of the same ilk, as the person he is mirroring. In the light of these points an interesting problem arises: as the fieldworker experiences feelings of discontinuity and identity fragmentation, where will he find a suitable mirror to reflect back to him a secure sense of his identity? The anthropologist is, by definition, adrift in a sea of foreigners; the eyes that mirror his soul are alien, unfamiliar. Is there any way that these alien eyes can be made more familiar and, therefore, less disturbing?

The most common solution to this problem may be for the field-worker either to use "naturally" qualified individuals or to make others become qualified to serve as narcissistic objects, that is, as objects that can be used to maintain, buttress, or retrieve one's sense of identity (Stolorow 1975). In practice, "qualified" here means some characteristic of an individual that a fieldworker may be able to seize upon as a means of restoring some aspect of his sense of identity; for example, the individual's temperament, intellectual abilities, or position in society may appear to the fieldworker to be similar to his own temperament, intellectual abilities, or position in society. This similarity may then enable the individual to provide the field-worker with a source of positive mirroring. As examples of "naturally" qualified individuals, those whose principal mirroring characteristics are genuine and not projected onto or into them by the fieldworker, I would cite the following two accounts.

Choong S. Kim (1977) is a Korean anthropologist who chose to do his fieldwork in the United States. In the following account, he is using an Asian couple as a narcissistic object:

> When I finally returned to my motel room, I was exhausted from the events of the day. I did not feel like eating anything . . . I was very frustrated and threw myself on my bed. Suddenly the motel recep-tionist called me and said, "Hey, the Yamamoto couple are here. They're waitin' for you at the restaurant." Frankly, I still had some special feelings about Japanese owing to the antagonisms that devel-oped while the Japanese occupied Korea during most of my boyhood. However, when the motel receptionist called me, I did not remember those old enmities at all. I was happy to know they were in Pinetown. I cannot give any adequate explanation of why, unless I figured we shared many of the same feelings because we were fellow Asians in an alien society. I rushed to the restaurant at once . . . I enjoyed eating my meal for the first time since I had come to Pinetown. (53)

Briggs (1970a) appears, on the basis of her own description, to have been a fairly volatile personality when she chose to study the re-markably unvolatile Eskimo. The problems this posed for her sense of identity are adequately attested to in the following passage, in which she demonstrates the value of a narcissistic object, a woman named Niqi:

> I never responded to her childlike antics, because they embarrassed me and because I feared to augment the rather considerable reputation

for childishness that I myself had acquired. But for the very reason
that I, like Niqi, *was* "childish" in Eskimo eyes, I eventually developed quite a kindred feeling for her. We were, in a sense, children together, neither of us able to maintain the behavior proper to an
Eskimo adult. . . . And both of us were subject to the same disapproval
from the rest of society on account of our reprehensible volatility. . . .
Another bond between us was the fact that I found Niqi's impulsive
actions reassuring and refreshing in face of the tremendous pressure to
self-control that oppressed me, a volatile alien in Eskimo society. It
was because her actions were "familiar" to me that I liked them; in
my world, too, people sulk or shout when they are angry, ask questions when they are curious, cry when their feelings are hurt—so I
empathized with Niqi when she did these things; it was as though I
were witnessing a fragment of my own culture, and it gave me relief.
(201)

I think that it is possible to maintain, with a fair degree of certainty, that these two descriptions represent naturally qualified narcissistic objects. In Kim's case, the critical feature appears to have
been the couple's status as Japanese, a feature of their birth, and in
Briggs's case, the independent evidence bearing on Niqi's status (her
household was built across a river and isolated from the main camp,
the ostracism accorded her by other Eskimo, and so on [Briggs
1970a:198–200, 203–8, 214–23]) is convincing. Except in cases such
as these, however, in which the evidence is remarkably straightforward, the dividing line between a naturally versus a projectively
qualified narcissistic object is often difficult to determine. I want to
reserve further comment on this point until after I have clarified the
nature of a projectively qualified narcissistic object.

There appear to be, essentially, two interrelated techniques involved in the creation of a projectively qualified narcissistic object:
projective identification and/or the establishment of a narcissistic
transference. In the former instance, the fieldworker projects and
deposits bits of his own self into the "ethnographic other," thus rendering him a most suitable source of mirroring; in the latter case,
whatever the particular variety of narcissistic transference developed (Kohut 1971; Kohut and Wolf 1978), the fieldworker turns the
ethnographic other into one of his own past significant others (self-
objects), often his father or mother or combination of both (but not
necessarily so), thus again rendering the native an effective source of
mirroring. Just as in the consulting room, so in the field, these techniques are often found entangled together. Probably, however, the
tendency toward projective identification is found more frequently

than a fully blown narcissistic transference; the latter requires, to develop fully, a carefully structured set of circumstances that are not likely to be realized in the field situation (Kohut 1971).

One of the most fruitful areas in which to investigate the effects of projective identification is anthropologists' descriptions of their principal informants. In the traditional fieldwork situation, when the student is alone in a foreign culture, one might expect that as the student experiences the fragmentation of his identity, he would turn toward those closest to him, often his principal informant(s), for support. And because this support is crucial for the maintenance of his sense of identity, must we assume that the student has left the matter to chance? I think not. From this perspective, is it any wonder that so many anthropologists (see Casagrande 1960) describe their principal informants as "social scientists without a home," "natural ethnographers," or "primitive philosophers"? Keeping the work of Thrane and Greenacre in mind, what better attributes could the initiate-anthropologist equip his native mirror with than those of a potential social scientist? This discussion should be kept in mind when considering the following descriptions.

All of the following, with the exception of Forge (1972), are drawn from Joseph Casagrande's (1960) fine collection of accounts by anthropologists of their principal informants. I will present each description in turn and then discuss all together at the end.

Raymond Firth (1960) has described his Tikopian informant as a man with whom he could find an "intellectual refuge," a man who could "discuss problems in general terms." Although somewhat naive about technology and the West, "he was sensitive and perceptive in his understanding of human relationships." Further, Firth "could discuss *any* problem with him frankly and freely, exposing my arguments to him with *all* the intellectual resources I could muster, and receiving from him question, comment, and elucidation on a *similar level*" (3; emphasis added). Firth's informant was "if not the best informed, at least the most systematically minded Tikopian in respect to ritual affairs" (5). "He could adopt a critical, experimental attitude. . . . He was particularly lucid in talking about human relationships and found generalizations easy" (6).

Thomas Gladwin's (1960) account is a true classic in this genre: "Petrus Mailo is a man secure, and therefore humble, in the certainty of his own wisdom. He is a statesman who, but for the setting and character of his tasks, could take his place among the historic molders of our common destiny" (42). He has a "magnetic personality,"

28

and yet "he is a man who seldom obtrudes himself into any situation, yet whose presence can somehow never be left out of account. . . . Petrus sitting in thought—withdrawn into himself, almost brooding—is inscrutable but vastly impressive. One waits in respect, although with some slight discomfort, before his dynamic immobility" (48). Petrus "is his own anthropologist, yet a far surer one than any outside student of his culture could hope to be" (61). Gladwin saw Petrus as a paternal figure and sometimes believed that "Petrus could never be wrong" (54).

James Watson (1960:130) saw his principal informant as a stranger,[2] a man caught between two worlds, an orphan in a cultural sense, who was "questing in an alien world."

With David Mandelbaum (1960) and his experience in India, we are back to the world-historical level again. Sulli, his informant, "stands forth bold and clear" (274) and "is eminently distinctive" (275), although or perhaps because he has suffered as an outcast, a loner, a stranger. He has an impressively "strong and determined character . . . [it is a privilege] to know a person of such force and character, whether it be a figure on the grand stage of world history or in the minute microcosm of Kota life" (279). "Sulli has the kind of integrating, abstracting mind which one may consider to be more properly the prerogative of the ethnological theorist than of the ethnologist's informant" (307).

Muchona the Hornet, Turner's (1960) interpreter of Ndembu symbolism, was a marginal man, "entirely unable to belong" (346), yet possessing the "bright glance of the true enthusiast" (334). Turner describes his meetings with Muchona in telling fashion: "In our 'seminars' . . . a new and exhilarating intellectual dimension had opened up to him as well as to myself. . . . At such times he had the bright hard eye of some raptor, hawk, or kite, as he poised over a definitive explanation. Watching him, I . . . used to fancy that he would have been truly at home scoring debating points on a don's dais, gowned or perhaps in a habit." Muchona was truly a "philosophy don" (355).

Finally, according to Forge (1972:257), "If any one thing has convinced me of the virtues of the British social-structure tradition of anthropology . . . it was the endorsement [it] received from Tswamung." Forge discussed these virtues with his informant in New Guinea "in a way sometimes rather like a seminar" (257). Tswamung, perhaps because he was a marginal man, became an "enthusiastic anthropologist" (269), whose "analysis of the symbolic properties and totems . . . was masterly" (270). "The need for two-way relationships in which the anthropologist has something to contribute of more than symbolic value can become intense. One can have many friends . . . but my side of the relationship was based on my pseudo-Abelam role—my existence before I arrived in the area was irrelevant. Tswamung [gave] . . . me hope in the worst of the early days" (272).

As Forge implies in his last statement, an anthropologist needs to develop a relationship in which his identity, his "prior existence," counts for something. I believe that one way this can be accomplished, as these passages hint, is through projective identification. That is, the anthropologist turns the native other into a person who can—in fact, who must (because the native is now a replica of the anthropologist)—appreciate the anthropologist's sense of identity for what it really is. There is also evidence, in the Gladwin passage especially, of the establishment of a narcissistic transference relationship. Gladwin describes his informant as the archetype of the "wise, old man" or as a cross between Buddha and Confucius. Such abnormal overevaluation (the world-historical imagery especially) is familiar to the modern analyst as the therapeutic remobilization of primitive narcissistic configurations characterized by the activation of omnipotent object representations.

In arguing these points, I am not denying that many informants are exceptional individuals. But it is precisely their special qualities that serve as the hook upon which the anthropologist can hang his projections; it is as if an informant needs to be something of an analyst for the anthropologist to turn him into a fully blown "philosophy don" and make that attribution convincing (see Searles 1979 for the hook metaphor). This discussion should also render clear my reasons for avoiding a strict division between naturally and projectively qualified narcissistic objects—each, in a sense, falls in with the other and contributes to the total image.

Some people might still argue, of course, and maintain that these informants really were as special as they were painted. Perhaps the seemingly overblown and exaggerated descriptions (again the world-historical imagery, the incredible sophistication in social theory of these individuals, and the like) are true to reality. Perhaps it is a mere coincidence that so many anthropologists describe their informants in like terms (see Casagrande 1960). And yet, even if such were the case, my ultimate argument would still be intact. The anthropologist would still have *found* a most perfect mirror; he would not have *created* one, however. And what would be the content of the reflections received back from such a mirror if not the image of the student-initiate as anthropologist?

In addition to projective identification and the establishment of a transference relationship, there is another and rather different defensive maneuver that the student may employ in an effort to secure positive mirroring. I am thinking here of what in popular jargon is known as "going native," or, in my terminology, secondary identification with the native culture. Contrary to the other defensive maneuvers mentioned above, in cases of secondary identification the student attempts to reconsolidate his sense of identity by internalizing various aspects and symbols of the native culture in which he is immersed. It is almost as if the student were operating on the principle that any sense of identity is better than none at all—at least temporarily. Secondary identification enables the student to feel that once again he has a place where he belongs, that he is again a member of a larger, more enduring whole. It enables him to experience the powerful and positive overtones associated with acceptance by members of the native culture. To borrow Morris Freilich's nice little phrase, secondary identification "regenerates the anthropologist's psyche" (1970:536).

The evidence of this secondary identification may take several forms, some of which I want to mention and illustrate here. I will begin this discussion with that "malady" very commonly observed among anthropologists newly returned from the field, reverse culture shock. Alan Beals provides an excellent example of this phenomenon:

> We could not understand why people were so distant, so hard to reach, or why they talked and moved so quickly. We were a little frightened at the sight of so many white faces and we could not understand why no one stared at us, brushed against us, or admired our baby. We could not understand the gabble of voices on the television set. When we could understand people, they seemed to be telling lies. The trust and warmth seemed to have gone out of life to be replaced by coldness and inhumanity. . . . Simple pleasures . . . did not exist. . . . Where in Gopalpur there was a feeling of stability, timelessness, and adaptation to nature, even the houses and buildings in the United States seemed to express instability, sterility. . . . We had returned to civilization. We were suffering from culture shock. (1970:55)

Reverse culture shock, that feeling of anxiety that results from losing all of one's newly familiar signs and symbols, is subject to the

31

same explanation as plain old culture shock. In either case, the innumerable identifications through which an individual seeks to maintain some sense of identity are broken apart. The only difference
between the two is that in culture shock, the identity that is being
attacked is primary, whereas in reverse culture shock, the secondary
identity is being attacked. To experience reverse culture shock, a
person must have experienced some degree of secondary identification with the foreign culture. In a similar vein, Freilich (1970:532–
36) has argued that the profound sorrow some anthropologists experience when leaving "their people" would be difficult to understand
without postulating some degree of secondary identification.

Reverse culture shock is a phenomenon that appears, by definition, once the anthropologist has left the field. There are a number
of other behaviors, however, that the anthropologist may produce
while in the field that indicate secondary identification with the
native culture. The following selections, ranging from a few lines to
a short vignette, illustrate these behaviors indicative of secondary
identification. "During my last week in Malaya, I had a nightmare
dream, in which I *was* a Malay peasant, a woman crouching over the
fire to blow up the embers for an evening meal. I awoke in terror,
momentarily confused about my own identity, Malaya woman or
English scientist. . . . To me, the experience of becoming an anthropologist includes that of learning to play a part so well that one may
occasionally forget whether it is a natural one or not" (Rosemary
Firth 1972:3).

Solon T. Kimball has related and interpreted, in brilliant fashion, a
truly strange experience that he underwent during his Irish field
tenure:

> This night was no different from the others. . . . Suddenly a figure ap-
> peared from the side street and stopped about three feet away. My first
> thought was that this was a member of the Civic Guard who patrol
> the streets at night and take the names of those who are out after
> midnight. I greeted the presumed guard with a "Hello," but there was
> no reply and I thought the figure began to move toward me. My sense
> of danger and my reaction were almost simultaneous. I kicked with all
> my force at the midsection of the approaching threat. But there was no
> connection with anything solid. Instead my foot went through the air
> and I was nearly thrown off balance. The figure moved backward a foot
> or two, and I had the sense that I had repelled what was intended to be
> a friendly advance. The figure then disappeared. In the meantime I had
> reconnected with the bell and was pushing with all my might. In a few

moments the porter arrived and opened the door. As I stepped quickly inside, somewhat shaken, I said in what I tried to make an off-hand manner, "I have just seen a ghost outside the hotel door." (1972:189)

After Kimball reported his experience, he found himself the center of much favorable attention. Further, he reports that he acquired a new status that had not been previously granted him and therefore no longer felt constrained in his dealings with the Irish; he now shared an experience with them (1972:190). His interpretation of the significance of these events is precise:

The specific problem is how far my ghostly encounter may be considered as some index or measure of the extent to which I had absorbed the Irish perspective and been incorporated in Irish culture. . . . But if one were to choose an identification with powerful and positive overtones of acceptance, it would be difficult to find an area that was more deeply embedded in the Irish past and present than belief in the supernatural. Is it possible that unwittingly in this precipitous and dramatic fashion I had declared a fully Irish cultural perspective? (1972:191–92)

Alexander Alland (1975:x) is equally telling, if somewhat more humorous, in describing his experiences among the Abron:

Early in fieldwork, I began to learn how and why things were done. After some time, I thought I understood, even felt, as an Abron might. I began to identify with "my people," so much so that during a trip to "alien" country my attitude toward the non-Abron villagers was colored by the sentiments expressed by my Abron companions. I thought that my feelings of mistrust and hostility must in some way be Abron. I am white-skinned, but after several weeks in the field, I forgot that I did not look like everyone else. Not shaving, I had little cause to use a mirror. As my identity became Abron, I turned black in my imagination. I tried to convert this into physical change by sunbathing. From the Abron point of view, it was probably one of my most idiotic behaviors. Their country is about six degrees north of the equator, and all normal people seek the shade at midday.

This passage is remarkable in that it appears that Alland, in his haste—indeed, his need—to assume an Abron-like identity, went beyond the pale of sensibility; he went overboard in his actions and, ironically, behaved in a non-Abron fashion.

The last example that I want to present in this chapter requires a somewhat more detailed presentation. This particular experience is derived from a paper in which an anthropologist, Bruce Grindal

33

(1983), recounts his feelings surrounding two funerals that he attended while in the field in Africa. Going to a burial ceremony is not an unusual occurrence for an anthropologist in the field. Grindal's experience is of great interest, however, for the remarkable intensity of his feelings.

Arriving in time to witness the preparation of the body for the first burial, Grindal describes the scene as follows: "The corpse of Ali was covered from head to foot with a large cloth and was lying on its side. Protecting the body from the dirt floor was a cowskin. The corpse was putrid, oozing juices from its body. . . . Even though the corpse had been washed about three hours earlier, the stench of the room was horrible. Finding it overpowering I turned away from the room." Later during the burial proper, "one of the *bukaliba* [gravediggers] took my hand and led me to the edge of the grave. He asked whether I wanted to go down into the grave and inspect their work. As I recall this moment, I was overcome by a most profound sense of revulsion, nausea, and trembling. The stench of Ali's corpse pervaded the yard and it seemed that I stood for an eternity on the edge of the grave. Then I became possessed by a most disquieting fear that were I to have gone down into the grave, the *bukaliba* would have used their iron hoes to smash my head . . . I bolted back." After the burial, and throughout the rest of the day, Grindal reports that "the putrid smell from Ali's corpse was on my clothes, on my skin, under my fingernails, in my hair. I reeked of death; it even filled the air of my dusty 1962 Volkswagon. Yet as I drove . . . I came to feel that the smells had become part of me." Grindal then recalls his impression of an abandoned village he had seen earlier: "It looked and smelled of death."

In the terminology of existential psychiatry, Grindal's world has closed and darkened. In terminology more in keeping with the thesis of this chapter, Grindal's identity had hit "rock bottom" (Erikson in Lichtenstein 1977:185), had undergone a "metamorphosis" (Lichtenstein 1977:184) and reached its ground or zero point. Grindal now feels the smell of death to be a part of him. He is symbolically dead. It is from such a zero point that Grindal will reemerge to build a new sense of identity.

The beginning of this rebirth can be seen in Grindal's comments regarding his feelings attendant on his presence at a second funeral, held a few days after the first: "The grave was not a solitary grave . . . but a communal grave which had been re-opened to receive the body of the Tumukuoro's drummer. I recall now that I walked to the brink of the grave and stared into the dark abyss which contained the bodies of generations in varying stages of decomposition. Unlike my experience at the burial of Ali, I was drawn by the odor of death which emanated from the dark and putrid bowels of the grave. I teetered on the brink of the grave, enraptured by the scent of death. Suddenly . . . Bajo embraced me tightly and told me to calm my heart." As D. W. Winnicott (1971) points out, there is a time for the analyst to keep silent and let the patient discover his own interpretations. As Grindal comments: "Death is an event of great power, to be experienced in accordance with the strength of one's heart. My witnessing of a death divination was in excess of this strength. . . . I had sickened. My heart had changed. I was no longer content to be a polite middle-class American anthropologist. Instead, I wished to let fall like a veil the whole condition of my upbringing, so that I could play and learn the secrets of those crazy men who divine over the dead."

Recapitulating these interpretations in my terminology, it is clear that Grindal had begun to reconsolidate his sense of identity, but along the lines provided by the culture at hand and not those of his own home culture. For this particular African culture, the role of *bukaliba* is one of great import—such men witness "many wonderful things." That Grindal had been able to consolidate, to some extent, such an identity can be seen in the increased strength and self-assurance with which he was able to confront the fact of death at the second burial. He now no longer trembled at death but was drawn to it as a "calling." Witness also his reaction to a threat of physical injury: "At the entrance to the inner yard [funeral site], I was stopped by an old man brandishing a battle axe. In a most rude way, he told me to get out, obviously threatening to strike me. I remained firm. I felt that I could care less about what he could do to me and stood boldly before him." In further support of this interpretation is an experience Grindal describes as an altered state of consciousness. During one phase of the second burial ceremony, certain ritual experts sing over the dead man in an effort to open a path for his spirit to the ancestor world. The success of such a venture is indicated by the corpse's movement, for example, dancing. Grindal witnessed such movement: "I cannot say when the experience first occurred. . . . The corpse, shakened by spasms, then rose to its feet, and in ecstatic frenzy spun around and danced with the *goka* [funeral singers]. . . . Then a most wonderful thing happened. The talking-drums on the roof of the dead man's house began to show a bright light which was so strong that it drew the dancers to the rooftop; whereupon the corpse picked up the drumsticks and began to play. . . . I remained for some time, trembling in the aftermath of the experience." In attempting to understand his experience, Grindal states: "Upon reflection, it does not seem strange that I witnessed the ancestors dance; . . . I *saw* the collective power of the drummer's household and the whole lineage of the chief of Tumu. I *saw* what the others around me saw: the passionate resurrection of the power of the ancestors." Grindal saw what the others saw because he was, in fact, one with them. He had sufficiently identified himself with the *bukaliba* to see what they all saw.

Grindal is now an anthropologist at an eastern university, however, and not a *bukaliba* in a small African society. His return to and rediscovery of anthropology as his "significant symbol" of transcendence was mediated by what I would describe as a transference relationship that he established with his principal informant, Kojo. In Grindal's words: "Kojo, when I knew him, was a quiet, a strong and proud man. A person of impeccable discipline. . . . Though I never asked I would have guessed his age to have been in the late 50's or early 60's. Age seems unimportant, however, for he struck one as timeless. . . . There were occasions when I was impressed, if not awestruck, by his physical strength." Grindal goes on to list numerous anecdotes, too many and too long to quote here, concerning Kojo's "mental and psychic powers."

The focal nature of this relationship for the solidification of Grindal's identity is highlighted during a three-day period following his witnessing of the two burial ceremonies. Apparently, the catalyst igniting these events was two comments made by Grindal—one recounting the threat he experienced when the man came at him with a battle ax, the other when he "spoke jokingly about how the *bukaliba* had invited him into the grave" followed by his consideration that "maybe I should become a *bukaliba*." Upon hearing these comments, Kojo became very upset and warned Grindal: "Don't you talk foolish. . . . Those men, they be doing nothing but . . . laughing and playing their tricks all the time. . . . They like you. They like playing with you." Grindal then comments: "What Kojo said impressed me profoundly. As the days passed his warnings set deeply in my heart. Again I felt the same sickness and shortness of breath. Kojo again watched my condition with grim concern."

Grindal is here having to deal with the realization of a threat to his symbolic rebirth and existence—that he had begun to reconsolidate his identity along the lines of a false identification. Compound-

36

ing this factor, if Kojo was a transference figure for Grindal, his admonishment would have inflicted a powerful narcissistic injury to Grindal's sense of self. After some ten months in the field, he, a researcher, did not know how to differentiate the possible from the impossible, the serious from the humorous.

Grindal's final breakdown, entailing the destruction of his false secondary identity and the beginnings of his true primary one, occurred just a few days later. Kojo had prepared some "heart medicine" (a "black pasty substance") for Grindal to ingest to cure himself. "I reached into the porridge with my fingers and tasted it. It was horrible! My stomach convulsed and I turned away, only to feel Kojo kneeling behind me with his hands on my shoulders. Momentarily, a feeling of calm set over me. Kojo then moved his hands slowly over my chest, and he said softly: 'Don't lose your heart here master. This is not your home.' I recall, I cried."

This is a brilliant demonstration of therapeutic empathy, coupled with a finely balanced understanding for the importance of a well-timed and well-delivered interpretation. And the content of Kojo's interpretation is easily translatable into my terminology. Restating those two lines here yields: "Don't lose your identity here. The roots of it lie within the context of your home world." It appears from this example that Grindal was finally able, if not to secure, at least to activate the potential for securing, an anthropological identity through the mediation of a transference figure/narcissistic object.

One final question concerning the various types of defensive/reparative behavior needs to be dealt with here: how effective are they? Can the activation of these behaviors halt or otherwise reverse identity fragmentation? The answer to these questions depends on the extent to which the student-anthropologist experiences feelings of self-dissolution and self-fragmentation. When these feelings only, so to speak, scratch the more superficial layers of the anthropologist's self, that is, when the structuralization of the anthropologist's self had proceeded without disturbance and cognitive clashing is less than maximal, one would expect these various defensive/reparative behaviors to be more or less effective in halting the fragmentation of the self. Naturally, this does not mean that the student will be rid of his "identity crisis" after a few letters from home or something of the sort. But it does mean that the student will be able to maintain his identity crisis within reasonable and controllable bounds. If, however, these feelings of fragmentation penetrate to deeper levels of the anthropologist's self-experience, particularly if the structuralization of the student's self has been disturbed and some degree of cognitive clashing exists, even the massive activation of defensive/reparative behaviors will not prevent the center from giving way, will not prevent the student from losing, in a vital sense, his sense of identity. In fact, in an individual with a vulnerable self-representation, the massive activation of defensive/reparative behaviors, particularly projective identification, may well aid or hasten the process of identity fragmentation. Feelings of "self-depletion" often result from massive projective identification. It is almost as if the self projects too many bits of itself away to coalesce again properly (M. Klein 1975:141–75; Robbins 1982). If the self is built on a foundation of shifting sands, hallucinatory wish-fulfillment, which is in essence the nature of the help provided by defensive/reparative behaviors, cannot stand for long against the overwhelming reality confronting the individual.[3] In cases of this sort, the initiate's sense of identity will largely collapse, only later to be reconsolidated through an identification with the discipline of anthropology as mediated via the creative work.

Or so we shall see.

Part II
Plain Old Everyday Fieldwork

3

The Typical Field Experience

The natives are superficially agreeable, but . . . they go in for cannibalism, headhunting, infanticide, incest, avoidance and joking relationships, and biting lice in half with their teeth.
—Margaret Mead, *Letters from the Field, 1925–1975*

The majority of anthropologists probably do not experience their fieldwork as a shattering rite of death and rebirth—there are no statistics on so subjective a topic. They do not generally experience the field as a searing and brutal attack against their sense of identity, as a major psychological trauma. Nevertheless, the same general constellation of themes that I isolated in the first two chapters as occurring in extreme instances also characterizes the "average" or "typical" field experience—the experience produced when an anthropologist with a reasonably stable self-structure encounters less than maximal cognitive clashing during fieldwork. In typical experiences, the anthropologist will undergo an attack against his sense of identity, will engage in defensive/reparative behavior to fend off that attack, and will identify with his work and with anthropology, although to a lesser extent and depth than in the more extreme situations. The differences between an extreme as opposed to a "typical" fieldwork experience are largely quantitative and not qualitative.

The difference in intensity of field experiences was first brought home to me when, in my quest to locate individuals on the extreme end of the continuum, I spoke with a great many fieldworkers who claimed and actually appeared not to have been significantly changed by their field experience. This is not meant to imply that such individuals breezed through fieldwork without any major affectual problems or responses, or that their experiences were of less value or not truly genuine. Rather, unlike the individuals to be discussed in Part III, these fieldworkers do not return from the field seeking, or better, driven to reorient and center their respective senses of identity

41

around the symbol of anthropology as mediated via their work. These people just don't say, "the experience in the field, it's me" *and mean it literally.* They undergo no such significant personality change.

To illustrate what does happen to the identity maintenance of anthropologists who undergo a typical fieldwork experience, I will present four vignettes taken from my interviews with fieldworkers. These four individuals were all without any trace of significant self-pathology, that is, there were no obvious vulnerabilities in their self-representation; they seemed well-adjusted (their psychological defenses were in good order) and happy with their lives. In presenting their views, I have tried to maintain an experience near, evocative style of writing and to stay as close to the actual interview format (Appendix A) as was possible. I have, however, routinely changed facts that I felt might compromise my informants' anonymity. In no case have any of these changes affected my interpretations.

Fieldwork in Northern Europe: Vignette 1

This vignette concerns the field experience of a young woman ("Karen"), age twenty-six, during her approximately ten-month stay in a small northern European fishing community. This particular interview contains some very fine material relating to the identity attack that anthropologists experience in the field. For example, in response to my question concerning her orientation to fieldwork, Karen responded:

> Definitely Malinowski school, definitely Malinowski school. The danger in that is going native. The great danger in that is going native. And the great danger in that too is allowing your own personality to disintegrate. It has to disintegrate to a certain extent, but you have to be constantly rebuilding it. In the situation you have to constantly rebuild it or you are going to fall apart. You walk into the field and you're an infant and they're going to restructure your entire adulthood for you if you let them. I got lessons in not being middle class. You know they told me what I couldn't say, what I could say, how I could act, how I couldn't act, by every movement and gesture, by every time an eyebrow rose, by every time someone whispered behind my back.
>
> Q.: You were very much an infant then?
>
> A.: Very much an infant. It's interesting because the group of people I associated with over the length of my research went from childhood friends, teenage friends, adolescent friends, to adult friends. Very much that type of progression. The relationships had been there all the time but the concentration, you see. The children, I spent most of

the time with the children on a daily basis in the first part of my fieldwork, and with my parents, my surrogate parents. In the second phase of my research, it overlapped slightly with teenagers. And in the last section very definitely I had my adult friends. And those people I turned to when [a friend in the United States] died, for example. That hit me quite hard. . . . That was the day when my adulthood in that culture actually started, definitely from that day. Because I went to one of my adult, to D. [a principal informant] and she got a bunch of brandy and we sat there for about four hours and just blathered. . . . We talked about the people that mattered in our lives that died. . . . It helped. . . . I definitely moved through a life span there, and I definitely had my personality broken down. Broken down and replaced with the way I see myself now. . . . Not a complete change, of course, but a shift in self-perception. I could never be [her former identity] again now. . . . It's part and parcel of the whole shift in self-perception.

These passages are interesting and suggestive. What Karen terms "personality disintegration" I refer to as identity disintegration. And she is able to specify the motivating factor behind this disintegration—the natives told her what she could and could not do, say, act, and so on. That is, the natives began to reflect back onto her their own set of expectations (mirroring) about what her sense of herself should entail. There is also a powerful suggestion that this mirroring induced in her a degree of secondary identification with the native culture; she moved through her own developmental life span and became an adult in the culture.

Approaching this question of personality disintegration from a slightly different angle revealed the culture shock imagery and negative feelings associated with it:

I was depressed. You know that depression that you get where you go down to being sad and then you go below that and you don't feel anything. I kept flipping back and forth between the sadness and the emptiness. I had left my family, I had left my country, I had left everything, and I was opening myself up. . . . I had to use all these things I was unfamiliar with. There were all these strange people, in a strange situation. Even though it should have been familiar because I had been there before. It wasn't. Everything was alien. I don't know whether that was me imposing that alien feeling on it or whether it has really changed that much. . . . I cut my nails, stripped them off of fingernail polish, took all my makeup off, changed my earrings to posts, put on my conservative clothes, and went in.

The last point mentioned here is a familiar one in that the identifications that are being given up or changed all relate to one or an-

43

other aspect of the body-self. As I have already pointed out, the image an individual holds of her body-self is an integral component of her total sense of identity. Therefore, anything that affects this image, for example changing traditional patterns of dress or adornment, affects the individual's sense of identity (Schilder 1950).

> **Q.:** How long did that initial feeling of depression last?
> **A.:** The curious thing was that after that initial fear, that initial depression, the "I don't care anymore" attitude, everything was uphill [?]. Complete optimism. Complete optimism, because of the way I was treated.
> **Q.:** Everything was uphill?
> **A.:** Well, you see that kind of psychological disjunction you have to deal with as the researcher. You have to deal with that. And if you don't have your emotional problems at least under control, if you don't have your problems solved, in that kind of situation you're going to fry. You're completely going to fry. I kept wondering why I wasn't cracking up. Because the pressures on me were intense.
> **Q.:** How did you manage to avoid losing control?
> **A.:** I didn't prevent it. I did disintegrate. The point is while I was disintegrating I was building up a whole other set of adult behaviors. I was one kind of adult when I went to the field. I was a graduate student. I had a philosophy of life that was rather silly at times, and at the same time, terribly, terribly serious about the important things, the important things. I went into the field frightened out of my mind and expecting to be rejected. Completely out of hand rejected. . . . And I came back from the field a different person.

It appears that some of the disintegration Karen experienced was prompted by her own attitude toward field research:

> I hit the field, and by that time I had myself completely opened up. In order to get good data you have to open up completely. You have to leave yourself completely and totally open. You can't have any defenses. . . . In the research situation I had to open up completely. It really was quite threatening.
> **Q.:** Why did you perceive the culture as one in which it was safe enough to open up completely?
> **A.:** It's very much like American culture. The language was closer; they spoke what they called English to me. . . . And the kids sing the same songs that we do here, like "everybody likes me, everybody hates me, go eat worms," that one. They have that.

These last comments concerning why Karen felt her fieldwork situation was safe enough to open up completely are of great importance here. On one hand, her answer makes it clear that she experienced minimal cognitive clashing; she perceived the culture as "very much like" her home culture. On the other hand, she perceived these cultural similarities as a link to or continuity-maintaining device with her home world; the kids sang some of the same songs there as they do here. These similarities functioned in a defensive/reparative manner to help stabilize her sense of identity.

Although the identity fragmentation Karen experienced was not catastrophic, nevertheless any experienced fragmentation calls out behaviors designed to halt that process. Aside from the children's songs mentioned above, she employed a number of other defensive/reparative behaviors.

> **Q.:** Can you recall anything about your dream life during field-work?
>
> **A.:** I didn't have any recurring dreams while I was there, which is different from my normal pattern. I suppose I had a lot of sexual dreams. I don't really remember much about my dreams though. You see, self-analysis is not part of the culture. . . . So that's another reason that I had to keep up with the cards.
>
> **Q.:** The cards?
>
> **A.:** Yes, Tarot cards, definitely. I had to. It's part of me. It's part of me. I took it up three or four years ago. It was under extreme circumstances and it's part of my life now. It's part of the way that I order my life now. Don't get me started on the Tarot. I could go on for hours. But I did need to do it in the field. And it turns out that S. [a principal informant] took it up. And she and I used to go and play cards together in the town for hours at a time.

For now, simply note that S., one of Karen's principal informants, took up reading Tarot cards. Shortly I shall present the evidence that confirms what we see being hinted at here—that S. was being used as a narcissistic object.

Karen's relationship with her surrogate parents was complicated by identity issues and defensive/reparative behavior:

> My one set of parents I had trouble with. That set of parents I had to see at least once a day. Unfortunately, they had no children. It was becoming a power play. After Christmas, talk about parent/child aggression, we eventually came to a point where I said, "I'm sorry, that's it." They immediately stepped back and apologized. I said, "You don't seem to realize that I am an adult woman, that I am an adult American woman." You see, by their standards a woman in her twenties is still a little child. They were constantly treating me like a child. My parents [in America] had never treated me like that. I've always been told to make my own decisions. When I was in a situation where I was

being given direct orders, the [her family name] rose up within me and said in great hostility, forget it.

Karen's surrogate parents reflected onto her a sense of her identity as a little child. Because this was in marked contradiction to Karen's own sense of herself, she responded, through anger, in a manner designed to restore her sense of identity as an independent, competent, fully mature woman.

When asked to describe her typical day, she produced the following remarkable passage:

> They normally get up very early, about seven o'clock in the morning. I *don't* get out of bed before eleven. This is something I reserved for myself. I didn't go out of the house before eleven. I wrote letters before eleven and people visited me before eleven, people who knew I was up before eleven, people who knew I was secretly up. I never put clothes on before eleven. . . . I couldn't sleep in the nude there. I was constantly being awakened, and the temperature was too cold. Because of that my sleeping pattern shifted. . . . I had a little plastic tub I bathed in in front of the fire. I got up in the morning and heated my water for bathing. I bathed every day. Again, atypical by local standards. But still I did, every day, because it's American to do that, and there were some things that I saved for myself. Murder mysteries and science fiction I saved for myself. When I first got there, I didn't have a TV but someone loaned me one and so I watched TV too. Television is a lot sparser there. . . . At twelve o'clock I always went home and watched the news to keep up on what was happening in the world. . . . I had to take up knitting again. I've always been a crocheter and an embroiderer, but I had to take up knitting again while I was there. They didn't approve of how I crocheted and I wasn't about to do it the way they did it because it was too hard. . . . I had to watch certain television shows that I never watch here in order to be able to talk with people. I had to watch "Dallas" and "Flamingo Road." I hate those shows. Soap opera shit. I hate them.

This account is a lovely example of the strength of defensive/reparative behaviors. Even though the people routinely begin their day at seven in the morning, and even though one would therefore expect the young and dedicated anthropologist to be up and snooping about then, Karen needed to maintain that link, in the form of a sleeping habit, with her home world. The daily baths, the reading, watching television, the refusal to crochet the way the natives did, and the taking up of knitting instead (a behavior she had performed earlier than crocheting in the United States) all seem to be serving continuity-maintaining functions. Even the hatred she felt over watching "soap opera shit" can be interpreted in this same manner. A good, genuine hatred for a dyed-in-the-wool American fad can forge a remarkably strong link to one's home world.

Karen commented that after arriving home from the field, one of the first things she did was to stop at a restaurant: "I had a salad. I missed American foods very much. They don't have salads there. They don't eat vegetables. They live on grease and starch. They live on grease and starch and desserts. . . . I had a salad. That's the first thing I ate when I got back. It was nice. Before the field, I used to eat salads constantly. I missed having one in the field. . . . And I really missed having a 'Big Mac.' Some of my friends in the field tried to make me one. It looked very much like the real thing, but it just wasn't the same. It lacked something." That sandwich masquerading as a "Big Mac" was in fact missing all the innumerable identifications that one normally associates with it and the home world.

Probably the single most powerful statement combining elements of Karen's experienced identity fragmentation and defensive/reparative behavior was generated in response to my question about whether she kept a diary in the field:

> I didn't keep a diary. I used to send tapes to other people in the field and these served as my diary.
> **Q.:** You found it necessary to send the tapes.
> **A.:** Absolutely, absolutely. You have to do that. You have to do it. When you're in another culture, even one not drastically different, when you're in the field, as much as you may be accepted by the people, as much as you may be loved by the people, and I was, you're not one of them. They don't understand the things, the "in" jokes. I could not say to anybody in the community, "I'm horny as hell." I could not say that. But to one of my friends elsewhere in the field, I could. I could make jokes, I could criticize. You can't criticize in the field, or make judgments. In my tapes, I could make judgments; I could judge myself and the people. . . . Everybody else could and did make judgments, but I could not. It was not appropriate. . . . I could be crude in the tapes. I could be, I could be American. I could say, "Don't you really want a bagel with lox?" Nobody there understands a bagel with lox. I wanted sour cream for my baked potato once, and they thought I was out of my mind. Things like that. The food differences, the clothes. The clothes I was allowed to wear. There were lots of things I took that I couldn't wear. The colors were too bright. And my hair. Do you know how many different hair styles I had there? Depending on who grabbed me, I had a new one for each person. You laugh, but that's

important. Earrings, shoes, stockings, which ones were right and wrong. Things like that. These things, and departmental gossip I could talk to other fieldworkers about.

In this long and beautiful passage, one can witness the difficulties Karen was having in trying to cope with the loss of those innumerable identifications that she had established with various elements of her home world. Her need for sympathetic positive mirroring of her experiences also comes through poignantly.

A last and more speculative example of a continuity-maintaining behavior—although it might be more correct to say that this example concerns a lack of behavior—centers around Karen's sexual life in the field. I had asked Karen to describe a most memorable aspect of her fieldwork:

It was a cloudy day and the men were all working in the harbor. You remember I talked about the, about all the free-floating sexual energy? D. [a principal informant] and her husband were splitting up. So she and I were both bothered by these men. Seriously, you'd just walk through and feel it all around you, like electricity everywhere. And you just had to walk through and grit your teeth. And as pleasant as that was, you just couldn't respond to it. . . . That is very interesting. Every time I made arrangements to go, to go someplace by myself, this is strange, to have an affair, which I kept trying to do, to have an affair, I became ill. There was no occasion in which I could get away from the community people. I would get physically ill. I would get sick. Which is a very curious thing that I still don't understand. I assume it has something to do with psychology. Because every time, you can look at my arrangement book, I made arrangements ahead of time, and then had to cancel due to illness. Illness would be scratched across it. Every time I made arrangements, I became ill. And by the time I got over the illness and made arrangements again for the month ahead, I would fall ill again. There was no way that I was going to escape. And I was making sure that I didn't. I still think that's it.

Karen was doubtless at least partially correct in her interpretation; this strange behavior does have "something to do with psychology." Rather than seeing it as a means of blocking escape, however, I see it as, in a sense, guaranteeing escape, in that she was "forced" to remain celibate and so direct her sexual frustrations outward and homeward. In so doing, Karen would forge another link with her home world.

When I asked Karen about her principal informants in the field, she responded with the following three descriptions:

48

Two of them were not from the area. A., the seventeen-year-old, one of my major informants, and his family, generally would tell me anything. He's seventeen years old. He was applying for colleges, and he was applying in physics. He doesn't have the background, and he's not going to make it. He's the first member of his family for generations ever to try and go to college. He was related to the T. family, which doesn't mean anything to you, but they were the Jews of this area. Extremely bright people. They're not into formal education, they're into experience and thinking. And A., right in the middle of this, will not go anywhere. And that hurts him. It was still recognized that his family had only been there five generations. They were still incomers. A. was going to make the break from the community. He and I were very close. I saw it very much in terms of a brother/sister relationship.

S. I would say S. was another major informant. She was from another part of the country, trained in social work, working with emotionally disturbed kids. She was twenty-nine years old. Half the experiences I had. She was very protected. This is the first time she had been away from home. But I was a totally new experience for her. I talked to her like I would talk to any American woman her age. I would swear in front of her, something I never did in front of anyone else. At the same time, we were both learning the native culture. She showed me differences between the other areas she had worked in and where we were now.

And there is another woman named D. This is the third informant. She came from outside the area also. She was doing the same thing. She moved to the area two weeks before I did. She belonged to a church that none of the other people belonged to. This was very unusual. That church was virtually dead for a long time. These three people knew me best. These are the people I would bounce the data off and say, "what do you think of this?" And I would get an explanation. These were the people doing the explaining. They were the people developing the theories. They were the people to whom I would say, "This is what I think is going on," and they would say "no, you're all wrong," or "that makes sense, let's go test it." And they would do it. . . . We literally went out and tested theories and ideas that we had devised, each in our own groups. A. went out and got me stuff; I was training him to be an ethnographer, just as in the past I have trained other people for jobs. . . . It's very interesting how some of my most interesting insights came from people who came from outside the community, who were actually also trying to adjust to the community. And so they were actually anthropologists as much as I was and giving me data. And they were giving me theories as well: "We were thinking this is how it works."

49

Karen's principal informants possessed qualities that are, by this time, entirely familiar. They were all marginal individuals trying in one way or another to understand and adjust to the community in which they found themselves. They were all anthropologists, developing and testing theories about the culture; they were all social scientists caught betwixt and between. Certain aspects of their individual descriptions also bear mentioning. A., with whom Karen developed a brother/sister tie, came from a family that downplayed formal education but emphasized experience and thinking (and what is fieldwork if not experience and thinking?). Further, she had trained A. to be an ethnographer, just as she had trained others in her home world to enter managerial positions in industry. Karen's father was an academic, and she sees education or teaching ("training") as her primary goal in life. In training A. to be an ethnographer, Karen was both maintaining a sense of continuity with an important aspect of her sense of identity ("educator") and creating a narcissistic object in the form of an alter ego. And finally S., her Tarot card–reading companion—the significance of which is now apparent—was a woman of roughly her own age with whom she could talk as if to another American woman. These people all functioned as mirrors, as narcissistic objects, for Karen.

There is also evidence in Karen's account of a degree of secondary identification with the native culture:

> **Q.:** Do you remember your feelings upon leaving the field?
> **A.:** That was the worst. Without a doubt. I did not pack my bags. I did not pack my bags. I had to leave—the government kicked me out. I did not pack my bags. I did not do anything. I already had my tickets. I had sent my money on ahead already. I had all my arrangements made. I did not pack. D. packed me. She packed me. I just refused to face the fact that I was leaving. I tried to face it but I just broke up. I tried to but I couldn't face it. I didn't see, say good-bye to a number of people. I couldn't face saying good-bye. I know it was rude. . . . I went immediately home after I got back. I needed to see my parents; I like them. They needed to see me. . . . I was so wrapped up with those people, so emotionally wrapped up; I gave myself heart and soul to those people. They gave me heart and soul. But the idea of them rejecting, oh, you have no idea how painful that is. Even now, they're still protecting me. No matter what I do, I have a home there. It's too safe though. I'm not going to develop there. . . . Am I making sense? I was giving up a whole lifetime of relationships. And when I got back home . . . I went into a very bad depression. I couldn't express it to my family for fear of being misunderstood and so I spent a lot of time reading

in my room, and oh, I got a cat. My dog and cat had died just before I left for the field. I picked up a stray that just wandered in. She got me through a lot of it. Because she was an orphan; she had been abandoned. I don't know if I could have gotten through it otherwise. She needed me.

Admittedly, in evaluating evidence of secondary identification with a native culture, it is nice to have the noisy, dramatic evidence that clamors for attention (such as Kimball's ghost and Grindal's dancing corpse, cited earlier). Nevertheless, it has to be admitted, with Freilich (1970:532–36), that one of the more parsimonious ways to understand the profound sorrow that Karen felt on leaving her field area is to assume that some degree of "going over the fence," of secondary identification, had occurred. There are two especially suggestive ideas in her comments that bear on this issue, one being the use of the word *home* to describe her field area, and the other her description of the stray cat as orphaned and abandoned. Whatever else home may refer to, and there are few more pregnant symbols in the English language, it is the place where one psychologically begins and feels secure; home is where one feels one's identity to be strongest and most vital. Finally, who can doubt that in the image of the cat, Karen was seeing a projected image of her own self, orphaned and abandoned once again, the result of the bonds of secondary identification being slowly snapped? In fact, much like a young child's imaginary friend, Karen's cat functioned as a transitional self-object aiding her in her attempt to reconsolidate her sense of identity.

What does all of this say about Karen's experience of fieldwork as a symbolic death? Is this a useful metaphor to describe her psychic experience during her ten months in northern Europe?

Symbolic death? See, I don't like that, the whole idea of death in this whole thing. I don't like it at all, because it's not appropriate, for me anyway. It was not a death for me, but a reconstruction, a ripping away of certain things and a rebuilding of certain things. I would say no to a death. I would say taking an old house and rebuilding it. Putting new beams in. As you take out the old beams, you put new ones in. You don't kill them. You don't strip them away and leave them. It's a replacement. . . . It's a replacement, not a death. I think it's highly dependent on what kind of research you do. I did not lose my identity in the community we're discussing here. My core, I was stripped down to the very core of my personality, true, and then a whole bunch of new behaviors started getting built up, as the old ones got pulled

51

away . . . but my core remained, remained completely solid. Solid as a rock. I think a lot of it depends on your position in your life when you go and do research. In the community under discussion, there was no symbolic death. The core of my identity was always solid, completely solid.

This is not the least bit surprising. Karen experienced minimal cognitive clashing in her fieldwork situation. In addition, it now appears that the structuralization of her self had proceeded relatively undisturbed. I take this to be evidenced in her statement that her core remained solid as a rock. An individual with one or another primary self-pathology (Kohut and Wolf 1978) could never make that statement, simply because for these individuals, the "core" of their selves has never solidified, has, in fact, never become a core at all. To be as solid as a rock at one's core is to possess a self secure in its primary foundations. The individual with such a securely anchored self will always be able to regress in the service of the self to a secure base of internalized object relations during times of loss of external support, isolation, and the like. This point is nicely illustrated by Karen's reaction to a traumatic incident early in her fieldwork:

My research was in jeopardy. My reputation was in jeopardy. . . . My feelings were very much like I was taking my life in my hands. Very much. I was taking my emotional life in my hands. This was during the early stage, remember, when I was back to being an infant. Where I could not be any of the things that I had ever been before. I had to be my basic personality stripped down to the core. And that is dangerous. You must have support to do that. I had nothing. I couldn't fall back on data or on anything I had ever read. I couldn't fall back on any of the experiences I had before, none. The only thing I had to fall back on was my own [natal] family. If I didn't have such a strong family structure, this whole incident would have done it. I was able to say to myself there are people who love me no matter what. I knew there were people in the world who loved me. They were always with me. I carried them inside me.

All that remains to be discussed here is Karen's response to the question of whether the field experience made her feel more like an anthropologist:

Well, yes, a little bit I guess. I mean I'm official now. I'll get the letters [Ph.D.] after my name and I'll be an anthropologist then. But mostly I remember the personal changes in myself. . . . I was terribly serious about important things before I left. But my criterion for important things has really changed now. What's important and what isn't. Time means a lot more than it used to, the time to just sit and relax and be your person. . . . One of the most devastating effects of the fieldwork experience on me is that I no longer have a clear perspective on anything. Everything is so relative. So incredibly relative. . . . Everything is so relative, so dependent upon circumstances, the environment people are in, and this has created real problems for me. I could once characterize myself as a biosocial anthropologist. I can no longer do that now. I always had the ability to see all sides, but I knew where the evidence was centered. Now the center keeps shifting.

This is a fitting passage to end with because in commenting on it an aspect of my ideas that has until now remained somewhat implicit will become much clearer. The fieldwork experience did provide Karen with some increased sense of her identity as an anthropologist. Aside from her direct statement, there is the speculative and suggestive hint contained in her emphasis on relativity, the need to view cultures from many angles and each in its own right. This sounds to me much like the tenet of cultural relativism, a belief in which was once, and in many places still is, the sine qua non of an anthropological identity. Whether a psychologically vulnerable individual or a "genital character," the mirroring that a student receives both during and after fieldwork will affect how that individual experiences her sense of identity. The evidence that Karen received this anthropological mirroring is strong. Aside from the already discussed use of her informants as narcissistic objects, there is the following passage (as well as the mirroring she is currently receiving from her adviser): "And right before I left, I got drunk with Colin. Colin is a marine archaeologist who has chosen to live in this community and yet is in the academic community, although not a member of the traditional academic community. He and I traded information that evening when we got drunk and it was like a confirmation of everything I had believed about the native community and the surrounding area. It was such an incredible confirmation of everything. I knew then that I was on the right track." The point here, then, is not that a psychologically vulnerable individual will "become" an anthropologist and a "genital character" something else as a result of fieldwork. Rather, the point is that the former individual's identification with anthropology will become the sole pivot of his life, the very foundation of his self; it will come to replace, in Harry Guntrip's (1968) poetic phrase, the "lost heart" of his self. For the individual with a more secure self-structure, the identification with anthropology will be less driven, less deep, more flexible, and form only one aspect of his total and larger sense of existential identity.

53

Fieldwork in Southern Europe: Vignette 2

This vignette concerns the field experience of a woman, age thirty-four, during her approximately thirteen-month stay in a southern European farming community. Of all my interviews, this one contains perhaps the clearest and most straightforward discussions of the difficulties that anthropologists face in maintaining their sense of identity during fieldwork.

In response to my asking for a description of her feelings surrounding entry into the field area, Cathy responded with the following long passage:

> At first, it was extremely difficult in ways that I didn't expect. Before I went I thought about it a lot. I was concerned about what I would do. One just goes to a community. How does one do fieldwork? How does one enter into their life? What are your reasons for being there? How do you explain yourself? How do . . . it seemed a real problem at the time. I'd rather go there and have a secretarial job, and have some sort of position in the society that makes sense to people, some sort of standardized interaction. What am I supposed to do when I get there, say here I am? . . . I remember when I came back for two weeks in January. The department was having a party, and I tried to talk to several people about what I was experiencing, in terms of loss of self-confidence, basically. Loss of self-esteem. I'm, I mean I always thought of myself as a very competent human being. At my age I've learned how to deal with things. I'm a good cook, I'm intelligent, I'm verbal. And here I was in this town, all of a sudden, where I was treated like a benign idiot. And far from thinking, oh here she is, wow, she knows so much, or anything, I couldn't communicate. I didn't know the language well. And I was, well, you know, sort of regarded as an idiot, but not only that, but going shopping with other women, and as a woman my role was sort of, well I had women's tasks to do, and I didn't know the first, the simplest things about shopping. I didn't know a good cut of meat from the worst. I could get taken in by the butcher without even knowing it. And not only that, but I ate mushrooms raw—how uncivilized! It was very hard on my ego. I thought I was a very competent human being. I made dinner for some people, but I didn't have one of the necessary implements. But I should have known that! My friend took over and made it into a genuine native meal. It was okay, but I never invited them over again. I remember distinctly that I started knitting, which I used to do in high school and hadn't done since. I had to do something other than cerebral work and learning the language, and besides the women all knit. I'm very good at knitting. This was during the early fall, in the rough period, when I felt I couldn't do anything, wasn't an intelligent human being. I am a competent

human being, why couldn't anybody tell? I took up knitting. I knit well, and I do it without looking at my hands. I just amazed these women. They do a lot of knitting but look at their hands. I remember sitting with some friends, knitting, and all of a sudden silence fell over the room, and they looked at me and said, "My God, she works without looking." Then P., a good friend, well she's like my mother, she said, "Well, these Americans are not too bright at most things, but there are some things they're pretty good at." And that was very significant. This was something that gave me credibility in their eyes as a woman and . . . I did very well. I knit unusual sweaters and picked up very quickly other complicated patterns and stitches. I got a great deal of pleasure out of this. They said, "She's so good at it." The rest of it, well, I was a benign idiot as far as they were concerned. Later I got the language down better, but I still felt the people were often gratuitously critical. They'd say, "Why don't you study more?" And I'd say, I do. And they would offer other suggestions to help me learn faster. There was just no understanding of what it took to learn a foreign language and to speak it. And the mayor of the town would always compare me to others who were learning to speak the language, and comment negatively. And then I would not be able to speak very well. I ran into this throughout the year, although a little less at the end. It was what I took to be gratuitous sorts of criticism. I was used to people who were very supportive and encouraging, and instead of this I ran into people who would just say, "Oh, what do you know?" Or, "Why don't you work harder, why don't you study more, and why don't you dress differently?" Or a number of other things like that. . . . I suppose this heightened my feelings of incompetency in the community where I worked. It was frustrating not to know anything about how to behave, how to do even the simplest things. It was, you see, the people didn't want to learn, were not eager to learn like so many in our culture. This is something that was very true. They were closed to alternatives, narrow-minded. This was the way to do things. Their way was right. But I had a sense of being competent too. Yet my ways, well, they didn't understand them or if they did, they didn't like them. I like eggs cooked in butter. But they would only eat eggs cooked in oil. There was only one way to be domestic. It was a real threat to my self-esteem. . . .About the other bad experiences, they were mostly with people with whom I was talking. I would make what I thought was a coherent statement in the native language, and someone would say, "Well, you still don't speak the language," or "Why don't you practice more?" "You Americans don't mind making fools out of yourself. If you can't speak correctly, you just open up your mouth anyway and talk." I said now wait a minute. . . . It just shows their ignorance.

The thrust of these statements seems to me to be remarkably clear. The attack on Cathy's sense of identity as a competent human being, including her sense of herself as a competent woman, is clearly enunciated. Her loss of self-esteem and self-confidence is mentioned in several places throughout this passage, as is the cause—the preponderance of negative reflections that she received from the majority of the people. One can also note that her knitting functioned as a defensive/reparative behavior. It appears that through knitting, and in particular through her own style of doing it, in which she had become proficient through long hours of practice in her home world, Cathy was able to assure at least some positive mirroring for her sense of competency as a human being (woman).

Throughout the interview, Cathy displayed a marked tendency to intersperse comments about the state of her sense of identity within the description of defensive/reparative behaviors, or vice versa:

I was also worried about my, I don't know what you call these people, my companion, my friend, M., who was back home. He's a professor so he wasn't with me. I was worried about how people were going to get in touch with me. I wanted a phone but was told it would take two years to get one. I set up a routine of being called by M. every Saturday, no every Sunday. Every Sunday he called. My parents were in Europe so I couldn't reach them. But they called once, as a surprise.

Q.: This weekly phone call, did you ever miss it?

A.: *Nooo!* No. Sundays I didn't go places. If I was going to change my plans we arranged it ahead of time, to reschedule the call. I was given a key to the house, I was family, and so I had access to the phone. I was lonely. Very tired a lot. Slept a lot. More than I do normally. I talked to other people who experienced the same thing. I think it has to do with the strain of speaking a foreign language, the strain of all the incoming sense data that you're not used to. And the effort of speaking a foreign language is very tiring. Relating to people when you're not sure how you're supposed to do it. And so I slept a lot at first.

Q.: How long did that last?

A.: Often [!] and on for most of the first, for most of the year that I was there [laughter]. . . . It's also interesting that M., when he read my field notes, kept picking up on some sort of hostility toward B., the daughter in my family [surrogate family]. Let me explain. I was so dependent. I was dependent. I felt dependent on the goodwill of other people. I felt dependent on their help in a very direct way to get anything done, because I didn't know the language and I didn't know the system. And I felt dependent on B. She was my contact with the family too. And B. is really a very nice girl, woman I mean [!]. I'm fond of her, but she is also very casual about a lot of things. And I thought we were going to have regular language lessons, but we didn't. I was counting on her for certain things, and oh well, maybe in two weeks or a week. Things kept happening and I would respond with a sense of, because I felt very dependent, I reacted as if it was a threat. I was hostile or scared, at least in my field notes, toward this self-centered, immature something or other. Yes, in thinking back I do remember the sense of dependency and helplessness, feelings which I don't think would be good for anybody. I thought well at least I'm a full-grown human being—what must it be like for someone in their early twenties, with all sorts of emotional problems anyway. You don't know how to deal with yourself anyway and then you're thrown into a foreign environment. My God, it's a wonder that most anthropologists don't just go bananas. I remember thinking that I just don't know how to behave.

Q.: You felt like an infant all over again?

A.: Yes, I think there's a lot to that. As a child you have to be taught the language. You have to be taught how to behave properly. As a child, well they were my family. They were my parents. P. is in some ways my mother. Very accepting and very compassionate. And I could be a child to her in ways she needed. She had raised a nephew who later married and behaved to her like a viper. In some ways, I was, in taking me in, she was restoring or reaffirming her faith in herself, as a good person. And she could be my mother basically. She's old enough. She could be.

Once again, this material is incredibly rich. The weekly phone call that could not be missed is a link with her home world and a source of positive mirroring. The increasing amount of time devoted to sleep is, proximally, related to the various strains Cathy describes in the passage. But ultimately, the underlying significance of this change can be viewed as a reaction to the loss of self-esteem and self-confidence and to the depressive feelings that inevitably accompany such losses. By sleeping more, Cathy removed herself from those most problematic human connections, from the negative mirrors so detrimental to her sense of identity. The analogy of being treated like an infant also makes its appearance here and in a context that makes clear its significance. It is one thing to be treated like an infant when you are one, but it is altogether different to be treated like an infant when you perceive yourself to be a "full-grown human being" and a competent one at that. There is always the underlying reflection conveyed by the image of a thirty-four-year-old infant: from the natives' viewpoint, anyone who is "grown-up" and yet still remains an infant, who cannot speak "our" (the) language or do the simplest things correctly, must be an idiot, or at best, a little deranged. Such reflections are apt to provoke questioning about one's sense of identity. And yet, humans being what they are, sometimes a positive gain can be achieved out of a bad situation. I am referring here to the possibility that Cathy may have established at least a weak transference relationship with her surrogate parents, P. and C. Within the context of a self-object transference, being treated like an infant, though not without its problems, does yet allow the individual to maintain a sense of identity through the receipt of positive mirroring from past significant others. Admittedly, the evidence for the existence of this transference relationship is not as strong as I would like to see it, but it is suggestive. Aside from Cathy's description of P. as her "mother," there are the following comments about P.'s husband, C.:

> He's sixty, solid. C. seems very solid, calm, very hardworking. It's true. He seems to be like a pillar, but he does contain a lot of upsets. C. is always very calm. . . . P. is also very modern in her attitudes, a liberal really, which surprised me. And I think that C. must be also. They let their daughter do a variety of things that I don't think were standard practice. . . . P. and C. were liberal in their attitudes; at least I was told that. They were not typical, I think that's true as well. They may even have been marginal to a degree as well. They were more liberal than most American parents even. P. said, who cares about what others think, anyway. Things change, and life's too short to think about all that. . . . I'm smiling because I was just thinking about M. compared to C. M. is very tall and thin, nervous, and extraordinarily intellectual, whereas C. is short, fat, somehow very down to earth, very solid. But it's interesting, C. reminds me a little of my father. I'm relatively close to my father; the relationship is uncomplicated. My father is laid back, intellectual, laid back, humorous. . . . He cares deeply about me, I know that. And in that fashion, C., I know C. cares about me and accepts me as a family member and worries about me. He is sort of like my father. I guess he really is.

In trying to clarify further the nature of her relationship to her "parents," I asked about whether they might be construed as amateur ethnologists (it was already established that they were marginal). Cathy's answer was interesting, but not because of my question:

> That's interesting. No, not at all. P. is not real good at observing. C. is not a social scientist, although a keen observer, yes. I think of him as knowing lots of specific information. We didn't theorize about everything. A lot of what I finally understood about the culture came from him, but only in terms of information. A real working-class view, but no theorizing. No, I had no coinvestigators, except M. when he came

to visit me from America. No, I felt this was a real problem. I would be writing to people, calling them. You just feel so isolated. I didn't feel abandoned, that's a different feeling entirely. But I felt so isolated; who could I talk to? I couldn't talk to anybody about these things. I was going to talk to a fellow graduate student, but she left the field without coming to see me. She just left and went home. In April, I was able to talk with a local anthropologist but was unable to make her see the importance of my project. She just said there were plenty of other things to look at. And one of the reasons I came back in January—this may be a justification, I really wanted to see M.—was to get some kind of feedback on what I was seeing.

Cathy's "parents" were not in any way to be considered social scientists—perhaps because, in a sense, these two people offered only those hooks on which to hang parental projections and not those of fellow social scientists (see Searles 1979). What is really impressive about this passage, however, is once again how it reveals the strength of her need for a positive mirror. She felt entirely isolated, with no one to talk to who could really understand her. Either of the two reasons she gave for coming home ultimately satisfied the same need—the need to talk to one who really understood who and what she was.

This passage also reveals a highly relevant aside to my ideas—that certain individuals in the field situation may, by virtue of one or another special characteristic, psychological or otherwise, serve as highly identity-dystonic mirrors. It is hard to imagine, for example, that the local anthropologist, who not only failed to see the importance of Cathy's area of interest but actually advised her to change her investigation, could have been anything but such an identity-dystonic mirror. This fellow social scientist, a person who should have been the paragon of a positive mirror, was unable to relate to Cathy's work except in a highly negative manner. Such a special or more problematic identity-dystonic mirror also appears to have been present in Cathy's relationship to B., the daughter of her "parents," P. and C. There was a hint of this relationship earlier in the passage I quoted on B. There Cathy's problems with B. were couched within the general framework of dependency. A closer look at B.'s characteristic features reveals more precise details:

It's sort of complicated. I used to think, it's very complicated. I thought she might be jealous because of my relationship with her mother. I was over there a lot, talking with her mother and being very supportive, and she lived about sixty kilometers away. It's complicated

59

because she is nice and bright and I like her, but we really didn't have a lot in common. At first it was the language, but I don't really think it was that. It's somehow just a very different range of interests. She was not interested in my work or in doing anything about it. She accepted me as part of the family and that was about it. She accepted me and then you don't have to worry about it anymore. She says that she has been lazy and not done what she has to academically to get her degree. I think that's probably true. In many ways, she is an extended adolescent, in that, well, for example, she has been going with her boy friend for eight years. He's an engineer and living at home, she's working and spends a lot of time at home. I asked her if she didn't want to get married. "Oh, no. Why would you want to get married?" "Well, don't you want to have children?" No, she doesn't want to have children. "What about a home of your own?" "I already have two homes, my apartment and my parents'." That would be the extent of the conversation. M. says she is quite vain. Quite self-absorbed. I used to think she was so inconsiderate. I found this very threatening at first, because I needed to depend on her. I needed her concern. I needed her to take an interest.

Although the dependency issue is raised again, other, more impressive reasons are revealed in this passage for the problematic nature of their relationship. To be blunt, nearly all of B.'s attributes represented a fundamental challenge to Cathy's attempts to hold onto her sense of identity. B. was not interested in Cathy's work, she was lazy and therefore did not complete her degree, and perhaps most serious of all, to sum up a number of additional characteristics, she was an extended adolescent, perhaps the very antithesis of a grown-up and competent human being (woman), the image that Cathy obviously held of herself. B.'s very existence served as an identity-dystonic mirror for my informant.

I have already presented some evidence bearing on the question of Cathy's use of defensive/reparative behaviors. I want now to concentrate my attention on these behaviors, documenting a number of the more familiar and useful ones. Her dreams make a good starting point:

Lots of heavy dreams having to do with the relationship to my mother. This was near the end of my fieldwork. Many dreams centered around M. and his marital situation. Fairly straightforward. Or around his wife. Well, I mean they were separated at the time. I remember that I was dreaming in the native language. This was probably about midway along in my field stay. Increasingly, the native language became more and more important in my dreams. And I remember a

60

dream where I was using the native language, French, and English and I said oh boy, come on, because I haven't had, even spoken French, since college. . . . I was very puzzled about why I was having those dreams about my mother. . . . I'm trying to defend myself. I was working out my relationship with my parents, or working it out again, while I was in the field.

The two points that require discussion here are the "heavy" dreams about Cathy's relationship to her mother and her dreaming in the native language. Regarding the first point, it would be well to keep in mind that any loss of a sense of identity exposes the individual to his own childhood conflicts. It is in these childhood conflicts and, more precisely, in the child's relationship to its mother and later other members of the household, that one's sense of identity is psychologically hatched (Erikson 1980:99). In recalling aspects of that early relationship, Cathy is literally calling herself back to herself.[1] Regarding the significance of dreaming in the native language, Michael Agar (1980:51) has argued, in summarizing Anderson's research (1971), that an anthropologist's dream life will initially focus on early life events; not until the anthropologist has established a "secondary identity" as a member of the native culture will he dream in the native idiom. Agar and Anderson are maintaining that the dream life reflects and parallels the fieldworker's initial sense of identity fragmentation followed by his activation of defensive/reparative behavior, including secondary identification with the native culture.[2] Cathy's dreaming in the native language would then indicate that some degree of secondary identification had occurred.

In response to my inquiry about the nature of her cravings, Cathy revealed the following:

Chinese food. I would have loved some. It's one of my favorites. I got bored with the food where I was. It was very good, but I just got bored with it. And I tried to make a blintz, but they had the wrong kind of vanilla and it turned the whole thing sour. I wanted to make lots and lots of Christmas cookies because that's important to me. I normally do a lot of baking around Christmas time. But they just didn't have the ingredients. . . . Oh, cravings, I remember some more. I craved seeing movies in English. That I really craved. I wanted to see good movies in English. I saw a lot of old movies on TV, but they were all dubbed. And reading English books and novels, I really missed them.

Q.: Did you experience any sort of sexual cravings?

A.: Absolutely. But there is no question as far as I can see. You don't have an option, you must remain celibate. Sexual relationships in the

61

field are going to be disastrous. There was no way that I was going to do anything there. It might be different for a man, but I don't know about that. It's hard to say really.

Q.: Did remaining celibate present any problems?

A.: Oh, sure. Sure. My vibrator had a transformer. And I was extremely horny. It went through phases, but especially during the first few months I was there. I was very conscious of these feelings every time I went to bed.

Q.: About your fantasies?

A.: My fantasies were always with M. I sometimes wondered about that. Why it was always with M. He was so very far away, in a different world really.

The various types of foods and the emphasis on English-speaking movies and books possess similar identity-maintaining characteristics. The comments about her celibacy and the problems it generated are, like any discussion of human sexuality, open to interpretation. But it cannot be denied that M. was very far away and in a different world and by directing her sexual frustrations and fantasies in that direction, Cathy was forging a powerful link with her home world.

The following memory was elicited in response to my asking Cathy for a description of her worst experience in the field. It is worth keeping in mind here that she is Jewish: "As to one particular event, there was a large religious ceremony that I remember. During the ceremony, I felt more like an outsider than ever before, a stranger. This was about three-quarters into my fieldwork. It was near the end. I was confronted with a sense of alienness. I was an outsider. I was just really confronted with the sense that this is an alien culture. It was an experience where I didn't belong. I thought how much I would like to be at a 'seder.' Just to listen, hear about the Jews and the Egyptians." During a ceremony in which Cathy is suddenly reminded of the existential reality of her situation—that she is a stranger, alone and afraid in an alien world—she rekindles a memory of an important religious ceremony from her own past and her own future, and so returns home. The recall of this memory provided her with a sense of that culture to which she belonged and would soon return.

Q.: Did you ever experience a period of emptiness during fieldwork, a sense that your work was meaningless?

A.: I had periods where I just ran out of questions, ran out of energy.

I didn't have any ideas. I went through dry spells and then I would get going again.

Q.: How did you get going again?

A.: Once it was shortly before I came back here in January, so that was a chance to refuel. Once it was before M. came to visit. Once it was before I went to see the local anthropologist. I wrote letters to people I knew back home, telling them to write me back. Often I would do something to remove myself from the field situation. And oh, sure, I used the weekly phone calls for that, and as an escape, a safety valve. I think it would be impossible to do fieldwork completely out of touch. Who do these people talk to; how do they avoid the isolation? The immersion was sometimes difficult. There was no privacy, no time to really escape. Sometimes my ears just hurt. I didn't want to hear the native language anymore. They just hurt. I wished for everything not to be puzzling. I wanted not to know not what things were. I wanted to feel comfortable, to not be assaulted by something strange.

I realize the importance of "distancing" in any situation when one is very close to the data and one is fighting for new ideas. But it is no mere coincidence that in distancing Cathy appears to have engaged in a series of behaviors that would have served as identity boosters (even the local anthropologist was, if nothing else, an anthropologist). Distancing is always away from and toward something; here it appears to be toward home and away from the native culture. The last few lines of this passage are poignant reminders of the anthropologist's desperate need to return home, even if only in his imagination.

It is now time to get Cathy out of the field—for real and not solely in her imagination:

I didn't want to go. There was something to be acknowledged, that it was some kind of liminal period, an in-between period. In some ways you were more free, but in others you were far less free, more constrained. You don't know what to do. You feel you can't afford to do anything wrong. You can't make any mistakes because you are so dependent on others for their help. You need to be accepted. By the end of the stay, though, I enjoyed the freedom. There was a lack of physical threat. I could walk anywhere anytime. There was no concern for the, for physical safety. I liked the tranquility, very pleasant. I liked the sense of community, the friendship, the family sense. The families do things together a lot. It was very different from the atomic, separated lives we live here. There's less of a focus on material goods, less a feeling of cheapness. I had no desire to leave, to come back here.

The second half of this passage appears to substantiate the earlier evidence—dreaming in the native language—for the existence of a degree of secondary identification with the native culture. The first half of this passage suggests the paradoxical quality, the ambiguity, associated with being betwixt and between cultures. And what does Cathy see as the effect on her self and her identification with anthropology of passing through this liminal stage of fieldwork?

I think it's very interesting. I think it is a rite of passage very crudely. To become an anthropologist you do fieldwork, to be validated. Most people had to do fieldwork in a foreign culture to know what's going on. I think that's true. There is some sort of deconstruction, or destruction of the self that goes on when you confront a different people. The subtle as well as the overt behaviors are all different. I think it's easier if you're in a place that's very different. You don't expect any similarity. But if you're in a place like I was, you think, oh it's just like the United States. And the differences can be very subtle and catch you completely unaware. They look like they dress alike but it's not quite alike. So when you dress, they think you look funny or just badly dressed. In terms of the liminal period, you are betwixt and between. . . . I talked about deconstruction of the self, maybe reformulation is a better term. Maybe not, maybe it's not a reforming but an adding on of secondary behaviors. There are a whole series of things I do here that I don't do over there. So maybe I didn't change, but just built up a second set of behaviors. But to the extent that there is conflict between the two, there will be some dissonance set up. Probably then one will be denigrated or both will be isolated apart from each other. I don't know. But I'm sure the dependency and the insecurity stuff are related to this need to tell yourself, "I'm really a competent human being." And as much as you tell yourself that this need is just a product of the different cultural situation, it still persists. I was confused over how I fit in the society. Did their cultural rules apply to me? I don't know. I was more free of the rules, that's what one person told me when I asked. Another told me to start dressing like a woman should, and not in blue jeans. It's one thing to be expected to behave like everybody else, but sometimes they don't understand that you don't know what that means. I think I was more constrained in the community. Here I know what I can do, how far I can go, who I don't want to offend. There I didn't. I had to care about everybody there. It's more complicated.

Q.: Do you feel yourself more of an anthropologist now than before you went to the field?

A.: Yes, although I have much less faith in anthropology. Most anthropologists treat their subjects like objects. I have problems with that. And there is another thing. I know how at times my insecurity, my defensiveness, affected the data I collected. Your relationship with your people is critical. And I know how incompetent some anthropologists are as human beings. I think I have more self-confidence now as an anthropologist, and toward other anthropologists, because I've been to the field. They can talk about their field experiences, but I have mine now. And that's what it's all about. Nobody can argue with you, about what you say. You are the only one to know your people. Part of the experience is also just getting through a really difficult situation. I did it. And it gave me a sense of validation as an anthropologist. It was a different experience in ways I never expected. My self-image, self-confidence, insecurity, survived some threat. I got through that. . . . Basically it's an individualized experience, people going through their rites of passage, experiencing different things. I don't think it's science. I don't see how anybody can. I think a lot of anthropologists are just frustrated novelists. . . . There are covert aspects to fieldwork also. Some of it is probably to see if you can go to Bongo-Bongo land and make it as a man. The effects on the self as a rite of passage are a part of fieldwork.

The attack that Cathy experienced against her sense of identity as a "competent human being" is linked directly to her heightened feelings of dependency, as well as to the dearth of positive mirroring that she received. Although the field experience appears to have heightened her sense of anthropological identity, it does not seem to have become the pivot of her existence. In fact, it is the validatory aspects of fieldwork that are principally emphasized, and in such a manner as to suggest that "anthropologist" forms only a partial aspect of her total identity. It is significant here that Cathy avoided using the metaphor of death to describe her experience; her self-image and self-confidence (the core of her self/identity) survived "some threats." There was an intact core to survive; in other words, the foundations of her self were fairly secure. I see this as also evidenced by her progression from a "deconstruction, or destruction" of the self, to a "reformulation" of the self, to, finally, a simple adding on of behaviors to a still intact self, as a result of the field experience. This last point suggests that some part of the self had remained solid enough to support the adding on of secondary behaviors.[3]

Fieldwork in India: Vignette 3

In this vignette, I will be analyzing the experience of a young Indian woman ("Rita"), age twenty-seven, during her approximately ten-month stay in a small village in India. This case is particularly important in that this woman experienced either a minor amount or none of the feelings normally associated with the field experience (identity disintegration, secondary identification, and the like). The absence of these experiences is, however, consonant with my understanding of fieldwork when allowance is made for the special circumstances surrounding Rita's fieldwork.

The nature of these special circumstances was revealed early in our interview. Rita had been married about ten months before leaving for her field site to an Indian graduate student in anthropology who was also preparing to do fieldwork in India. Although they worked in different areas in India, they were able to meet twice during their respective field stays. Of more consequence, Rita's father had just retired from his post as an administrator in the same state in which she was planning to do her fieldwork. The significance of this point was not lost on Rita: "That was a big help. Before he retired, he had worked as an administrator of sorts, with many of the people that I had to work with. That was why my interests, how I became interested in studying those people. I knew them to an extent before I left to go into the field, indirectly, through my father." Even at this early juncture in the interview, I began to wonder further about the "closeness of fit" between Rita's field site and her home world. The following comments are verbatim from this section of the interview:

Q.: Were you working in the same area that you grew up in?

A.: Not exactly. I did my work in a neighboring state. It's a culture, a tribal group—that's what they call them in India—it's a culture that is geographically very close to my own community, culturally very close also. But we do have different languages. We are considered different tribes. Although there are many similarities, I don't think I really studied my own culture. It was a different culture.

Q.: Did you have to learn the language then?

A.: The language is different, but there are some similarities. So I had a kind of passing knowledge of that language. But I did have to hire an interpreter; I couldn't converse fluently with them myself.

Q.: The ten months you were in the field, was that a continuous period?

A.: Yeah, more or less continuous. I did go out once in a while to my home. My parents weren't living in exactly the area where I was, but they were not very far away. I did manage to escape the scene once in a while, to rest up a bit. But I was there most of the time. . . . It's hard to say how many times I left the field. I didn't think about it. You see, sometimes I went for a week, sometimes for ten days, sometimes just for a day or two, a weekend even. It's very hard to count these times up.

Q.: Please describe your feelings on entry into the field.

A.: I was very excited in the beginning. I had written my proposal, had all my exams. I was thinking about my dissertation, dreaming about the field. And I was aware of the kind of people I was going to meet. I wasn't ignorant about the area where I was going. I was very excited about the whole thing. When I went to the field, I stopped off at my parents' house first because, as I already told you, my father knew the people and the area. In spite of retiring, he still had some influence in the area. So he was able, through relatives, and through other junior administrators, to get maps of the area and to pinpoint a village where I could work. My father was a big help in these matters, in making the initial decisions. And he also managed to find an interpreter for me, who also became a good friend.

Q.: There were no caste problems where you were working?

A.: No. I studied a tribal community, and many tribal communities in India do not fall under the caste system of the Hindus. They're outside the system. In fact, I belong to one of those tribal communities, so I know we all look down on this caste system the Hindus have. We like to consider ourselves a very egalitarian community. So since I studied a tribal community, there were no caste problems.

Rita's situation is entirely different from those of the two individuals discussed earlier in this chapter. The community she studied is "very close" both geographically and culturally to her home world. Even though the people speak a different language, she had a passing knowledge of it, as well as an interpreter to aid her. Caste presented no problems, nor did her entry into the field, engineered as it was by her father. Finally, it appears that her natal family was close enough to her field site to allow her to take several vacations, ranging from a day or two to periods of seven to ten days. This does not sound like a world in which Rita would have any grave difficulties in maintaining those innumerable identifications that composed her sense of identity. Nevertheless, this similarity in cultural worlds need not mitigate against a limited degree, however minor, of identity disintegration; any two cultural life-worlds, no matter how similar, are also different, and this difference may present small identity problems. There is perhaps a hint of these small problems in the following passage:

Q.: Did you ever feel yourself psychically isolated?

A.: Yes, when I went to the village. But not all the time. Sometimes I really enjoyed myself. The whole experience wasn't a nightmare. I did, though, feel isolated quite often. We did have different ways of thinking about things. When I felt isolated, I tried never to show it. I would try and bring myself down or up, whichever, to their level, and try to understand why they were behaving as they were. Very often I had to, for instance, if my friend, my interpreter and I came across something and she would explain it in a manner different from mine, frankly if I felt she was being ignorant and stupid in her belief about something, I would try and forget my own explanation for it, which I felt was more correct and more scientific, and maybe sometimes act more stupid, and try to understand it like she did. I would agree with her even if I didn't really agree with her inside. I went home a lot when I felt isolated. And when it was very rainy, or when the people were too busy to be bothered about my questionnaires, I would often go home and take a rest. Coming back from home, I felt very rested and refueled. I felt that I could tackle another ten days or a month. . . . The main thing I missed by not having my husband around was his company, somebody to talk to who shared my beliefs. My informants were there every day, and I tried hard to think like them, but I couldn't. So often I wanted to relax and just be myself. I didn't want to always try, try, try. I just wanted to be myself. That's why I wanted my own kind of company, someone who's had my kind of experience.

    Q.: You wanted to be yourself?

    A.: Most of the time I was myself. But sometimes, as I mentioned, I had to act a little stupid in order to be accepted. I had to be ignorant about certain things in order to be accepted. I never did find an intellectual companion in the village. I took my frequent trips out of the village to the local libraries and even to home, to see my father, who was a good companion. He was so knowledgeable about those people. It was nice talking to him about it. And even old friends I had left behind so many years ago. I would meet them and discuss my experience with them. And the local librarians.

As I said, there is a hint of some small identity problems here ("I just wanted to be myself"), but that is all they ever are or remain—small problems. Any time she really needed a booster, a refueling, any time she really needed to be herself, she either went home to see her parents, her old friends, or the local librarians. There was a familiar world to be found just around the next turn. Despite her disclaimer to the contrary ("I never did find an intellectual companion in the village"), she does appear to have used her interpreter, and especially the latter's husband, as an intellectual mirror:

I told you that I worked with an interpreter. So she was the main person that helped me and her husband. They were a young couple.

Her husband was the first college graduate in the village, and he was graduating that year. That meant they were educated. They were able to understand what I was trying to do and what I wanted to ask. The girl was actually my principal informant, although I found it easier to work with her husband. Maybe because he was educated he understood what I was trying to get at. He could grasp the problem I was after. Generally, they were both very helpful. And in a sense, they were different from the rest of the villagers. They were both young and educated, as opposed to the rest; the majority of the villagers were illiterate.

With this field situation, I did not expect Rita to engage in much defensive/reparative behavior; there was, after all, not much to defend against or repair. Her responses to my questions concerning typical examples of these behaviors are interesting, however, for the additional information they provide concerning her field situation:

Q.: Did you do much reading in the field?

A.: I brought some anthropological stuff with me. Not much theory but books on the people in the neighboring areas. And I read a few novels in the field. There were times when I got bored. There was a boy there who had a collection of novels and magazines, things I would never normally read, stuff about movie stars, anything to keep my mind occupied. It's not that I had a preference for them. They just happened to be there. Always when I got bored I would read or contact my father and go home. More often the latter, I think.

Q.: Do you remember anything at all about your dreams in the field?

A.: I really don't remember anything about my dreams. I was very lonely in the field. My mother was there sometimes, and she would cook for me because she thought it was very hard for me to come back from a day spent in the hot fields and cook for myself. She felt sorry for me, and so she came and gave me company and cooked for me. Then she would quickly go back home because my father needed her there. Very often she would be with me five days of the week and then go home on weekends. Sometimes I would just go with her then back home.

Q.: Any particular food cravings?

A.: My diet was fairly similar to what I was used to. I had a small room where I stayed in a nearby town. It had a small attached kitchen, and I could cook for myself. Plus my mother did a lot of the cooking for me. She was there most of the time. I had the kind of food I was used to, and so I didn't have to adapt to their food.

Q.: About your husband being so far away?

A.: Well, I craved to be near my husband. I really wanted it to be over. I was lonely and was just dying for it to be over. The heat and the leeches. I was getting tired of everything.

Admittedly, hot weather and leeches can create an uncomfortable situation, and certainly being lonely is no fun. And yet whatever loneliness Rita did experience, it was unquestionably different in degree and largely in kind from that described by my two earlier informants. It was certainly not a loneliness that leads one to question the integrity of one's sense of identity. It was impossible for it to be so in this situation; her mother was with her "very often" for five days of the week, and then when she finally did leave, Rita often went home with her. It certainly seems that in going to the field, Rita was returning to her home world, quite literally.

On the basis of this analysis, it should not be hard to predict Rita's response to leaving the field, as well as her response to my question about identity loss as a symbolic death:

Q.: Can you remember your feelings on leaving the field?

A.: I was happy that it was over. I think the experience would have been better for me if my husband had been with me. Or if I had some friends to talk with who were doing similar kinds of work in similar villages. Some companionship. I was relieved to get away from that village. I went home after I had finished and then left with my husband to come back here.

Q.: Do you think that fieldwork involves some sort of symbolic death?

A.: No, not really. I did perceive a lot of change in me during my fieldwork. I tried so hard to understand how the people were thinking, to try and think like they were thinking, that that brought about change in myself. And I did mature a bit more. But I don't think it was a death of an identity. No, I don't think so. When I say I changed during the field, I think I became more tolerant of many things. I had a friend who visited me for a week when I was in the field. I think I must have behaved like her when I first got into the area. I changed a lot from that; I became so tolerant. For instance, tolerating the people and the dirt. I saw a lot of dirt around the place. Village life is dirty. Cow dung everywhere, human dung. You just have to skip through it and keep smiling. My friend was so squeamish about it. I must have been in the beginning too, but after a while, I didn't even see it anymore. I just kept walking. That tolerance, it was mostly resignation, I think.

Q.: Do you feel yourself to be more of an anthropologist now than you were before you left for the field?

A.: Yeah, yes. I guess so. There are many problems that one reads about and can't really understand without having done fieldwork. I've gotten my hands dirty now. I know what it actually means now.

It is not surprising that Rita considers symbolic death to be a less than useful metaphor for describing her field experience. Nor should it be surprising that, in admitting to feeling more like an anthropologist after her field experience, she cloaked her response in purely intellectualistic imagery; the depths of her self remained virtually unaffected as a result of the particular conditions of her experience. The only point that I do wish to comment on here is her increased toleration of the "dirt" associated with village life in India. Although at first glance this might appear as evidence of secondary identification with the native culture, I think that a more correct interpretation would be to construe this attitude—note her choice of words, "toleration" not "acceptance"—as, in her words, "resignation," or in my words, the result of habitual exposure. Secondary identification, conceived of as a merging with the native culture, is prompted by the experience of identity fragmentation and is always accompanied by some affectual response, typically a profound sense of belonging or acceptance. In Rita's case, there is no or very sparse evidence for any identity fragmentation and certainly no evidence for any affectual response, except perhaps a negative one in relation to her experience of the villagers' way of life. Rita grew more tolerant of the dirt because it was always there, not because of some intermingling of her sense of identity with that of the villagers. She was never, at heart, a villager.

The results of this analysis have their parallel on the cultural-historical level. Just as Rita was able to maintain the innumerable identifications that composed her sense of identity by returning home, so it is also true that with the increasing Westernization of the world's many cultures, other student-initiates may very well not experience such a radical severing from their links with the home world. How long will it be before Coca-Cola and designer jeans invade the interior of Brazil or the highlands of New Guinea? In overstating this issue, I am not implying that the student will experience no psychological discomfort; New Guinea is not and never will be the United States. But the total amount and intensity of discomfort may very well be less than in an earlier epoch, when "Western culture" was still largely confined to the West.

A particularly pronounced instance of this phenomenon was that of the British neocolonial fieldworkers. This tradition of fieldwork operated from within the context of the "Britishization" of the local culture. Traveling to many parts of Africa, India, or a myriad other places during the neocolonial period was, in a very real sense, like never leaving home; the innumerable identifications were all there to be found. In fact, the relative lack of psychological discomfort experienced by the British neocolonial anthropologist may well be the reason why Meyer Fortes (1963:433) was able to remark that an anthropologist's psychological adjustment in the field is largely a "peripheral" issue.

One might also make these same points about the modern American "Indianists." Robert Lowie (1959:60), for example, reports a conversation with a Crow Indian in which he was trying to explain exactly what he did for a living. After a momentary hesitation, the Indian replied: "Oh, I see, you're an ethnologist!" Alice Marriott (1952:60) reports a similar experience with a knowledgeable Indian. As she began to draw a kinship diagram, her informant remarked: "You're going to use the University of Chicago type of diagram then." On today's reservations, stocked as they are with natives who know all about ethnologists and University of Chicago diagrams, and whose distance, culturally and geographically, from the mainstream culture is very small, it should not be surprising if the students who go there return relatively unchanged psychologically.

Fieldwork in Southeast Asia: Vignette 4

In this vignette, I will analyze the field experience of a man, aged twenty-four, during his approximately ten-month stay in a small hunting/gathering society in Southeast Asia. This individual ("Sam") had been to the field about sixteen years earlier; he was forty years old at the time of the interview. After leaving the field, he had worked as an anthropologist in an academic institution. This vignette is especially important for two reasons. First, it appears that, although Sam experienced some identity problems with the natives, far greater identity problems arose in his dealings with the local missionaries (he was living on a mission station during his fieldwork). Second, it appears that Sam entered the field already firmly convinced of his status as an anthropologist, and this enabled him to halt or otherwise curtail the attack on his sense of identity. Fieldwork was a job that one simply had to do.

Beginning with the former point, I asked Sam whether he would consider his life with the missionaries a real field experience:

Absolutely. Absolutely. More so than with the natives. Especially because I was prepared for the natives. You don't know what you'll find with the natives, but it will be challenging. So you're set. But the missionaries, I didn't even think about them. I had a friendly relationship with one man, which was helped a lot by the fact that we looked on each other as intellectuals. But most of the missionaries were from the rural areas, and mostly anti-intellectual. They're not actively anti-intellectual, but they are distrustful and suspicious of anyone who presents themselves as an intellectual. That was a considerable problem. The missionaries were, let me put it this way. There was no time in working with the natives that I felt my fieldwork was at stake, but I can't say the same about the missionaries. I felt I had to control myself constantly with the missionaries. With the natives it was etiquette. I was living with them on their land. But the missionaries, who the fuck are they? . . . The missionaries posed special problems, totally unexpected. I remember saying to myself before I left that you're going to have to make some adjustments in your life toward the natives. But I was completely unprepared for the missionary culture. I never thought about them. I wasn't working with them, so why bother. What I found was that there were certain grounds on which I felt uncomfortable with them. For example, I am quick to use obscenities—not in anger, but more as a figure of speech. I say "God damn it" a lot, but you don't say "God damn it" in front of a Methodist missionary. I picked up on this, but it really cut into my speech. I say "God damn it" a lot. I was very uncomfortable with the missionaries over this propensity to swear. I deliberately censored my speech. I remember that feeling very well. This did not happen with the natives. They picked up the English swear words very quickly, and I felt free to use them in their presence. Saying "fuck" to the natives was never a problem. It's that sense of freedom of speech that I had with the natives and not the missionaries. I was totally unprepared for it. It was certainly a strain. I felt a sort of circumspection around the missionaries that I didn't feel around the natives. I just wasn't prepared for it. I went to the field telling myself to watch out. I didn't know the people's sense of proper behavior, the natives' that is. Now I would make the same statement about the missionaries. It seems so trivial now, but it wasn't then. Especially my propensity to swear. . . . It's not that they had me on a rack. I wasn't suffering from that perspective. Yeah, but I think the strain on me—I'm quite sure, there's no reason to speculate—the strain on me was very considerable. The pressure was keenest, I would emphasize, from the missionaries particularly. Watching what I said.

73

These comments illustrate the identity problem Sam experienced in his daily life with the missionaries. The missionaries resented and distrusted intellectuals. Because of them, he felt forced to alter his habitual speech pattern, which seems to have presented great difficulties for him. And very importantly, Sam was completely unprepared, psychologically, to make these adjustments, a point that he makes three times in the above passage. The strength of the problems presented by the missionaries is strikingly revealed by Sam's description of his reaction to two particular incidents:

> There is one memory, you can make of it what you will. A young female missionary was interested in me, and I must admit I was interested in her. But she had a tendency to keep badgering me about my dedication to my work. She badgered me about this and about why I didn't particularly care to socialize with the missionaries. I don't care to have people questioning the way I lead my life. My private life is mine. As it does not hurt anybody else, I choose to live it the way I want. I believe that I have a right to do that. One night, and I did this deliberately, note at night, she was visiting me. She commented about my reclusiveness and my work. I asked her to move closer and I punched her in the mouth. I pulled my punch so I wouldn't do any real physical damage. I shocked her, and I said, "This is my life and I'll live it as I choose." I got plenty of respect after that. I really shocked her. She fell on the ground, just shocked. I thought I'd throw that in as a more memorable missionary experience. I remember a second one, an explosion with a missionary that if I had gone through with it would have ended my fieldwork. He was intolerant of the natives, had no respect for them, didn't have any knowledge of them. An ignoramus's disrespect really. Didn't have much respect for anything really. We shared the latrine. Well, I piss like I assume most guys do, standing up. Well, a couple of times some of it got on the top of the seat. He made an issue of it. Now this is a sensitive subject under any condition. But certainly the thing to do, if he wanted to bring it up, was to do it privately. But he made a public issue out of it, public meaning in front of his wife and a female guest. I took him aside and told him he had better talk to me about it in private. I was really furious. This to me is virtually grounds to kill somebody. I found what he did totally unacceptable. Sure enough, it happened again. He did it again in public. I got up to go for him—at this time it would have ended my fieldwork—but I got up anyway. X. [his principal informant] came by and stopped me. One of the most unpleasant personalities I ever had to deal with. I have no doubt that if the matter came up again, I would react in the same way. . . . It's funny, but as you recall these events the feelings come back so strongly. Generally, I was very careful. I always knew

that my anger, my swearing with the natives, would not hurt my field-work. With this guy, I was so furious that I was prepared to do something that would have almost got me thrown out of the field. I was really furious. That was the low point of my fieldwork.

Q.: Why do you think you felt so angry?

A.: Discussion of a personal matter like body eliminations in public. I just will not tolerate that. I consider it the height of bad taste. If that guy were to do it right now, I would just put one of these coat racks through his head. I consider it grounds for virtually murdering somebody.

We can see, in these remarkable descriptions, Sam defending certain deeply felt aspects of his sense of self against inroads by the missionaries. In the first instance, the female missionary appears to have been attacking his sense of himself as an intellectual and as an independent person with rights of his own. The second instance, though psychologically more opaque in that the ultimate reasons for this extreme intolerance about discussing body eliminations are not transparent, is equally telling. Whatever the underlying reasons for Sam's intolerance about these matters, his reaction does indicate that the missionary was attacking some very deeply felt aspect of his sense of self, here expressed as a matter of propriety. He was willing to forsake his fieldwork, possibly even to murder this man in a fit of rage, to correct this attack. In both these cases, it is as if Sam was proclaiming, "I am what I am," that is, "this is my life and I'll live it as I choose"—a statement of his sense of self/identity.

Although Sam's principal identity problems arose in response to the missionaries, this is not meant to imply that life with the natives was without any problems, was completely identity-syntonic. Feelings that he experienced among the missionaries, for example, psychic isolation and separation, were also felt among the natives:

It was there with the natives too. There were just certain things I couldn't share with them. For example, they have no notion of class inclusion. You can't say that something is within a larger whole. I remember the sheer frustration, I remember going through a copy of *Time* in the bush with a native man. There was some photo of the New York skyline, and I said, gee, that's New York, that's where I come from. And his response was "I thought you said you came from America." I remember the feeling of culture shock then. How could I, how could, how could I possibly point this out? I couldn't get the point across. It would be pointless to try.

75

I missed company that I had a lot in common with. To say that I made friends among the natives is certainly true, and even among the missionaries. But it's one thing to have a native friend who shares a few parts of your life with you, and it's another to have a friend who is a larger part of your life and can share more experiences with you. There was nothing like that. I really felt the loss. My best informant was a good friend, but there were some things, because of our different backgrounds, that I just couldn't share with him, things that I could and did share with someone who had a similar background, at home for example. That was . . . that was real difficult. I did correspond with such friends by mail. Once a week a plane flew in with mail. So there was that kind of correspondence and it was terribly important to me. But the special friends, the ones who are really important in your life, there was nobody like that there.

The dominant theme of these two passages is identical. In both, one can almost feel the isolation that Sam was experiencing. There was no one with whom he could communicate as an equal, no one who shared his own experiences, no one who really knew about his life. There was, therefore, no one who could mirror onto him a positive sense of his identity.

In addition to this lack, he had to make a major adjustment in relation to the natives' use of time, or rather, their lack of use of time:

I would take a nap after lunch. Everybody slept then. I found it to be virtually essential for my well-being. I don't want to make it sound like I was that busy. In fact, the greatest problem in the field was boredom. Some days would go by, well I don't know about days, but a day would go by where there wasn't much to do. Boredom was by far the most massive problem. When I got out into the bush, the problem was compounded. The people have a much slower pace of life than mine. They and I spent large parts of the day sleeping. The boredom was massive. I would emphasize immense chunks of time with nothing to do.

Q.: Sleep was essential to your well-being?

A.: Well, after lunch, the missionaries would sleep too. I'm quite certain there was a physical aspect to it. It's certainly more than likely there was a psychological aspect to it too. I just needed a rest from the strain. The strain primarily of not having a strain. It's not that there was no strain, but life there was just not strenuous enough.

Q.: I am impressed by the great activity in your life before the field.

A.: Yeah, active, yeah. As a graduate student certainly, always work to do. Yeah, as a private person always trying to keep myself occupied through either a chore or a hobby. Including sports. I was physically active a lot. I've always hated just having empty time. I pride myself on filling, on using, time well.

Q.: How did you handle this boredom in the field?

A.: I had some books with me, a batch of novels. I'm not sure I had any novels when I first went, but I sure as hell learned to get them whenever I had a chance. Especially a book by Roth. What's it called? *Call It Sleep*, that's it. That was my favorite book in the field. It still is one of my favorites. Novels and various magazines; magazines like *Time* and various football magazines. Really I think I would have gone up the wall without novels and magazines. . . . I really got a lot of satisfaction out of reading *Time* magazine, even if the copies were six months old. Yeah, *Time* was pretty important! You got to do something.

The point that I want to emphasize about Sam's difficulties with boredom is their identity-relevant features. He admits, in his life before the field, to hating "empty time," to feeling a sense of "pride" over his ability to be constantly active. Certainly, an individual's characteristic use of time, his typical pace of life, forms one of those innumerable identifications that compose his sense of identity. When an individual is then thrown into a situation in which his sense of time is disrupted, as Sam's obviously was, he will experience that disruption as a threat to his sense of self-continuity. From this perspective, Sam's reading of *Time* and various football magazines takes on a defensive/reparative function. Not only did this reading transport him back home—he was and is a football fanatic—but it also plunged him directly into the hurly-burly of the modern world, a world in which there is constant activity and always plenty to do to fill up time. Sam grew up in New York City and thrives on that fast pace of life. These identity-relevant aspects of boredom may very well apply to many Western anthropologists, and all others for that matter, who, for one reason or another, lead a fast-paced life and then do their fieldwork in a much slower-paced culture—or vice versa, depending, of course, on the individual.

It is also no accident that Sam's favorite book in the field was Henry Roth's *Call It Sleep*. Set in New York City, this book is a powerful psychological novel depicting a young Jewish boy's search for identity. Sam found in it both a concrete symbolization of his current difficulties in solidifying a sense of identity and a continuity-maintaining link with his past; he was the Jewish boy growing up in the streets of New York City.

77

Aside from the reading of various magazines and books, Sam engaged in other behaviors that had, as one of their multiple functions, a defensive/reparative one. The following passages, in response to my questions concerning holidays he celebrated and cravings of various sorts, make this point in a manner now familiar to the reader:

> Oh, well, I celebrated, well maybe celebrated is not the right word. I recognized New Year's Day. New Year's Day, my celebration for it, if you want to call it that, consisted of recognizing it in my head. The missionaries didn't mark it, and certainly the natives didn't either. I observed it in my head. I recall saying to myself that it is now 1966. For a while, although I've stopped in recent years, I used to recount to myself where I'd been on each New Year's since 1950. Yeah, I did that in the field. I recognized the years changing and the places I had been. My birthday, I remember marking somehow, something in my notebook. It's hard to remember.
>
> Q.: Did you experience any particular cravings in the field?
>
> A.: Oh yes. Foods, sex. The thing I missed most, and I mean this quite seriously, was seltzer. More generally, carbonated stuff. My main drink is seltzer. It was that sense of not having something carbonated around that bothered me a great deal. I drank a great deal of carbonated stuff when I was growing up. Yes, a thousand times. Kids say they were raised on mother's milk; I can say I was raised on seltzer and soda. I was really dying for something carbonated in the field.
>
> Q.: You remained celibate in the field?
>
> A.: I jerked off but I didn't have any sexual partner.
>
> Q.: Why was that?
>
> A.: Why didn't I have a sexual partner? Well, because of the tactical advice I was given before I left for the field from my adviser. . . . I certainly had the opportunity, some of the women were willing. Several times I was approached by native women, but I decided I better not risk it. So I didn't.
>
> Q.: Did you then have much of a fantasy life?
>
> A.: Sure, but my partners were not native women. I was not turned on by native women. Most of the women were probably from the states. I wasn't particularly interested in the women in that area at all. By and large not appealing. Probably the women back home mostly. Yes, definitely.

The continuity-maintaining features in these accounts seem clear. On New Year's Day, Sam recounted to himself where he had been on that same day over the past sixteen years, that is, he was the same person who had been in those places on New Year's Day in the past.

78

He missed, in terminology so blatant one could almost trip over it, his "mother's milk," which was seltzer. Carbonated beverages were a part of his life from his earliest days to the present. About his celibacy and sexual cravings, the familiar fantasies about women "back home" make their appearance again, as does the lack of interest in native women. Again and again, human sexuality is an enormously plastic phenomenon, undoubtedly capable of serving many different masters—but one master it does serve is the person's sense of identity (Lichtenstein 1977). The link forged with the home world, out of the furnace of sexual renunciation, is a powerful one indeed.

In addition to these behaviors, Sam employed his principal informant as a narcissistic object. In fact, as the passages below show, his relationship with his informant might almost be considered the type specimen of narcissistic object choice:

I had a best informant, X. Extremely extroverted, extremely willing to talk. Friendly, trustworthy. Yeah, trustworthy. Intellectual too. One of the great joys in fieldwork, and it is a joy, is the joy of discovery. I really discovered things. I solved problems. I cleared up controversies. There was real joy in that, an intellectual joy. And this is a man who appreciated the intellectual life. I mean he was a thinker. That was one of his most memorable qualities. I remember very clearly his verbosity. I don't mean that in a negative sense; quite the contrary. Unbelievably verbal. . . . I don't know his exact age. Clearly, I guessed he was in his seventies. In fact, I can be reasonably certain of that. This old a man is a little unusual. He certainly wasn't typical though. Far more verbal, far more aggressive. And open and honest, I should add that. Talks very easy about his personal life. He was unusual in all these respects and for his concern with the intellectual life. His physical prowess was really remarkable for a man his age. I like him very much.

Q.: He sounds to me something like a social scientist.

A.: Yeah, yeah. Definitely a social thinker. In fact, this was the impression I had of a lot of my informants. Very clearly involved with intellectual issues concerning social classification and I think appreciation of me because I was similarly involved. . . . I saw a lot of myself in X. Yeah, the verbosity again, without being negative. The friendliness, the interest in the intellectual life. Also he was an athlete. He was an incredibly skilled dancer. He was one of the few men who really danced well, and a good swimmer as well. I'm not a particularly good dancer or swimmer, but I am very much a physical buff in other ways. I had a sense of him as a man of the body and the mind, something I see myself as. When I met him, he was not only verbal, but he was aggressive. Many people stayed away from me the first few days, but he came right up. He was quite aggressive and approached me quickly, which is also something that I see in myself. I'm not particularly intimidated by people. That's the kind of guy he was. Really open and aggressive in a pleasant sort of way. When I say he was aggressive, I don't mean pushy. In fact, he had a really good sense of social space, something I like to think I have. My impression was that he was very concerned about dealing with other people, that he respected other people's privacy. He allowed me a certain privacy and space, something I try to allow others as well.

Obviously Sam was dealing with no ordinary man. Not only was X. a "wise, old man," but more specifically, he was a verbal, pleasantly aggressive, athletic, sensitive social thinker with interests paralleling those of my informant. Point for point, characteristic for characteristic, X. was a mirror of Sam's perception of himself.

An incident that bears on Sam's use of X. as a narcissistic object took place about six months into his fieldwork:

I remember once I went with my informant and several other men to an island. That's where my informant was raised and so he has strong emotional attachments to that area. He, being always so active either physically or intellectually, had gone there officially to help clear an airstrip for a small plane. I remember one day, in the middle of the day after the afternoon nap, he had, he and I had gone to work on the clearing of the airfield and the rest of the guys stayed in camp. We waited, then started work, assuming they would come. At least I did. Then when I saw they weren't coming, I went back to the camp and I screamed at those guys in the native language, you guys ought, you guys are sitting on your asses while that old man works, it's really disgraceful. I really felt that. When I hollered at the guys, I was more myself, felt it.

   Q.: In hollering, you were more yourself?
   A.: Not so much the hollering; it was that he was working. He was an old man working while the others just sat around, younger men. I was taught as a kid to defer to older people, and I generally still do, unless I'm given a very good reason not to. I certainly felt it appropriate, from my own background, not to allow what I considered a discourtesy to this guy. There was a factor that I should have taken into account but I didn't. Because of certain kinship obligations, X. owed these men some labor. He was the indebted affine. I recognized this, but when it came to clearing the airstrip, I was pretty angry at that. I thought it disgraceful they weren't doing anything.

Although Sam was aware that the younger men did not have to help X. with the work of clearing the airstrip because of certain kinship obligations, lessons from his "own background" intruded to color the situation. Sam was projecting his own conceptions of proper behavior onto the younger men in yelling at them for their "discourtesy." This projection might then be construed as a defense against the implicit attack on an aspect of Sam's sense of identity, his belief that older people deserve some measure of deference, an attack produced by the seeming disregard of the younger men for the older man. Sam also probably saw this "discourtesy" as a personal slight. In looking at X., Sam was looking into a mirror, was seeing himself, and therefore a discourtesy to X. was a discourtesy to him.

As a last tribute to the character of X., I offer the following passage taken from Sam's discussion of his other informants:

> B. was a really bad informant. I asked him once about ritual names, which I already knew something of, and he gave me a five-hour disquisition that was pure bullshit. I shouldn't malign him so much, but when it came to, when I gave this problem to X., he just cut through it like a hot knife through butter. B. was not that bad. He was useful as an informant in some ways. I did feel for him as a marginal man. Both of us were marginal men in a sense. . . . But X. could give me the rules, the underlying constructions, of the problem.

Although B. was not completely without use, and although he was a marginal man, he was never able to attain X.'s status, that of a full-fledged anthropologist.

For certain specific reasons not relevant to my concerns here, this informant was not able to return home directly after completing his fieldwork. His comments on leaving the field provide, however, another and last example of defensive/reparative behavior:

> The place where I came back to presented a lot of problems. It was a very conservative little town. I felt like I hadn't left the bush. You wind up always doing the same things with the same class of people. But I like to diversify my life, to mix with all kinds of people. It felt very confining. I need some tension in my life. So what I did was to go to a larger city in that area. I felt happy then. I went to a larger town for a while. It felt like New York. I felt kind of pleased about that. It was a positive feeling, a sense of relief. It was my favorite place in the area, especially one place in particular, that reminded me of a cross between Forty-second Street and Greenwich Village in New York. I had something of the life I always enjoyed. After the field, I needed this, some freedom. It was the equivalent for me of New York in this country.

The first town that Sam stayed in upon returning from the field appears to have disrupted the continuity of his sense of identity in a manner analogous to his life in the bush. In both cases, the slow pace of life and the almost rural atmosphere seem to have clashed violently with Sam's own sense of his past life. In remedying this clash, he, in a sense, did manage to return home to New York City, if only in his imagination. He was able to locate (create) an area in a larger town that rekindled memories of two of his favorite places in New York City, an area in which he could have "something of the life" he had "always enjoyed."

Sam was unique among the people I interviewed in that he went to the field with a secure sense of himself as an anthropologist and that this feeling helped to prevent extreme identity deterioration. That Sam did feel himself to be an anthropologist before he went to the field is a point that he insisted on: "The sense of myself as an anthropologist was already there before I went to the field. I had already published, had my M.A. degree. I didn't think of fieldwork as establishing me as an anthropologist. That wasn't the question. It elevated my already established position in anthropology. I was not simply an anthropologist when I returned. I was the young star of anthropology in that area. I was treated accordingly. Everybody in the department, including the faculty, looked up to me. And in other departments as well." Although the discoveries that he made in the field and the positive mirroring that he received about them heightened his sense of identity as an anthropological star, the foundations of that identity were firmly implanted before fieldwork; he had an "established position" as an anthropologist before undertaking fieldwork.

This identification with anthropology, as mediated by his work, helped Sam through the worst times in his fieldwork. This point is illustrated by his response to my question concerning his most memorable experience during fieldwork:

> The discovery I made. That was a real discovery. That was a discovery of great importance in this area. I got it. I felt like hitting the roof. I had cracked the code, solved the major theoretical issue in that area. The general discoveries and the fitting into a pattern gave a tremendous high in the field. It really made all the difference. I remember one lady, a wife of a missionary. She was having trouble adapting to the field. One day she asked me, "How do you keep going, how do you keep it from getting to you? How do you stand it, tolerate it?" My answer to her, which I felt very genuinely, was, well, my work makes all the difference. The discoveries were the tremendous high. I don't know what words to use. They made all the difference. I knew the importance of what I was finding. I had cracked the code; there was no

doubt of that in my mind. It's that sense of discovery that's so profound. It makes up for a lot of suffering. It really does.

Sam was the only one of my informants who, in responding to my question concerning one's most memorable experience during fieldwork, emphasized an experience the significance and meaning of which was primarily determined by and in relation to his own home world; my other informants emphasized experiences whose locus of meaning was within the native culture. I take the outer-directedness of this person's experience as an indicator of the strength of his identification with anthropology. Even in the worst of times, he was always able to look toward home, to draw support from the knowledge that he was an anthropologist doing his job successfully.

On the basis of the analysis offered here, it is understandable that Sam's response to my question concerning whether his fieldwork entailed his undergoing a symbolic death was negative:

> No. There was nothing like that. I guess that behind all my endeavors I always felt a sense of myself and the idea of losing myself I generally won't allow or something like that. Experiences where I felt myself under water, drowning, which is the quickest metaphor I can think of for self-loss, because as a kid I almost drowned a couple of times, I never felt anything like that. I always felt that behind what I was doing was me, a living me. At times I felt overwhelmed or under the weather or frustrated, but there was always me there to feel overwhelmed. I always felt there was an agent, if not in command, at least trying to swim. That's something I try to stick with in my life generally.
>
> Q.: Did the field change you at all?
>
> A.: I'm not sure it did. It gave me some extra credentials, but that's external. Did it affect me as a person? Not radically. It gave me a sense of pride and confidence to know I had discovered these things. I don't mean to dismiss the experience as having had no effect on me, but in comparison to other things, it means relatively little.

Unlike the young woman who went to India, Sam remained relatively unaffected by his field experience, not because in going to the field he was going home but because in going to the field he brought his home, in the form of a strong identification with anthropology and his work, along with him. It was that identification that enabled him to withstand attacks on certain parts of his total sense of identity.

The preceding four vignettes have served to illustrate the variety of identity-dystonic effects associated with "normal" fieldwork. In all of these accounts, we can witness the many challenges that anthropologists experience in relation to their sense of identity during fieldwork. The defensive/reparative behaviors mobilized to stem or halt this identity disintegration are also apparent and in all their many guises. In all these cases, the individuals' field experiences were not brutal or traumatizing. But what of those, probably few, anthropologists about whom we cannot say the same? What happens when the center cannot hold and psychological chaos is unleashed?

Part III
Fieldwork as a Study in Extremes

4

A South American Odyssey

Naked and alone we came into exile. In her dark womb we did not know our mother's face; from the prison of her flesh have we come into the unspeakable and incommunicable prison of this earth. Which of us has known his brother? Which of us has looked into his father's heart? Which of us has not remained forever prison-pent? Which of us is not forever a stranger and alone?
—Thomas Wolfe, *Look Homeward Angel*

One of the major difficulties associated with investigating extreme experiences of fieldwork is the relative paucity of accounts with which to work. Understandably, those anthropologists who found their fieldwork a shattering and brutal rite of death and rebirth have not tended to write about it—or at least to publish very much about it—which generally amounts to the same thing in the end. There is a way out of this evidential dilemma, however, and that is the personal interview. The principle here, in theory, is simple: if you way-lay enough anthropologists, sit them down (individually, of course), get them talking about their fieldwork, and listen carefully and empathetically, then sooner or later you will find an extreme fieldwork experience. This way of doing business may not be the most efficient, but as the following vignette illustrates, sometimes it works out rather nicely.[1]

In this vignette, I will analyze the field experience of a self-described "small-town girl," age thirty-one (at time of entry into the field), during her approximately eighteen-month stay in a small community in South America. As with the material in the preceding chapter, I have tried to stay as close as I could to the interview format in presenting Sue's account. Because of the nature of this case, I have had to make certain routine changes in my informant's comments to secure her anonymity. These changes have not affected my interpretations in any substantial way. As with any interview, so with this one, I began at the beginning:

Q.: Sue, please describe your feelings on entry into the field area?

A.: There were a couple of things that really cluttered up the fieldwork experience for me. One was I hated being, after being out in the world as a grown-up, I hated being a graduate student. I hated being a student. Suddenly I wasn't quite grown-up. I felt disfranchised in all sorts of ways. I felt like I had been through an enormous hazing process trying to get through those exams. I hated my entire university career here. I was emotionally drained when I finished, almost like fighting, almost like I had been fighting against some force all the time. Swimming upstream, fighting all the way. So getting out to the field was getting away from that. And right before fieldwork, just before I left, I broke up with my boy friend. That was completely finished.

I mean it's an odd experience to pop down into a foreign culture and deal with it, with all the strangeness of it, and I felt, because of my particular approach to the field, that the support systems at home had been cut off in a shocking sort of way. I went determined to feel, to see fieldwork as a personal quest, a personal odyssey. Quest and odyssey are ideas that I carried with me all the time. This is what is giving it meaning for me. The first cause about this is not the dissertation, not a hypothesis, not a thesis, it's not just going after data. One of the compelling motives for me was how will I do under these circumstances. My idea comes from the old adventurer type of stuff I used to read when I was younger. It's the very old and out-of-date romantic quest. There was a lot of questing and testing going on. The one question that I carried with me was how will I do when I'm put down in a strange place with only myself as a resource. And how will I come out of it at the end? These things were very much on my mind. When fieldwork begins, I remember saying, now the quest begins. Now the journey begins. These were the types of metaphors I had for it. My whole orientation to fieldwork was to try and make it, to heighten the emphasis on it being a solitary quest. I wasn't sure I had any empathizers at home to bounce this stuff off of. I should add, in regard to testing myself, that I made a conscious decision; I decided no matter how bad it might be for the fieldwork, I want to know how I'll do. I made it a part of the circumstances—I went without virtually any linguistic skills. Almost none, and I did it on purpose. Because I had to know. My motive for this was no so much what you can learn about the culture, but what you can learn about yourself. That was really important to me. I guess I felt that if I didn't carry out this odyssey in a really extreme way, I would always have to ask the same questions again in a different experience. Fieldwork was a personal quest for me. I wanted to know, when everything was stripped away, what was essentially left. I wanted to know what was available at the core. I wanted to test my limits, to ascertain my boundaries.

Q.: You felt psychically isolated in the field then?
A.: Yeah, yeah. I felt cut off. I think that would be truly fair to say.
Q.: How did you handle that?
A.: To overcome that sense of being cut off? Well, not for a long time. I just added that to part of the quest. I just took it to be one of the extremes, and I developed quite an interest in extremes as a result. The isolation made me enter more fully into the community and stand more apart from what I had left. I didn't try to find any helpful Americans in the area, or find a companion in the field to help me. I took a very austere, almost a personal trial approach to the whole thing. I really couldn't think of anything to do.

These passages are profoundly suggestive of several facets of Sue's experience. First, she was the only one of my informants whom I was able to detect experiencing identity problems before entering the field. This situation is reflected in her sense of "disfranchisement" during graduate school, although it is perhaps more powerfully represented in her imagery of fieldwork as a quest or odyssey. Such imagery suggests that Sue was searching for a meaning framework within which to secure her sense of self. My impression of these passages is also that of a self trying to "reenergize" itself, to overcome feelings of self-inauthenticity. Before undertaking fieldwork, Sue had been in therapy to work out her "feelings of estrangement" from the world. She apparently meant fieldwork to be an opportunity to solidify her sense of self, that is, to find "what was available at the core," to "test limits," to "ascertain boundaries." Sue was unsure of the foundation of her self—note the interrogative form, "what was available"—and was seeking to reaffirm (rebuild) it through fieldwork.

Also, in purposely neglecting to learn the native language (a variety of Spanish), in failing to try to locate some means of handling her psychic isolation, and in her entire "austere" approach to her "solitary quest," Sue was, in essence, heightening the cognitive clash between herself and the natives. She was exaggerating the potential for culture shock, for identity fragmentation. Despite her strength in planning this highly austere approach to fieldwork, however, she did feel the need to break out of this highly dangerous isolation; "I really couldn't think of anything to do" implies its opposite, that she had been trying to think of some way to lessen her extreme isolation.

That this austere approach to fieldwork had begun to accomplish its goal of stripping away the "less essential" aspects of her self is nicely illustrated by a brief passage that Sue tacked on to the end of our interview: "I thought very little about anthropology in the field. Once I asked myself to name two great works of anthropology and I couldn't think of anything. The more I was there I was into the experience, into the people, into my field notes. I was taking field notes, but I wasn't thinking how this relates to so and so's theory. There was a period of amnesia in there when I couldn't remember who any anthropologists were. I couldn't even name my own dissertation committee members. I really couldn't."

Although several of my informants reported not thinking much about theory while in the field, no one before or after Sue had ever reported not being able to name two great works of anthropology or any anthropologists and certainly not to be able to remember their own committee members. These failures suggest a marked break in Sue's sense of continuity with her own immediate past. And it is this sense of continuity that provides the backbone for an individual's sense of identity.

None of this is meant to imply that Sue produced her own identity crisis out of herself, so to speak. Admittedly, she did bring a personality structure (feelings of self-inauthenticity) into the field that tended to encourage such a crisis. But it also must be admitted that the natives' life ways and manners of perceiving her encouraged this tendency. Under the category of life ways, for example, I cite the following passage, in which Sue details her reactions in trying to adjust to the loss of one of those innumerable identifications that compose one's sense of identity:

> The most torturous aspect was visiting informants who weren't there. You would make an appointment and show up and they wouldn't be there. You would feel shut out then. You've wasted valuable time, and you wonder if there's something going on that you can't understand. The culture is like that. There are no schedules. People don't make appointments. I'm the stupid person trying to do that. I could see that the culture operated that way, but it is still terribly frustrating and aggravating to someone who operates according to a time schedule, who has a sense of time. It was terribly frustrating. Whole days would pass with nothing but waiting. The vast majority of time one spends waiting, feeling unproductive.

As impressive as this passage may be, it pales in comparison to the following:

Being a woman in a community where I wasn't understood, well women don't behave like you have to. They don't live alone, they don't even dress the way you do. They're not intellectuals. They don't carry little notebooks around. They have children—so what's the matter with you? Everything about my experience, the environment I went into, served to heighten my sense of being isolated. I mean I did pick up relationships with the natives and with their families and became a member of one family where I felt comfortable. Still, though, I had to keep up a lie most of the time about having a fiancé back home because I had to seem like some kind of normal human being. One important aspect of fieldwork was that I had to become sexually neuter. In their eyes, I wasn't what a woman is. I couldn't quite be what a man is either, and so I was a neuter. I was a neuter in role and over time in that identity as well. Really, I felt asexual in my inclination. I just lost my sexuality. I was nothing. The only way you could be a woman was to have four kids and a husband and I didn't have those things. It turned me into nothing.

Q.: About celibacy in the field?

A.: It wasn't at all a problem. It may have had to do with the whole self-image problem I was struggling with, the neuter status which I had acquired. I think I saw myself as neuter. I didn't have sexual needs. I just didn't have them. When I went into the larger city in the area, I could have met an American man, one of my own kind, but I didn't care less. I couldn't engage myself at all on that level. It disappeared. The fieldwork state is a study in neutrality. You're a neuter. You're not quite anything to these people. You're womanlike in some ways, manlike in others, and so you never quite fit in anywhere.

I have already mentioned the importance of one's perception of one's body self for the maintenance of a stable sense of identity. It seems probable that Sue, in being neuterized, experienced a powerful attack on her sense of existing as a fully grown-up woman. "What's the matter with you, no kids, no husband?" She became not merely an anomalous creature, both man and woman, but a "nothing." Such a powerful attack against one's sense of identity cannot go unredressed by any individual, and Sue was no exception. A relatively undramatic response to this attack is already hinted at by Sue in her interestingly ambiguous statement: "I had to keep up a lie most of the time about having a fiancé back home because I had to seem like some kind of normal human being." To whom exactly did she have to seem like a normal human being? For whom was this sham maintained? Was it for the natives or perhaps for her own psychological well-being? Actually, the dichotomy I have proposed here is false. Sue had to seem normal to the natives so as to receive back from them the reflections of her competency as a woman. In trying to convince the natives of her normality, she was trying to convince herself of it. Her lie, then, was functioning in a defensive/reparative manner; it was an effort to hang onto her image of herself as a fully functioning young woman.

If a lie could serve as a defensive/reparative behavior, imagine how much better an actual flesh-and-blood fiancé would be. It appears that some such train of thought must have unconsciously occurred to Sue, for when an old boy friend came to the field to visit her, she turned him into her fiancé:

> In December, after I had been in the field about six months, I took him to my community with the express purpose of introducing him as my fiancé. I had told everybody, I had invented him earlier. This was a source of difficulty for me. The women had always been asking me about marriage and children and so on, so I told them that my fiancé was back home with a full-time job. When he came down then, I told him he was going to be my fiancé. It was an elaborate role-playing and it greatly relaxed the people about me. The problem was that it became, was more than a put-on. Women would constantly stop me, this was after he had left, and ask me how he was doing, when he's coming back again, how many children are you going to have, where are you going to live, etc. They would ask me for these details. I, of course, gave them detailed answers. That near killed me. That was hard. It was far from harmless, which is how I first thought about it. They saturated me about this, and it was always very difficult. They had this image of him in their minds, and I had to carry out the scenario. It put a strain on me all the time. It wasn't the truth, it was fictitious. Psychologically, I should have just invented the whole scenario, brought a picture with me, just invented a whole stupid scenario. I just kept replaying a scenario that wasn't true, and I was conscious of the lies in all this. That was an enormous psychological burden.

As this passage amply illustrates, the most clever plans often go astray in unpredictable ways. Far from relieving her identity problems, this flesh-and-blood fiancé appears to have aggravated them. Now women were constantly stopping her for information, and she was forced to construct elaborate lies about some aspect of her past and future life that had not and never would exist. Such a charade would hardly serve to heighten one's sense of continuity with one's own life.

There are a great many other stunning examples of defensive/reparative behavior in Sue's comments. For example, in the middle of a discussion about her interactions with the native people, the following exchange took place:

> I was generous. Generosity is not the rule there, and I thwarted the rule. I was generous in personal little ways. And in my work with the sick, I would always try to look in at them after a talk. And maybe give them some vitamins, or pick up some weird jungle root for them. And that kind of thoughtfulness is not part of the culture, it's not part of the culture, it's not a rule in that culture. I chose to violate that rule. I was anomalous in that way.
>
> Q.: Why do you suppose you violated that rule?
>
> A.: I don't really know. I suppose it might have had to do with my upbringing. I was always taught to be generous. That reminds me, I had an odd experience in the field, a peculiar kind of déjà-vu. It's not something that I expected to have at all. But I kept finding myself in certain community or family situations or scenes of life, you know "ethnographic moments," these are the people on the way to their fields, and they reminded me of when I was a kid in my hometown in Georgia, growing up. I'd be in a kitchen late at night, and there'd be a kerosene light, a cup of tea going around, and a kind of peace and simplicity, and I grew up in a kind of humble, I mean I was the American peasant. And I kept having these uncanny moments, a sensing of familiarity. And this odd continuity, this déjà-vu from my own world, this really simple peasant life, would give me the oddest sense of security, continuity, and understanding, and a genuinely shared moment. . . . The day before I left I went out to the fields to say good-bye. Just sit on the ground and talk. And suddenly, I was reminded of the same thing at home. That was a thread throughout, and it was always relieving, refreshing, and helpful when it showed up. It gave me a chance to rest, to relax, into a moment. That went on a lot. . . . The déjà-vu was always surprising. It was always surprising. Maybe it did have this we're not so different after all quality about it. I guess subconsciously we're all looking for what we share, have in common, with everybody else. . . . This familiarity may have been how I was defining my belonging, it may have been. You latch onto anything that seems familiar. You have to, something has to mark your space, to mark where you are. You can't go totally out to sea.

In the middle of South America, Sue was suddenly transported home, during an "uncanny moment," her "sensing of familiarity" providing her with feelings of "security" and "continuity." These moments were always "relieving" and "refreshing," refueling to her sense of identity. These moments always gave her a feeling of continuity in experience between her life in the field and her early childhood. She needed something to help her in "mark[ing] her space," to prevent her from going "totally out to sea," that is, to organize her experience in relation to her own sense of past identity. This déjà-vu is a textbook example of defensive/reparative behavior.

In response to my question about whether she celebrated her birthday in the field, Sue responded:

> I was sick in a larger city with typhoid at the time. But I did celebrate Thanksgiving. I was with a group of Americans, with the Fulbright commission actually. The cultural attaché put on a large Thanksgiving dinner. I had gotten word that this was going to happen, and I decided that this was an important holiday. I went in there and there were all these Americans, turkey, the whole thing, and that was important to me. I had thought about trying to do that in my community, give somebody a Thanksgiving dinner, but I didn't have the facilities to carry it off and they didn't have any curiosity about my world. It would have been awfully hard to get any shared enthusiasm. Thanksgiving is my favorite holiday. If we wiped all of them out, it would be Thanksgiving that I would want to keep. I like autumn; I like feasts; I like the sense of families feasting together. No complicated trappings, no tinsel, just a whole day together eating and talking, watching football. It's really my favorite moment for holidays. I guess I really said I just want to be with my own kind for Thanksgiving, and I arranged to do it. . . . Thanksgiving is for me a sort of time marking. I'll do it before next Thanksgiving. It's got some continuity, it gives continuity to my life. It's a personal ritual. My New Year's Day is Thanksgiving.

Thanksgiving is her favorite holiday, a "personal ritual" that gives her life some degree of continuity by "time marking." And she felt the need to celebrate the holiday with those of her own kind, with those who could reflect onto her a sense of shared understanding of the meaning of the ritual and so affirm her link to her home world.

Sue described another incident that seems to be related to an aspect of this Thanksgiving experience, as well as to the déjà-vu experience cited earlier:

> One evening, Ray invited me over for a big feast. They roast a lamb and potatoes, it's really very good. After the feast, we went for a walk and came back to the house exhausted. We all sat around in the kitchen, passed a bottle of beer around, and then Ray's wife fixed this humble potato soup, and we ate the soup. A bunch of little kids came in and fell asleep all around us, and we sat crowded around a burning

candle. And we sat there, in this adobe room, sort of crowded, with kids sleeping all around, sitting all around, with two guys playing the guitar and singing really beautifully. It was a deeply peaceful, cele- bratory kind of sharing, in the humblest way. Sort of an uncluttered moment. I wasn't notetaking, wasn't researching. It stands out like a photograph in my mind. It was one of those times when you get a really deep sense of the people you're with.

This occasion sounds very much like a transplanted Thanksgiving feast. In addition, I think I can detect the same continuity with the simple peasant life of Sue's childhood in this experience as in the déjà-vu and Thanksgiving day descriptions. All three of these de- scriptions have the same almost folksy, mellow tone about them. Although she does not characterize them as such, I think that it is reasonable to see in the two descriptions the same linking with her small-town background as in the more explicit déjà-vu experiences.

Behaviors that serve to link the individual to her home world may also carry with them an emotional backlash. In establishing this link, such behaviors may indicate to the individual just how far from her home world she actually is and, in so doing, generate a profound affectual response:

One interesting event happened while I was there. A man from Cal- ifornia, who was a buyer of certain native goods, stopped by while I was there. Three times in all. I remember when he saw me he was surprised—"My God, a woman here!" He left me a few goodies the first two trips. They were really a treat. And he was very sympathetic to the people and the culture. The third time that guy came was not much before I left to go home, and he had two Americans with him. They had brought a shortwave radio, and it was World Series time. I hadn't thought about any of that. We sat around, smoking some mari- juana and listening to the World Series in my room, and I just, I guess they were in a room next to mine, and I just went back to my room and wept. Something about home just washed over me. All this famil- iarity, this is what's going on at home. I hadn't thought about the flow of time. Here it's World Series time. I just broke apart. I had been holding a lot together. That was it. I was emotionally, physically, men- tally spent.

Sue also recalled precise details about certain general themes of her dream life:

I did have several dreams where I was with this lover friend of mine [he lived in the United States]. We would be together doing something.

95

Dreams of intimacy and closeness in communication. I remember those now. I would wake up from them emotionally devastated because it wasn't true. Maybe they were wish-fulfillment dreams, for companionship, intimacy, and love and the things you don't feel in the field even if you're very close to the people. I really care about those people deeply, but they never knew me. I knew the world they came from, but they couldn't even ask questions about mine. How did you get here, on a plane? Do they grow potatoes in your country? Everything was oriented to their life. They weren't curious about me, except in their terms. Companionship and shared moments were themes running through my dreams. I was really stuck there. Dreams of familiarity, sharing, and companionship—that was a recurring theme in my dreams.

On one hand, it is possible to see in these dreams an attempt to repair the damage inflicted on Sue's sense of herself as a competent young woman; in these dreams, presumably her lover sees her as attractive and desirable. Her body self has been replenished and reaffirmed. On the other, it is possible to detect in these dreams the same themes of sharing and familiarity as in the earlier-cited Thanksgiving day memories and the déjà-vu experiences. In this case, these themes appear to be a direct response to the lack of understanding (mirroring) on the part of the local people. These people, however much Sue might like them and vice versa, were, from the point of view of her identity needs, always and by necessity to remain strangers ("cracked mirrors").

As interesting and important as these dreams are, they cannot even begin to measure up to the significance of and the suggestiveness conveyed by the following dream:

I had one dream after I went down to the missionary's house, to get hot water. It was very cold where I was and cramped, and so I could never get really clean. I would go there and wash my hair and just pour the hot water over me. My muscles would relax, almost to the point where I couldn't stand up. I would fall asleep instantly. I would fall into this deep, almost fetal sleep. It was sleep and relaxation like I never had before. I had slept deeply at times in my community, and I always felt they were escapes. Crawl in and pull the bag shut around you, wall yourself off. Almost a drugged sleep. In this case, I was dreaming. I kept dreaming of my mother and my grandmother. This womanly warmth, this motherly, nurturing warmth all around me. They were making a cake for my birthday. It was this comfort and nurturing, sparked by suddenly finding myself clean and warm and comfortable and resting. I just felt like I had found the womb again for a few moments there. A deeply nurturing feeling.

This is a powerful dream. Sue's imagery is precise and correct: she was in a "fetal sleep," she had "found the womb again," for in her dream she was returning to the place and the time of her psychological hatching. She was back with her "mothering ones," back to where the roots of her identity first took hold. Nor should the significance of the birthday cake be overlooked; celebrating one's birthday is a powerful "time marker" and a reminder to the individual of her sense of continuity through time. Also of importance are the now familiar themes of nurturing, comfort, and the like, although special emphasis should be laid on the context of "womanly warmth" in which they are situated. This latter point may reasonably be seen, again, as a defensive/reparative reaction directed against those threats to her body self that Sue was experiencing.

As I listened to the recounting of this dream, and particularly to the emphasis placed on birth imagery and "womanly warmth," I began to wonder if it was merely the pleasant surroundings and hot water that had triggered it off. And so I asked Sue to describe the missionary to me. Her response is lovely in its directness:

She's just a fully energetic, very intelligent woman. Energetic, very independent woman. She had lived in the native culture for years and knew the people well. She knew, we shared a mutual respect for one another's experiences in the native world, for one another's effort to do whatever we did. The independence of it. So in her I found someone who knew in some sense what I was doing. None of the people at the Fulbright commission, the people responsible for my being there, had a clue about what I was doing. But she did. We shared some experiences. She had lived with a family in a remote place—for only six months—but she had steeped herself in that experience the same way that I was doing in mine. She had a sort of anthropologist's understanding of the culture. As experience, she had, in a sense, been there. She was in her mid-forties and quite mindful of taking care of herself, of being healthy. When I went there, she was incredibly aware of some of my needs that I wasn't even aware of. She was unique in that she shared that experience [fieldwork] with me. She cared deeply for the people, and so did I. This woman was critical for me, an unspoken sharing of the experience, an appreciation of it.

It seems very likely that Sue was using the missionary as a narcissistic object/self-object to bolster her sense of self. The mission-

97

ary was a very energetic, very intelligent, very independent woman, who understood, through shared experience, what Sue was going through. She had an anthropologist's understanding and appreciation of the native people. All of these characteristics would have rendered her a most suitable mirror for Sue. And perhaps it is also possible to maintain—note the caretaking reference in relation to the missionary's recognition of her unconscious needs—that in the missionary, Sue had found a "mothering one."

This use of an individual as a narcissistic object was not confined to the relatively alien (nonnative) presence of the missionary, however. One of Sue's principal informants also appears to have functioned for her in an analogous manner:

> One of my most important informants was this little old lady. She was seventy-one years old, bilingual, although her second language was about as bad as mine. Her feet were much more firmly planted in the traditional side of life there. She had been widowed in her early thirties and had then gone on to become a healer. Once I understood the culture more, I was inclined to say that she was very sympathetic, very compassionate with the old people. I mean she needed her payments to survive, but she also cared. I found that neither her needs nor her compassion outweighed the other. She was doing it because she needed to but also because she was a compassionate person, because she was bent in that direction. I came to really love her. Once I broke through, she took me on as a little daughter. Again, there was compassion. She reminded me of a few old ladies in my hometown in Georgia. She really did. That's one of those déjà-vu experiences I already told you about. Sometimes the setting, just sitting around the kitchen talking, the simplicity, it was very much like home. Yeah, that déjà-vu, definitely with that old woman.

Working with this old healer in the middle of South America once again brought Sue back home to Georgia through a déjà-vu experience. Sue's description of this healer's mode of relating to her is also interesting: the healer took her on as a "little daughter." Perhaps, if Devereux (1967) is right that often the most informative part of any statement is that which is left unsaid or implied, it is fair to say that this old healer treated Sue as a "little daughter" because Sue needed and therefore treated her as a "mother." To the extent that any daughter reflects her mother's characteristics, it is not surprising that just as this old healer worked because she needed to (to survive physically) and yet she exhibited great compassion, so Sue did fieldwork because she needed to (to survive psychically) and yet she exhibited great compassion (her generosity and thoughtfulness).

To explore further the range of defensive/reparative behaviors that Sue engaged in, I sought answers to questions about more mundane matters, for example, food cravings:

> Well, I craved protein. I wanted meat, and eggs, and peanut butter. I probably needed protein. The missionary made me some peanut butter once when I went down there. She sent it back with me. I had about a three-hour walk back to the village, and I would stop pretty frequently and just eat some of the peanut butter. It was just wow, it was almost erotic, an exciting experience! I couldn't get enough meat. The first thing I would do when I went into the city was to go to a steak house and eat a whole steak. I couldn't deal with the world until I had eaten this steak. It was on my mind so, this ritual steak. I would sometimes cook some eggs and make a whole meal out of them. I suppose they were familiar, you know I wanted, needed familiar flavors and textures.

I especially like Sue's answer here because it allows me to do away with an old bogey that surrounds this and my earlier interpretation of certain food cravings as providing a link to one's home world. I have little or no doubt that Sue did need protein, and I have little or no doubt that this physiological need underlay her cravings for protein. But this simple fact does not preclude the using of these cravings as a solution for other, psychologically based problems. Any piece of human behavior undoubtedly serves multiple functions in an individual's life (Waelder 1936). In this case, whatever the ultimate reason for her food cravings, Sue admits that she wanted "familiar flavors and textures," flavors and textures associated with her home world.

Continuing on with these mundane matters, I asked Sue about her reading and letter-writing habits while in the field. Her response was telling:

> I finally found great relief. It was humor; it was a real escape away from there; it was flights of fancy; it was liberation from some of the terrible day-to-day constraints, by reading one or two Tom Robbins novels over and over again. I would read one paragraph out of *Still Life of Woodpecker*, close the book, and read the same paragraph the next night. I just savored words, and paragraphs, and phrases, quirks of thought. I acquired these books from somebody in the Fulbright commission. One I wrote to my uncle for, and said, for God's sake, mail that book down here, I have to have it. In the end, that was the greatest pleasure. . . . I wrote a lot of letters, because I didn't have to see so

well for that. I used that as a real important tool. There are people around here who will talk and talk about my letters. I really poured myself into them. When I wanted someone to talk to late at night and wasn't ready to go to bed—you know everyone there goes to bed at 8:30—I needed this transition period, this period for myself. There was no TV, and I didn't have a radio for a long time. That was part of the extreme personal quest emphasis, so I wrote letters. I loved writing them and I would pour things out. To write about the hilarity, the events, my inner self. I also kept diaries. I got really interested in my diaries. I wrote a lot of letters as a venting device. I would get mail only every two months or so, and it was really important to me. I finally got a radio though. I felt a need to know. I borrowed a shortwave set from the Fulbright people. I had taken isolation to the limit at that point. I had been there almost a year, and the stress was building up steadily. I finally decided I needed relief from it. The radio made a lot of sense. I started to think about reentry into the U.S. and I saw the radio as a means to pick up a few threads of continuity with home, what was going on. Just hearing English and the kind of music you hear on the radio. I really got into the radio. I could crawl into my sleeping bag and just turn the radio on and listen. That was a form of companionship.

Again and again and again, Sue reiterates the same points that I have emphasized in my theoretical discussion on defensive/reparative behaviors—they serve to link the fieldworker to her own home world of shared meanings and understandings. Her reading of Tom Robbins's books gave her a sense of escaping from the field. And, of course, as one always escapes toward something as well as away from something, I would mention that her escape was toward home. In her letters, Sue was talking about her life and inner self, with people who could understand her, who knew who and what she was. I have already interpreted diaries as a means of maintaining order and continuity in one's relation to the world and to oneself. And finally, after a year of shattering isolation, Sue got a radio, through which she was able "to pick up a few threads of continuity with home." The familiar sounds of English and music provided a "form of companionship." The radio, letters, diaries, and books all were functioning in the same defensive/reparative manner.

The material relating to defensive/reparative behaviors that I have reviewed here is quite overwhelming. It is almost as if Sue was the prototypical, or better yet, the archetypal example of these behaviors. And yet such a massive activation of these behaviors suggests that Sue was engaged in a real life-and-death struggle to retain her sense of self/identity. That she may not have been completely successful in this struggle, that she may have felt the need to dissociate from her old and inadequate, inauthentic self, is indicated by the following extraordinarily rich passage:

I did have an interesting experience. I was looking into illness behavior, and further, into how these people view their own world. They [my experiences] weren't exactly dreams. Maybe they relate to my own problems in dealing with the existence of evil. Well, whatever, there was a crash pad in a nearby town that I could go to when I felt I needed it, run by a missionary. She was an expert in the language and had some experience living with the native people. She had told me that I shouldn't stay up there [in her village] too long without a break, that she could see it in me. It was more strenuous than I thought. Every couple of months I would show up on her doorstep for a shower, a hot shower. And she would cook a meal, with vegetables and meat. I would sometimes stay there for the night. I started looking seriously at her faith, at her religion, and I wondered how it empowered her, gave her faith. I developed a spiritual quest of my own. I was sitting up one evening writing field notes, with a candle burning for light, and I was worn out, was too tired to go to bed, and I closed my eyes and got a vision of myself. This image just showed up in my head. It was this dense mass of black, dense matter. It was like a black hole. It gave off no light. It was dense. It was very heavy. I recognized this black wad of stuff as me. I was quite shocked by it. And then you start to think about blackness and death. Later I went down to the larger city in the area. I was drained at this point; I had let the stresses build up without relief. Physically I was run down. I let all this stress build up. I had to see a nurse there to get shots. On the way out, she asked me how everything was going, some simple innocent question like that, and I burst into tears. I just fell apart. I was exhausted. I just burst into tears. She was a born-again Christian. She asked me to stay a few days and to go with her to church on Sunday. I didn't have anything to do, I was alone, and I felt that as I was alone in the field, I just didn't need that now, so I said okay. I said I just need to be with my own kind again. . . . There was a time for silent prayer in the service. But I was swimming in confusion and disorientation and didn't know what was going on. I started having this vision again, and it was like the vision I had with this black, dense mass, this center. I saw myself out on the patio of the building vomiting black stuff. This black stuff just kept pouring out of me. It wasn't a dream. It was psychically revealing. You're under enormous stress, you're broken down, you don't love yourself. I internalized all this and went against myself. I didn't have any support networks. Then there was the pressure of the field, wondering if you got enough data today, if you understood everything. Did I measure up today? But, of course, there's no standard to measure yourself by. And never are you up to the task. I was psychologically unhealthy. And in both visions, I recognized that it was me, that it was my inner self that had been, that had been distorted. I knew that I had to do something about it.

This is a striking and powerful passage. Sue's concern with local illness beliefs and her spiritual conversations with the missionary can both be seen as the catalysts, or triggering events, that gave body and content to the inner form of her experiential world. Sue's visions were materializations of her experiential world while she was in the field. As such, these visions are powerful indicators of the crisis in identity that Sue was experiencing in the field. Her self had become black and dense; like a black hole, it gave off no light. Her center or core was black, and she began to expel it from within her: she vomited her core self. This imagery suggests a self that has decayed past its point of usefulness. It is a self that no longer illuminates her life and actions; it is a dying self that is no longer experienced as authentic: "you're broken down, you don't love your self." Apparently, on the basis of this analysis, her quest or odyssey to strip herself down to the core was successful. But the core as it was finally revealed was damaged. It was an inauthentic core that needed to be recharged, put back together again in more suitable fashion. Her feeling, after the first vision, that she needed to be back with her own kind again was profoundly correct, although it appears to have come too late. By that time, the more superficial layers of her self-structure had already been stripped off, revealing her inauthentic core. Lacking an authentic core, however, is a difficult and painful predicament for any human being; as Sue comments after seeing her inner self revealed as black and inauthentic, "I knew that I had to do something about it." And what was she to do about it? A hint is provided in this last passage. She looked seriously at the missionary, a narcissistic object/self-object, wondering how her faith in her religion "empowered her," that is, gave her life meaning. Sue then developed a "spiritual quest" of her own, a quest to locate something that would give her life a new anchor.

Where might she have looked for such an anchor? Or better yet, where else? Where else than to her work and to the discipline of anthropology? Here I must begin at the end, with Sue's feelings on leaving the field:

A SOUTH AMERICAN ODYSSEY

My biggest concern was that I failed as a fieldworker. That I didn't really understand the people. A sense that there was so much I didn't know, and yet I couldn't ask any more questions. The turning point for me was when I recognized that I was getting the same old information over and over again. I was too tired mentally to force the next step. I had to get out. I couldn't get the distance to be creative. My health was terrible. I said time to go take care of yourself. I left feeling I had done a poor job in the field. I wasn't fully digesting anything; I wasn't writing enough stuff up; I should have done more analysis in the field. I was at an impasse. I didn't know if I had done any valuable fieldwork for a period of weeks near the end. I knew that I needed to get home. I had my odyssey, kilos of field notes. I was phased out. It was time to pull the plug. I felt I had spent myself. It was time to go. I felt a great dissatisfaction with myself. I wasn't coming home triumphant, you know, she did it! I didn't have that feeling. Later that feeling came many times in many different ways. Very rewarding sense. But then I was too spent. And I realized that I was really hungry to be with my own kind, to be relaxed again in familiarity, to let go of so much effort. To stop playing roles. There was so much still to do though. When the guys came with their World Series and the marijuana, and I realized that I needed to be with my own kind, I went to the larger city and made arrangements to leave.

This hardly seems like a promising backdrop from which to develop an argument concerning Sue's identification with anthropology. She had returned from the field "phased out." She was spent, physically and psychologically. And although there is a hint of better experiences to come ("very rewarding sense"), she appears very far away from such feelings at the time of leaving the field. She lacked an authentic core at this time. The following description of her arrival home illustrates this point precisely:

I went home for a time, to see my family. It was hard just getting back. The clamor of culture. I felt that I was in a daze. And when I got back home, I practically ended up in a fetal position. I started crying. When I went home to my mother, I felt like a piece of elastic that had been all stretched out and had no snap. I may have had a pulse, I don't know. About all I could do was periodically cry. Just a zero response. When I couldn't recognize myself, I went around saying to myself and my friends, well, I'm not like this. This isn't really me. I'm not usually like this. I don't normally do things like this. I just didn't even recognize myself for a long time. Many of my behaviors were unsound, not characteristic for me. People talk about culture shock and a couple of months of adjustment time. I expected a month or two, but the whole

103

thing just went on and on. Well, gradually I realized this is not culture shock, this isn't that. This is a whole new statement of self, and a whole new way of dealing with myself. There was a lot of integrating that had to be done.

She had no pulse, felt like a worn-out elastic band, emitted "zero response"—these are all images of a self dangerously lacking in vitality and purpose. She did not recognize herself because her old sense of self was no longer there to be recognized. And is it not fitting that in putting together this new statement of self, in being reborn, Sue should use biological imagery again; she landed in a fetal position upon arriving home. And just as it is with any young infant, so it was with my informant that her new statement of self would depend on a nurturing and warmth mirrored onto her from new significant others: "One thing that has been really nice is the reaction I'm getting from specialists in the area where I worked. I went down to talk with a few of them last week, and they were impressed with my findings. They wanted to know how I had been able to get the kinds of information I had. Nobody else had been able to get into the ceremonies that I had. They said, 'This is so good, how did you get this material?' That made me more confident in my work, made me feel good."

Following this point, I wondered whether she did, in fact, perceive herself to be more of an anthropologist as a result of her experiences (fieldwork and positive mirroring): "Certainly do. *I certainly do.* I don't feel like a student now. I'm writing up my research. It doesn't have anything to do with the university structure, and with Ph.D.'s and what goes on there. *It's my stuff.* I'm an anthropologist now. I don't have to wait for the Ph.D. to be one, for an academic job. That's immaterial. I am one now. And the fieldwork, that's why."

I do not exaggerate here when I say that her certainty about her identity as an anthropologist and the importance of her work were emphasized in the interview. The significance of her stridency in tone was made crystal clear in her response to my question concerning the applicability of the phrase "symbolic death" to her experience of self while in the field:

Yeah, I do, without question. It was very much a religious experience for me in some sense of that term. This personal quest sort of orientation, that's a deep thing. That was motivating me before I ever got to the field. It was part of what brought me into anthropology. I was looking for some kind of thing, some kind of meaning for my life. There

104

are elements of personal ritual passage in the experience. I think I was always aware of that. It is these elements that make anthropology, that give it a particular kind of understanding. We anthropologists are not philosophers, historians, economists. We're a species unto ourselves. And the fieldwork experience is one of the critical reasons why. That fieldwork for the anthropologist is a rite of passage is no figure of speech. . . . I think I got the quest out of my system, the quest that's been motivating me for a long time. Some of the key questions for me, not just for anthropology, but for me, about what I'm made of, the personal quest element, I lived it out. I think it's laid to rest a certain kind of restlessness about unanswered questions about myself. I have an enormous sense of peace about having done all that. It's wrapped up something that I've been pushing for for many years. I've come through it, but I don't dismiss it. The whole thing [fieldwork] goes on with me. But there is a feeling of closure about the great restlessness I always felt. I do feel this peace and closure and a growing sense of confidence about what I can do and what I've got. I'm interested now in myself, in the question of what makes us human. From a deeply personal perspective, I have come to appreciate that we are relational. The isolational aspects and my deprivation during fieldwork, which were part of my quest, served to deepen and heighten my appreciation of the relational aspect of humans. I value it highly. It kind of has a sacred quality about it. It's something that sets us human beings apart in a real special sort of way: we are relational. I place a real high value on that. I'm more content with balance now. I've always played a bit with extremes and gotten a lot out of it. I've always been hungry for unknowns, for experiences. My attitude has been one of taking in. And now, not because of the dissertation, my focus is on gathering up all that I've taken in and presenting it. My concern is with the expressive now. My expressive self is really important to me now. I don't have to have end-to-end experiences to say to myself that I'm alive. I don't have to struggle against challenges, against obstacles, to know that I'm alive. There are other ways that I want to know about. This definition of self, or fulfilling of self, or being convinced you're alive, for me does not depend on constant experience any longer. It's all a building onto, not a cutting off, of my experience in the field. I'm very pleased with my odyssey; I think it worked. There are many ways you grow that you never expected. I feel like there will be many more satisfactions coming from my experience, even if I don't get a job as an anthropologist, because there aren't any. The experience in the field, it's me.

This long passage is so incredibly rich that it is hard to do justice to it. Sue went to the field sensing that her self needed completion,

105

that she needed to find "some kind of meaning" for her life. In fact, it appears that before going into the field, Sue was fighting feelings of self-inauthenticity and self-inadequacy through engaging in "end-to-end experiences," through struggling constantly against challenges and obstacles (collectively, what I would call, following that great tragedian, the "Don Quixote syndrome"). It is as though the internal void in herself could be defended against through endless activity. Presumably, if such constant experiences were needed to maintain a feeling of self-vitality, then when her experience bogged down, her self would feel as if dead. Her "religious experience" of fieldwork, however, apparently rendered these considerations obsolete.[2] That aspect of her life appears to her now as having closed; her odyssey has apparently led to an Ithaca of sorts. She has learned much from her experience. For example, Sue now deeply appreciates the "sacred quality" of human relatedness. She appreciates that a part of her humanity, of being human, is being relational. These views are understandable considering that it was a disturbance in her sense of relatedness to other human beings that drove her to lose a part of her humanity, that is, her sense of identity. Or again, she has learned that her self need not be hungry for and devouring of experiences to feel alive. Rather, her primary concern now is with her creative work, that is, her "expressive self." This should hardly be surprising to readers of this work. None of this is meant to imply that Sue has simply learned a few lessons from her field experience and then forgotten about it. She mentions twice that she has not dismissed the experience; rather, "the whole thing goes on" with her, serving as a foundation to build upon. The hint conveyed by these brief statements, that she has internalized the field experience and therefore the identification with anthropology and her creative work as the anchor for her sense of self, is powerfully confirmed in her last statement: "The experience in the field, it's me."

5

Trauma in the Field:
Reflections on Malinowski's Fieldwork

But if the pieces of your mind do not come together again, the currently fashionable ideal of "fragmentation" resolves into a horrible condition. The unreborn individual remains inside a wrapping with cracks in it. There can be nothing much more terrible than to remain in this diffuse state of being. Only the sensation of being born again brings the victim or the remote, smiling child back to unitary consciousness.

—Alan Harrington, *The Immortalist*

Sooner or later this analysis had to take account of Malinowski's diaries. Any attempt to understand the field experience, and more particularly, the extreme field experience, has to come to grips with these documents. If a set of ideas pertaining to the psychology of fieldwork cannot help to illuminate Malinowski's diaries, if they cannot suggest a new perspective from which to view them, then their originator—the theorist of record—had best pack them up and retire from the field. Malinowski's diaries are that important.

One of the reasons for the immense importance of these diaries to the psychologist of fieldwork, aside from their being the work of an anthropological "founding father," is simply that they were diaries. Unlike the current spate of personal accounts of fieldwork, Malinowski never intended his diaries to be published. As a consequence, his writing tends to be less polished, less inviting, less well structured, but also more off the cuff, more direct, and more psychologically revealing than any other account of fieldwork with which I am familiar. Malinowski's diaries contain a certain pristine and wintry psychological clarity that is truly impressive.

Although it is fairly easy today to agree on the importance of Malinowski's diaries, such was not always the case. It would be fair to say, without much exaggeration, that the original publication of these diaries marked a low day for anthropology in general and certainly for British anthropology. And for Malinowski's many followers, his anthropological brethren, the day was not merely low, it was catastrophic. The Malinowski revealed in the diaries is not the Malinowski around whom the myths had grown up. For in the diaries, Malinowski is revealed, not as the archetypal fieldworker, friend of the natives and intensely interested in their every behavior, but as a man of almost "monstrous" sexual desires and lusts, a man who freely dispensed such descriptive terms as *savage, boy,* and *nigger* in reference to the "ethnographic other," a man who was nearly mentally paralyzed by longing for his own culture, a man of enormous, almost awesome ambitions.

Naturally enough, these revelations generated a storm of controversy (see Stocking 1968). And yet, when this at times vicious (and frankly humorous) controversy finally subsided, when all the smoke had cleared, surprisingly little understanding of the diaries had been achieved. As late as 1979, Francis L. K. Hsu (1977), a well-respected psychological anthropologist, could see in the diaries evidence only of Malinowski's ethnocentrism, of his attempt to flee from "hated human connections." One anthropologist who properly understood, or at least partially understood, the psychological significance of Malinowski's diaries was Forge (1967; see also Crapanzano 1977). In his view, Malinowski's diaries reflect one aspect of a struggle that every single anthropologist partakes of during his fieldwork: a struggle to maintain some sense of identity in the face of a confrontation with an overwhelmingly foreign reality. Needless to say, I agree with Forge here about the diaries as a record of an identity struggle on Malinowski's part. Yet something is still missing, a certain key to unlock the particularly desperate and almost tragic nature of Malinowski's identity struggle.

The search for this key need not detain us long. It is to be found, as Abram Kardiner and Edward Preble (1961:177) realized, in the nature of Malinowski's peculiar personality structure. To be more precise, Malinowski suffered from a marked vulnerability in his self-representation. The exact nature of this vulnerability cannot be specified more precisely because, strangely, there exists no detailed biographical study of Malinowski, "the most eccentric and controversial figure ever to enter the field of anthropology" (Kardiner and Preble 1961:160), in English (see Gross 1986). The exact specification of the nature of Malinowski's self-vulnerability is not, however, necessary for my purposes here (see Chapter 6 on this point). Rather, it

108

will be sufficient to demonstrate the similarities between Malinowski's characteristic attitudes and feelings and those classically and clinically associated with cases of self-pathology (Kohut 1971; 1984). In what follows, then, I will pay close attention to those behaviors that indicate disturbances in the structural cohesiveness, temporal stability, and affective coloring of Malinowski's self-representation.

Malinowski was born in Cracow, Poland, in 1884. His parents were both *szlachta*—landed gentry and nobility. His father was a college professor and well-known Slavic philologist. The little that is known of this period of Malinowski's life is suggestive. He was an only and lonely child, whose father died when "he was still a young boy" (Kardiner and Preble 1961:160). Following the death of his father, Malinowski and his mother grew extraordinarily close: "A lifelong attachment between mother and son began at that time. Until they were separated by the war, Malinowski's mother moved with him wherever he went and watched over him with affectionate care. His introduction to anthropology was from her lips, for she read to him for an entire year when an eye operation made it impossible for him to read at the very beginning of his career in anthropology. His mother's death . . . was a tragedy from which he barely recovered" (Kardiner and Preble 1961:161).

Although this relationship appears to have been mutually satisfying, there is a teasing hint in the diaries pointing to somewhat darker possibilities: "I recall the countless occasions when I deliberately cut myself off from Mother, so as to be alone, independent— not to have the feeling that I am part of a whole—furious regrets and guilt feelings" (297).[1] It appears that the closeness of the relationship to his mother presented a threat to the autonomy of Malinowski's nascent and developing self. Malinowski may have been experiencing some problems in self-object differentiation, in setting up and maintaining the boundaries of his own developing self. On those "countless occasions" when he sought his independence, Malinowski appears to have been fighting against self-loss through merger in the object image of his mother.

That the boundaries of Malinowski's self were weak and tenuous is a conclusion borne out by several incidents described in the diaries. After visiting a small island, Malinowski returned by boat to his base camp. His description of that trip is telling: "Had the feeling that the rattling of the ship's engine was myself; felt the motions of the ship as my own—it was *I* who was bumping against the waves

109

and cutting through them" (33–34). A second and ultimately more telling example: "Supper at English's. Before supper I walked on the veranda and had moments of concentration and spiritual elevation, interrupted by violent surges of sexual instinct for native girls, for English's servants. *I dissolved in the landscape"* (82; emphasis added). This latter dissolution of Malinowski's self occurs in the context of violent sexual longings, a point about which I will have much to say later in this chapter. For now, suffice it to say, in Malinowski's words, that "physical intimacy with another human being results in such a surrender of personality that one should unite only with a woman one really loves" (260).

The preceding discussion, though suggesting the possibility that Malinowski's self-boundaries were weak and tenuous, is speculative. From here on, the evidence grows far less speculative and far more convincing.

One point about which nearly all of those who worked closely with Malinowski agree was his hypersensitivity to slights. As George P. Murdock (1943:442) phrases it: "The key to an understanding of Malinowski's personality . . . would seem to lie in his acutely sensitive nature. Essentially humble beneath a surface vanity, he craved warmth and appreciation. . . . He found it difficult, however, to brook unfriendly criticism—a trait which sometimes embroiled him in acrid controversies." Raymond Firth (1957:1) and Ashley Montagu (1942:147) together add an important consideration to Murdock's ideas; they both point out that, in reacting to criticism that he did not think was tempered by personal loyalty to himself, Malinowski would often try, and be, "simply devastating" toward his opponents, and in a manner unmarked by any concern for the effects of his excesses.

Malinowski's hypersensitivity to perceived slights is marked throughout his diaries. I cite here only a few of the many convincing examples:

At 10 I went to Teyava, where I took pictures of a house. . . . On this occasion I made one or two coarse jokes, and one *bloody nigger* made a disapproving remark, whereupon I cursed them and was highly irritated. I managed to control myself *on the spot,* but I was terribly vexed by the fact that this *nigger* had dared to speak to me in such a manner. (272)

I handed out half-*sticks* of Tobacco, then watched a few dances; then took pictures—but results very poor. Not enough light . . . and they

110

would not pose long enough for time exposures. At moments I was furious at them, particularly because after I gave them their portions of tobacco they all went away. On the whole my feelings toward the natives are decidedly tending to *"exterminate the brutes."* (69)

Over-all mood: strong nervous excitement . . . combined with inability to concentrate, *superirritability and supersensitiveness of mental epidermis and feeling of permanently being exposed in an uncomf. position to the eyes of a crowded thoroughfare: an incapacity to achieve inner privacy.* I am on a war footing with my *boys* . . . and the Vakuta people irritate me with their insolence and cheekiness, although they are fairly helpful to my work. Still making plans for subjugating Ginger, and still irritated with him. (253)

In addition to these passages, Hsu (1979:518) reports sixty-nine instances in which Malinowski expressed feelings of high irritation, anger, and hatred toward the natives. The image I get from these quoted passages and from the earlier cited views of Murdock and others is that of an individual with a shaky sense of self relying very heavily on the receipt of positive mirroring from trusted others to maintain the integrity and boundaries of his self-representation. The vicious and devastating responses made to others, who criticize, in one sense or another, are attempts to negate the threatened self-loss precipitated by that criticism. And note here, for purposes of my later argument, that the criticism referred to primarily concerns Malinowski's work (compare the last quote, in which Malinowski's response is tempered somewhat because the natives had been helpful to his work).

With someone who was as hypersensitive to slights as Malinowski, it comes as no surprise to find that, recalling Murdock's point, he often found himself embroiled in "acrid controversies." The manner in which Malinowski dealt with these controversies is telling. Kardiner and Preble (1961:165) relate the following incident: "On one occasion, for example, he and his daughters were embroiled in a bitter quarrel five minutes after they met for the first time in a year and a half. At the height of the argument, which had to do with whether they should go to some fancy place to eat, as the girls wanted, or to a quiet place, where Malinowski could have all their attention, he withdrew himself and calmly analyzed the argument in terms of their respective, hidden motives." Firth (1957:9) had made this same point about his own and other students' relationships to Malinowski: "And if a crisis arose—because one could argue fiercely with him at times—he had a most disarming way of suddenly putting aside all emotion, and spreading the whole thing out on the table . . . for analysis of his own motives as well as those of the other person." Malinowski appears to have "practiced this motive hunting in all his personal, as well as professional, relationships" (Kardiner and Preble 1961:165).

In considering the significance of this depersonalization, I am reminded of a discussion by R. D. Laing (1965) about a young schizophrenic's inability to finish any argument in which he was engaged. Much like Malinowski, at the high point in the argument, this individual would suddenly withdraw and cease speaking. When prodded for a reason, he remarked that, in losing an argument, his opponent would lose only an argument, whereas he would lose his very self. Although this is an extreme example, the general point—that individuals with vulnerable self-representations often resort to depersonalization as a means of warding off self-loss in highly emotional or stressful situations—is a commonplace in psychoanalytic thought (Fenichel 1945). It appears that Malinowski was attempting to remove his self from the many arguments in which he got embroiled in an effort to maintain his integrity and stability.

In continuing to develop this point, Kardiner and Preble (1961:165–66) have argued that "this capacity for objective, unemotional analysis was the fulcrum for two emotional extremes in Malinowski. Although usually charming, witty, and optimistic, he was subject to moods of severe depression. He imagined himself besieged by illness and disease, and defended himself with ritualistic diets and exercises." Even Firth (1957:10), who generally tried to downplay Malinowski's personality foibles, had to admit that "exercise was one of Malinowski's fetishes." These hypochondriacal preoccupations are revealed throughout the diaries. Again, here are only two of the many convincing examples:

> I cannot say that I have felt really fit physically. Last Saturday [a week ago] I got overtired on the excursion with Ahuia, and haven't quite recovered since. Insomnia (not too marked), overtaxed heart, and nervousness (especially) seem so far the symptoms. I have the impression that lack of exercise, caused by an easily overtired heart . . . is at the root of this condition. I must get more exercise, especially in the morning . . . and in the evening. . . . Arsenic is indispensable, but I must not exaggerate the quinine. (13)

> Around Monday–Tuesday I was super-energized, and I stopped taking quinine. Last night a certain sluggishness, sleepiness, today too;

moreover I have a slight sore throat. Today I feel that heaviness in the head and body. . . . In any case, I took arsenic again this morning, calomel in the evening, and inhalations for my throat. Last night I probably caught cold because I felt the breeze even under my mosquito net. (126–27)

Throughout his diaries, Malinowski is revealed as a man constantly beset by supposed physical problems. He resorts to hot compresses, enemas, and the taking of numerous medicines, including calomel, arsenic, quinine, and iodine, to ward off these problems. This behavior is directly relevant to my argument here, for hypochondriacal worries are a principal diagnostic feature found in individuals suffering from an extreme vulnerability in their self-representation (Kohut and Wolf 1978). Hypochondria is often the surface expression of a more deeply felt concern that various parts of the body self are no longer securely anchored within the total self; the individual begins to experience an "apprehensive brooding" concerning the fragmentation of his sense of self.

In a man with Malinowski's self-structure, with a keen sensitivity to slights, and particularly to those directed against his sense of his own importance, it should not be surprising to find a deep undercurrent of envy directed against those who would pose a challenge to that sense. As evidence of this point, there is Malinowski's reaction, early in his fieldwork, to a visit by Alfred Haddon. Haddon, of course, was by that time an anthropologist of great repute. His very presence would have posed a challenge to Malinowski's self, would have served as a slight to his sense of self-importance: "In the village Haddon and his daughter loafed about. . . . I forbade hymn-singing, annoyed by Haddon. . . . We went back. . . . Passions and moods: hatred for Haddon for annoying me, for conspiring with the missionary. Envy because of the specimens he is obtaining." (36–37)

Logically, Malinowski could have seen this visit as a measure of his own importance. After all, Haddon did choose to visit him. It is possible to speculate that he might have appreciated the visit had Haddon not tried to collect museum specimens on his own and thereby deprived Malinowski of a share of the glory he so craved. Also, surely Haddon's bringing his daughter along, as if it were a pleasure trip and not of profound scientific importance, did not help.

The last point that I wish to consider before turning to Malinowski's fieldwork is his reaction to periods of crisis in his life. Otto Kernberg (1970:82) has argued that in times of stress or crisis (for example, loss of external supports, loneliness), the normal, reasonably healthy individual will be able to "regress in the service of his ego." That is, the healthy individual will be able to activate and draw upon past internalized object relations as a means of internal support, as a means of maintaining a firm and stable sense of self. The "emotional wealth" that surrounds these early object relationships serves as inner consolation and buttresses the individual against psychic collapse. The individual with a vulnerable self-representation, however, does not have this ability; he cannot regress in the service of his ego (self) because of a disturbance in the primary foundations of his self—a disturbance in early (self) object relationships. There is nothing solid to regress to. There is an internal void.

Malinowski faced more than one crisis in his life, and his reactions to at least two of them are significant, particularly in light of the above discussion. Malinowski's wife had been sick for some time when he wrote the following in a letter to Firth: "The times, full of hope and anticipation, and of that new start which my early teaching gave me—all this seems ages ago. It is a different world in which I live now, at best hopelessly gray and meaningless, at worst a nightmare beyond endurance. Of course, I *do* work, and even amuse myself and pursue my ambitions, hates, etc.—but it all is a thin surface, threadbare and unpleasant to touch, and beneath a horrible void" (1957:12). His work provided for Malinowski the support he needed to hold his sense of self together. Apparently, there was nothing but a "horrible void" underneath that work, a void at the foundation of his sense of self.

In response to the death of his mother, a crisis of unparalleled proportions in Malinowski's life, he states: "Feelings and thoughts: sadness and grief permeate everything. . . . I know that I have a black abyss, a void in my soul, and with all the emotional pettiness peculiar to me, I try to avoid the abyss" (293). This feeling of "inner emptiness, when inner resources are insufficient" (112), is a clear statement of the inability of an individual with a vulnerable self-representation to regress in the service of his ego.

The inability to regress in the service of his ego, the deep undercurrent of envy in many of his relationships, the hypochondria, the hypersensitivity, the depersonalization, and the probable disturbance in the mother-son relationship all point toward the conclusion that Malinowski was suffering from an extreme vulnerability in his self-representation.

Before considering Malinowski's field experience, two brief points

114

need to be made. First, although the primary thrust of this chapter has not been psychobiographical, in the sense that I have not relied on the dominant thematic concerns expressed in Malinowski's anthropological works to pinpoint the nature of his subjective experiential world (see the next chapter for more on this technique), such an approach does help to explain certain aspects of his theoretical concerns. I have documented that the critical personality problem for Malinowski was his failure to consolidate a stable and unified sense of self. His self-representation always remained weak and tenuous, liable to dissolution through absorption into some larger whole. With this in mind, it should come as no surprise that Malinowski would write: "My whole ethics is based on the fundamental instinct of unified personality. From this follows the need to be the same in different situations" (296). And from this, following directly, one can see the reason why Malinowski had to be the father of a theory of individual functionalism. What is Malinowski's functionalism if not a theory explaining—postulating—the individual's integration, both within himself and within his family and larger society?[2]

Second, I have had, by necessity, to concentrate my attention on the dark, unflattering aspects of Malinowski's personality. These should not and must not be taken as a picture of the whole man. From the point of view of the general psychiatric public, Malinowski had as many "good" points as "bad." If I have not dwelled on Malinowski's more admirable qualities, this is not because they did not exist but because they are not essential to my argument. Finally, it is important to note that Malinowski was able to use constructively some of his personality attributes that would have been potentially debilitating to others. It appears, for example, that Malinowski's hypersensitivity enabled him to detect very subtle nuances in the behavior of others that most people, including other fieldworkers, overlook. Malinowski was particularly sensitive to the underlying motives of other people and keen to ferret them out and subject them to the light of analysis. In addition, Malinowski's strong and persistent belief in his own greatness and in the importance of his work enabled him to continue to lead a productive life through the remarkably difficult and trying period of his later life. Malinowski's Trobriand ethnography, with its incredibly fine and rich descriptions of native life, is a monument to his ability to use certain aspects of his personality in a creative and constructive fashion.

In the Field

In this section, I will be concerned with the effect of Malinowski's personality structure on his experience of self while in the field. More precisely, Malinowski engaged in a desperate and near tragic struggle to maintain his sense of identity through the activation of massive amounts of defensive/reparative behavior, which served to link him to his home world and therefore to solidify his precarious sense of identity. This subjective awareness of the attack on his sense of identity took the form of, and intruded into his thoughts as, death. Finally, Malinowski achieved some semblance of security for his sense of identity through a self-immortalizing identification with his work and with anthropology.

There can be little doubt that Malinowski had great need to engage in defensive/reparative behaviors while in the field. That he was having trouble maintaining the boundaries of his self-representation is a conclusion borne out, at least partially, by evidence I have already presented (for example, the merger of his self with a ship and the dissolution of it into the landscape; see page 63 of Malinowski's *Diary* for a second example of this latter type of self-loss). In addition to this early evidence, there are at least two very telling passages in the diaries. After he had been in the Trobriand Islands for about six months, Malinowski commented: "At moments I feel like writing the story of my life. Entire periods already seem so remote, alien. Boarding school; Slebodzinski . . . Chwastek and the preparations for the doctorate—these things seem almost to have nothing to do with me" (63). About two years after this statement, Malinowski offers the following: "Three boats returned. . . . I went to the village. . . . Speculated whether I am myself or my younger brother" (145). I think that both these statements, taken together and with those quoted earlier, indicate a disturbance in Malinowski's sense of experiential continuity.

On the subject of Malinowski's use of defensive/reparative behaviors, a staggering amount of material is available. I do not exaggerate when I say that nearly every page of the diaries contains examples of one or more of these behaviors. Malinowski had pointed this out himself, although naturally in different terminology: "When I feel fairly well physically, when I have something to do, when I am not demoralized, I do not experience a *constant* state of nostalgia" (67). This statement clarifies my point considerably; since Malinowski

116

was a hypochondriac, since he rarely filled his days with activity from start to finish, and since he was so often demoralized, he was constantly nostalgic, that is, he was constantly engaging in defensive/reparative behavior. And even at those rare times when he was not plagued by one or all three of those problems, he still experienced nostalgic feelings, only not constantly. In an effort to order my interpretations, I have broken these numerous defensive/reparative behaviors into ten categories: diary/letters, dreams, books, names, scenery, food, music, narcissistic objects, sex, and mother/girl friends. In what follows, I will present examples from each of these categories, avoiding much commentary unless it is necessary for clarification.

Diary/letters. Diaries can be of great help to the anthropologist in the field as a means of maintaining a sense of his identity. This is what Malinowski is implying when he states: "This morning . . . it occurred to me that the purpose in keeping a diary and trying to control one's life and thoughts at every moment must be to consolidate life, to integrate one's thinking, to avoid fragmenting themes" (175). Malinowski wrote his diary in Polish; the use of and associations with one's native language are a powerful identity booster.

That Malinowski was using his diary as an identity-maintenance device is illustrated by a remark he made near the end of his diaries: "*My birthday*. . . . Evening at Raf.'s; discussion, first on physics; theory of origin of man and totemism in Trobriands. It is remarkable how intercourse with whites (sympathetic ones, like the Raffaels) makes it impossible for me to write the diary" (244). After interacting with sympathetic whites, Malinowski had no reason to write in his diary because he had been receiving positive mirroring of his sense of identity. The Raffaels talked with Malinowski about physics, the subject in which he was trained at the University of Cracow and for which he received his Ph.D. (with the highest honors granted by the Austrian Empire), and anthropology, the profession he was bent on following. There can be no doubt that these people and the topics they discussed formed a powerful source of positive mirroring for Malinowski. The effectiveness of this mirroring was compounded because it took place on Malinowski's birthday. Birthdays are a powerful identity marker in the life of any individual; the emphasis given to his birthday in his diary entry partially indicates that Malinowski was using its recall as an identity-maintenance device.

I have selected two passages that illustrate Malinowski's use of letters as identity-maintaining devices:

In the evening, characteristic dissatisfaction and restlessness, associated with mail day—this craving for strong and complicated impressions, *feeling for points of contact with the absent ones. This sudden rush of presence, need for a condensed dose of a friend's personality.* (194)

I was eating taro when someone brought me the mailbag. . . . I sorted the letters: Mother first, then the less important ones. . . . Moment of longing for N.S. [a former girl friend]. I read her letters last. . . . Slept badly. . . . In brief, I was entirely shaken. . . . I am transported—entirely, in a trance, drunk—the *niggers* don't exist. I don't even want to eat or drink. (178)

Upon reading his letters, Malinowski is transported, as if in a drunken trance—to his home world, where he is able to meet his need for a "condensed dose of a friend's personality," that is, where he is able to meet his need for identity-syntonic mirroring.

Dreams. Before singling out two dreams for further discussion, there are several general points that need to be made. In all of Malinowski's dreams, the natives are conspicuous by their absence. Instead, Malinowski reports dreams whose content consists solely of aspects of the European culture and people that he left behind. His dreams focused on Cracow (233), a white friend C.R. (195), his former girlfriend N.S. and his mother in Poland (202), marriage with T., another girlfriend (71), E.R.M., his fianceé, and a friend of hers (204), and so on. The closest he ever came to dreaming about the natives was "about the possibilities of research in New Guinea" (73). I would interpret this outreaching focus of his dream life as an attempt to maintain continuity with his home world and with his significant others. He describes the first dream as follows: "Strange dreams. In one I dreamed that I was re-experiencing the chemical discoveries made by . . . Gumplowicz, and that I was reading their works or rather studying them from a book. I was in the corner of a laboratory. . . . I saw an open book before me and I read his studies" (70).

In light of the above discussion, it is sufficient, in commenting on this dream, to point out that Gumplowicz was a Polish chemist friend of Malinowski's and that his (Malinowski's) first field of study upon entering the University of Cracow was chemistry. Malinowski is drawn home in his dreams, back to a time and place where he felt at least reasonably secure of his place and identity.

The second dream is far more significant and of central importance to my argument here: "Today . . . I had a strange dream; homo-sex., with my own double as partner. Strangely autoerotic feelings; the impression that I'd like to have a mouth just like mine to kiss, a neck that curves just like mine, a forehead just like mine (seen from the side)" (12–13).

The projection of his double—the materialization of the grandiose self (Kohut 1971)—by an individual suffering from a vulnerable self-representation has long been familiar to psychoanalysts as an attempt to maintain, retrieve, or bolster a threatened sense of self/identity (Elkisch 1957; see Kohut 1971, 1984 on the alter-ego transference). The double "personifies narcissistic self-love" (Rank 1971:86). In addition, Rank (1971:83) was one of the first depth psychologists to draw attention to the projection of the double as a means of combating the fear of death associated with self-loss: "Primitive narcissism feels itself primarily threatened by the ineluctable destruction of the self. . . . The fear of death . . . is denied by a duplication of the self." The projection of the double represents, then, an attempt to combat self-loss and the fear of death that it generates. And how better to combat these twin worries than by self-fertilization, a reenergization of the self with "life force."

Books. One of the functions of Malinowski's almost obsessive reading of novels and magazines is revealed in the following passages to be a defensive/reparative effort to maintain his sense of identity:

> Yesterday a week had passed since my arrival in Mailu. . . . I finished *Vanity Fair*, and read the whole of *Romance*. I couldn't tear myself away; it was as though I had been drugged. . . . I was under the spell of Tunnell, whom I had been reading for hours on end. I promised myself I would read no novels. For a few days I kept my promise. Then I relapsed. . . . Moments of severe moral collapse. Once again I read. Fits of dejection. For instance, when reading Candler about India and his return to London, I was overcome with a longing for London, for N., how I lived there the first year in Saville St. and later in Upper Marylebone St. I find myself thinking about T. often, very often. . . . In my mind's eye I go over and over the moments at Windsor and after my return, my complete certainty and feeling of security. . . . I also kept remembering the later times after I came back from Cracow. (16, 17, 20–21)

> I would start reading the moment I got up. I didn't stop while I was eating, and I kept on till midnight. Only at sunset did I drag myself from my couch and went for a short walk. . . . My head was hum-

ming . . . and yet I read, read, and kept on reading without letup as though I were reading myself to death. (62–63)

With the benefit of psychoanalytic hindsight, I would point out that far from reading himself *to* death, Malinowski was reading his self *away* from death and back to his home world.

Names. Under this rubric, I am thinking of two interrelated tendencies of Malinowski, which were originally drawn to my attention by Hsu (1979:519). On one hand, although Malinowski often specified the Trobriand name for the natives he worked with, he appears, in actually working with them, to have used, or to have preferred to use, only anglicized nicknames that he or other whites gave them (such as Ginger, Janus, and Sixpence). On the other hand, in referring to the Trobriand Islanders as a whole, Malinowski seems to have preferred terms like *niggers, boys,* and *savages.*[3] I see these tendencies as two sides of the same defensive/reparative coin. On one side, Malinowski was attempting to dress the natives in a more familiar, Western image, whereas on the other side, he was attempting to denigrate the natives in an effort to distance and isolate himself from those "human" connections so dangerous to his precarious sense of identity. In this light, it is significant that the one and only time in the diaries that Malinowski unequivocally talks about the natives as friends of his (51), he refers to the individuals concerned by their anglicized nicknames, Janus and Sixpence.

Scenery. Again, Malinowski's concentration on the scenery in the Trobriands reveals itself to be a means of rekindling past memories and associations from his home world:

Sailing down the river reminded me of the excursion with Desiré and the other "Assoc's". . . . Mountains rise from a plain. I looked at them through binoculars; they reminded me of the Saturday excursion to Blackall Ranges. (5)

Next day we left the fjord. The trip was fairly calm. . . . This part of the trip reminds me most strongly of cruising on the Lake of Geneva. (23–24)

I thought of E.R.M. [his fiancée]. I feel a mystical link between her and this view, particularly because of the line of breaking waves. I am happy at the thought that I'll live here. (157)

There are times, however, when Malinowski's need to maintain continuity with his home world and his sense of identity grows too strong simply to read into the local scenery memories of other times and places: "Toward the end of the day's work hidden longings come to the surface, and visions as well: yesterday I saw the western end of Albert Street, where the broad boulevard cuts across it toward Lonsdale St. Longing for E.R.M. *follows*. . . . I felt the need to run away from the *niggers*" (175). Malinowski's use of the local scenery as a projection screen upon which to focus his needs and feelings is also reflected in the following two passages. Here, however, the aspect of his internal experiential world that is projected is considerably darker; death-related concerns intrude into Malinowski's awareness:

> In the distance the white breakers smashed against the coral reef. In the west, scarlet spots on the dark clouded sky—strangely gloomy—like the flush on a sickly face, marked by death (like the flush before death on a diseased, agonized face). (39)

> Among the palms smoky vapors swirling as in a cauldron. . . . Took a short walk. . . . Half-dreamy mood. Through the swirling monstrosity of this Turkish bath flit memories of morbid moods in Omarakana. Then I felt a certain relief: began to look at all this—through all this—from outside. . . . But if *this* were to be the end—feeling that I am choking, that the claws of death are strangling me alive. (191)

Food. This is probably the one topic upon which the available evidence is most open to question; Malinowski commented very little about his cravings for food or related items. The following passage, however, is suggestive: "Introspection . . . my desire for the bottle of *ginger beer* is acutely tempting; the concealed eagerness with which I fetch a bottle of brandy and am waiting for the bottles from Samarai; and finally I succumb to the temptation of smoking again" (17). Although I would not want to push this point too hard, I do see here the possibility that Malinowski was using these foods and their accompaniments (smoking) as links to his home world. As regards smoking, this is the first mention of Malinowski's reverting back to a habit that was originally acquired in a European context.

Music. As with "naming," Malinowski demonstrated a peculiar split regarding his feelings toward music. Thus, although, for example, he was deeply moved by his remembrance of the "Prize Song," "Marche Militaire," and "Rosenkavalier," he seems to have felt almost nothing for the native music; there is only one entry in which Malinowski comments positively on a native melody (37). I think the same interpretation fits this split as fits the similar one related to Malinowski's use of names. He was attracted by or to that music which suggested his home world and was repelled by, or at least indifferent to, that music which suggested his great distance from that home world. This musical linking to the home world is illustrated nicely in the following passage: "I went for a walk along the foot of the hill. . . . Overcome by sadness, I bellowed out themes from *Tristan and Isolde*. "Homesickness." I summoned up various figures from the past, T.S., Zenia. I thought of Mother—Mother is the only person I care for really and am truly worried about. Well, also about life, the future" (52). As Malinowski found it necessary to visualize, or rather, hallucinate certain scenic elements (for example, Albert Street) in an effort to maintain his sense of continuity, so he also found it necessary to create his own music: "In the afternoon I leafed through Shakespeare and had a headache. In the morning I looked through Norman Angell and Renan. In the evening . . . I did not read anything. I had moments of wild longings to hear music and at times it seemed to me I was actually hearing it. Yesterday, for instance, the 9th Symphony" (63–64).

Narcissistic Objects. Malinowski spoke relatively rarely of his narcissistic object choices, that is, of his relationships with those individuals who functioned to maintain or buttress his precarious sense of identity. There are, however, several deeply suggestive passages:

> I always keep in mind Bill's basic problem: his marriage with Marianna [a nonnative woman]. . . . He treats Marianna as a native, stressing her bronze complexion. . . . At times I try—or rather have a [tendency] to feel in him an echo of my own longing for civilization, for a white woman. (148)

> Raffael—young, with a nervous, intelligent, pleasant face. Amiable, sincere and straightforward. Talked about politics and the war. His views are similar to mine. Invited me warmly to visit them, even to stay overnight. I have the impression that he is the only man whose company *would bring me in contact with civilization*. I find him extremely sympathetic as a person, as well as his views and manners. (214)

> Since Thursday I have been in a state of utter distraction. I must absolutely stop this. It is caused by too violent and too passionate contact with people, by an unnecessary communion of souls. There is no doubt that the presence of an intelligent fellow with a Parisian background is very important and full of charm for me. But I mustn't make

this my *main subject*. We may talk evenings, but should be silent during the day. . . . At bottom I am living outside of Kiriwina, although strongly hating the *niggers*. (264)

Again and again in these passages, Malinowski speaks tellingly of those individuals with whom, by establishing contact, he could maintain some continuity with the world he had left behind. Some measure of the strength of Malinowski's need for this continuity-maintaining contact can be gained from the last passage quoted above, in which Malinowski has to fight against his desire to allow himself to be preoccupied—to commune constantly—with a Parisian fellow. Finally, it seems probable that Raffael, the young man whom Malinowski found "extremely sympathetic," and who, as we have already seen, liked to talk with Malinowski about physics and anthropology, was Malinowski's most important narcissistic object during his early fieldwork.

Sex. Malinowski's sexual needs, longings, and desires form an essential part of his diaries. Needless to say, it was partially these longings and desires that so shocked the pure and chaste anthropological community; their god had a body! I will quote a few passages to illustrate the nature of Malinowski's longings:

A pretty, finely built girl walked ahead of me. I watched the muscles of her back, her figure, her legs, and the beauty of the body so hidden to us, whites, fascinated me. Probably even with my own wife I'll never have the opportunity to observe the play of back muscles for as long as with this little animal. At moments I was sorry I was not a savage and could not possess this pretty girl. (255)

Kenoria is pretty, has a wonderful figure. Impulse to "pat her on the belly." I mastered it. (153)

Yesterday, under the mosquito net, dirty thoughts: Mrs. . . . Mrs. C. and even Mrs. W. . . . Dirty thoughts about C.R. The doctrine of this man . . . that you're doing a woman a favor if you deflower her. . . . I even thought of seducing M. Shook all this off. (156; the women referred to here are all Europeans)

Leaning heavily on the first passage cited, Hsu (1979:519) has argued that it was Malinowski's ethnocentrism, his sense of racial and cultural superiority, that "stopped him cold," or made it psychologically impossible for him seriously to consider having sexual relations with a native woman; Hsu does not detect this same feeling of impossibility in Malinowski's fantasies about white women. I admit that I would welcome this argument—it would fit in easily with my already proffered interpretations concerning Malinowski's denigration of that which is native and his longing for that which signifies home—if only it were correct. Unfortunately, it is not. It appears that Hsu has let his fear of ethnocentrism sway his judgment here. In the second and third passages quoted above, I can detect about as much of a sense of "impossibility" in Malinowski's "I mastered it" as I can in his "Shook all this off," that is, precisely none. Hsu (1979:518) himself seems to forget that just one page before he began his diatribe on Malinowski's sexual ethnocentrism, he had pointed out that Malinowski's lecherous thoughts "even led him to paw native women" (p. 256).

It seems to me that Hsu, in concentrating so heavily on Malinowski's supposed ethnocentrism, missed the forest for the trees. I think the key point at issue here is why Malinowski remained celibate in relation to any and all women in his field area. Even if my earlier arguments are wrong and Malinowski did not feel the same restraints regarding native and white women, why did he not engage in sexual relations with any white woman in his field area?[4]

The answer, or at least a large part of it, has already been given by Forge in his brilliant discussion of Malinowski's fieldwork: "This self-imposed celibacy is a strange phenomenon, and each anthropologist has his rationalisation . . . the reason of most of us I suspect is again partly the need to preserve one's own identity. By directing acute sexual frustration and fantasies outside the present environment the anthropologist forges a strong and ever present link with the culture from which he came and to which he will return" (1967:224). Forge meant this explanation to apply to most anthropologists, and for that reason he did not fully realize how special Malinowski's case was. For Malinowski at the time of his fieldwork, sex presented the ultimate problem—the problem faced by many an individual with a tenuous self-representation—of self-loss (compare Malinowski's statement, cited earlier, that sex results in a "surrender of personality"). If Malinowski was going to risk his self, it certainly would be with a suitable mirror in a suitable situation, that is, with E.R.M. in his home world:

> I must not touch a woman with sub-erotic intentions, I must not betray E.R.M. mentally. . . . Preserve the essential inner personality through all difficulties and vicissitudes. (268)

About Elsie [E.R.M.] I think constantly, and I feel *settled down*. I look at the slender, agile bodies of little girls in the village and I long—not for them, but for her. (253)

That lousy girl . . . I shouldn't have pawed her . . . strong guilt feelings. Resolve: absolutely never to touch any Kiriwana whore. To be mentally incapable of possessing anyone except E.R.M. (256)

All the time: problem of maintaining inner purity in relation to her [E.R.M.], clearly realizing this can be done. . . . I resolve to watch myself right down to the deepest instincts. On the other hand, my deep, immensely tender and passionate love for her crystallizes into a strong feeling of the value of her person, and I feel that I really desire only her. (181)

This loyalty and dedication are commendable. But alas, the loyalty is based on his need to preserve a link with his own home world, to preserve his precarious sense of identity: "I felt I wanted her [E.R.M.] the way a child wants his mother" (241). "At moments almost unbearable longing for E.R.M.—or is it for civilization?" (190).

Mother/Girl Friend. The final category of defensive/reparative behaviors that I wish to consider here is Malinowski's memories of and longing for his girl friends and his mother. Once again, I will cite only a very few examples from the diary. The almost overwhelming number of available examples has made my selection particularly difficult.

I slept well enough; my dreams took me far away from the Trobriands and ethnography. . . . This brings me closer to E.R.M. . . . I often long for culture—Paul and Hedy and their *home* (almost brings tears to my eyes); E.R.M. and M.H.W. and that atmosphere. Will those happy days in E. Malvern ever come back?—Beethoven's melodies. (150)

I still think about and am in love with T. . . . The sandy beach at Folkestone and the cold, piercing glow of that evening. Memories of London and Windsor. . . . I have moments of general dejection. Themes from walks with Kazia and Wandzia, memories of Paris and elements of France. . . . At last I begin to feel a deep, strong longing for [Mother] in my innermost being. (27–28)

Main interests in life: Kipling, occasionally strong yearning for Mother—really, if I could keep in communication with Mother I would not mind anything and my low spirits would have no deep foundation. (41)

Malinowski's relationship to his mother was unusually close and tight, although not, of course, free of conflict. She followed him wherever he went, watched over him, treated him when he was sick, encouraged him when he made the transition from physics to anthropology, and so on. Whatever else may have conditioned Malinowski's recall of his relationship to his mother—and surely this, as well as the relationship itself, was overdetermined—certainly the need to maintain his sense of identity was one factor.

The following two passages reveal the intrusion of much darker, death-related, aspects of Malinowski's experiential world into his memories of home:

> A Russian dance tune comes to mind: vision of Juliet and Olga in the E. Malvern Studio. Yearning for what used to be. . . . E.R.M. is always with me. . . . Then thought of her under the mosquito net. Will I ever go back to Cairns and walk along the parade? Will I ever see E.R.M.? *Death, the blear-eyed visitor I am ready to meet.* (173)

> I thought of . . . N.S. and suddenly felt that I was deserting her. . . . I also thought of E.R.M. and in my nervous disarray I told myself: "*the shadow of death is between us and it will separate us.*" My betrayal of N.S. confronted me in all its starkness. . . . Death—all this is like an ebb tide, a flowing off into nothingness, extinction. . . . For the first half of the day I was dejected and almost did not believe in the possibility of health. Then I *buck up* and *I hope.* (192)

On the basis of the evidence presented so far, I think it is possible to offer the following conclusions. Malinowski suffered from an extreme vulnerability in his self-representation. Consequently, he experienced the field as a brutal and searing attack on his already precarious sense of identity. How, then, did Malinowski survive the field experience and go on to produce so much anthropological work? Or better yet, if the field experience was so painful for Malinowski, why did he do so much anthropological work on it?

It seems to me that the answer to this last question is basic—because he *had* to work. I mean by this simply that Malinowski survived the field by achieving a self-immortalizing identification with his work and with anthropology. In this manner, he was able to achieve some sense of stability in relation to his sense of identity and protect against its dissolution in both an immediate and ultimate sense. Such an identification is suggested by Malinowski's almost uncannily intense approach to his work (Firth 1957; Kardiner

126

and Preble 1961; Montagu 1942). Audrey Richards (1943:3), in her obituary of Malinowski, points out that "work absorbed him and possessed him"; the image of the self absorbed and possessed by, that is, fused with, its work is highly suggestive here. But is there any evidence from the diaries—the evidence that would really count—that Malinowski was concerned with these sorts of self-immortalizing problems, that he had in fact begun to identify with his (future) work?

Up to this point, I have let Malinowski speak for himself and build my argument for me. In the following discussion, I shall continue that policy and simply steer the argument, which will consist of a series of passages from the diaries, to its logical conclusion. So, Malinowski writes: "As for ethnology: I see the life of the natives as utterly devoid of interest or importance, something as remote from me as the life of a dog. During the walk, I made it a point of honor to think about what I am here to do. . . . Must concentrate on my ambitions and work to some purpose" (167). Is it possible to clarify the nature of these "ambitions" any further? "I analyzed the nature of my ambition. An ambition stemming from my love of work, intoxication with my own work . . . ambition stemming from constantly seeing oneself—*romance of one's own life*; eyes turned to one's form. . . . When I think of my work, or works, or the revolution I want to effect in social anthropology—this is a truly creative ambition" (289). Or: "I thought about ethnogr. work. Also, thought with pride about my work: better than Sp. & G.'s [Baldwin Spencer and F. J. Gillen], better than all the others" (215).

Malinowski is intoxicated with his work, which he sees as being the best currently in existence, and with his ambition, both of which appear to derive from "constantly seeing" his self or form reflected in that work. Malinowski is also very concerned that he and his work (an unnecessary dichotomy, of course) receive their proper and respective recognition: "External ambitions kept crawling over me like lice. F.R.S. [Fellow of the Royal Society]—C.S.I. [Companion of the Order of the Star of India]—Sir. Thought about how one day will be in *Who's Who*, etc., etc." (291). These worldly honors cannot, however, fully satisfy Malinowski's self-inflationary needs: "Concrete formula of life: *Mate with her, beget children, write books, die*—what is it in comparison with cosmic ambitions" (219).

These passages have certainly primed the pump, so to speak. The identification with his work and its ramifications for the achieve-

127

ment of symbolic immortality ("better than all the others," "*Who's Who,*" and the like) have been suggested. But something firmer than mere suggestion is needed here: "I am now so healthy and in such good spirits that I feel no desire to break the continuity of work by reading novels. I don't even wait for letters and I don't want the time to go by too fast! *I simply live in and for my work*" (272; emphasis added). And what does Malinowski now hope will be the result of his work? "I am wasting time, while it is my duty to her [E.R.M.] and to "our children" to work as hard as possible and to achieve a "position" in relation to myself—to be someone who really accomplished something; *make my mark in this world*" (278). And now, when all is said and done, when all the niceties are packed away, why did Malinowski seek to make his mark in the world, what did he hope to gain by so doing? "I tried to control myself and to remember that *I worked with immortality in view* and that paying attention to this crew simply banalizes my work" (112; emphasis added).

The thrust of these statements is remarkably clear: Malinowski survived the field through a self-immortalizing identification with his work. Landes's elegant comment certainly applies to Malinowski: "Are we supposed to shatter ourselves? It is easy to say no, certainly not. But some have done so, leaving work as a monument" (1970:134).

Closing Thoughts

As a consequence of an extreme vulnerability in Malinowski's personality structure and the clash between his own and the natives' cognitive maps, he experienced the field as a shattering rite of death and rebirth; he returned from the field fused with his work—a self-immortalizing fusion that was to provide immediate and ultimate security (symbolic continuity) to the stability of his self-representation. As long as Malinowski had his (potential) work, he had a bulwark against the ultimate danger of complete self-fragmentation/death.

I hope also that I have been able to offer an alternative interpretation of Malinowski's field experience. There might be elements of ethnocentrism in Malinowski, as there are in every anthropologist, and perhaps he could not really establish "truly human relations" (Hsu 1977:806) with the natives, but are these traits really bedrock? Must we be content with them? I think not. I think we can try to understand Malinowski's diaries for what they really are—the record of a man desperately trying to rescue his self from death. But I would caution here against going overboard and falling into the opposite extreme, which Malinowski suggests in the following passage: "The problem of heroism. Strong feeling of dejection. . . . At moments sad because I cannot subject myself to a test. . . . Then thought about myself. . . . For a moment I looked Destiny in the eyes. . . . Now: place my everyday life in that heroic frame; be ruthless in relation to appetites and weakness. . . . My love for E.R.M. can be, must be, based on the feeling that she has faith in my heroism. . . . And I too must have faith in myself, otherwise I won't get anywhere. To fight, to keep going, to be ready at any moment, without depressions and premonitions" (179–80).

As I said, we must guard against falling into the other extreme, the extreme that views Malinowski's struggles as heroic. His struggle was desperate, but it was also a reflex of the terror associated with self-loss and death; it was not heroic. The psychology of the creative narcissist is self-sacrificial. To win, he must lose; every change must be a sort of death.

6

Death and Rebirth in Fieldwork
An Archetypal Case

If he makes me wait much longer, the great friend, death, then I shall set out and seek him. . . . Without hope of the end life would be unendurable.
—"Ellen West" in Ludwig Binswanger, *The Case of Ellen West*

For one who is interested in examining the relationship between an anthropologist's personality structure and his experience of fieldwork, as I obviously am, working through the more recently published personal accounts of fieldwork can be frustrating indeed because the vast majority of these studies report only half of the story—that which immediately concerns the fieldwork experience. We are told much about the logistical difficulties of fieldwork, about the weird habits of bush pilots and native administrators, about good and bad informants, and also, of course, about the anthropologist's feelings during fieldwork. We are generally told very little, however, about the other half of the story—that which concerns the anthropologist's personality functioning before fieldwork. We never, or virtually never, hear about the anthropologist's unusual love for his mother or father, hatred for his siblings, bad marriage(s), and the like. In a word, we never hear about the psychological dirt, about the events, feelings, and actions that are necessary to piece together a full-bodied psychological picture of the anthropologist. Or at least we seldom do. In 1982, however, a young German-Canadian anthropologist by the name of Manda Cesara (a pseudonym) published an extremely psychologically revealing account of both her early life experiences and her experiences during fieldwork. This account contains sufficiently detailed material to enable one to determine the relationship between her personality structure and her experience of fieldwork.

The general format of this chapter will be identical to the preced-
130

ing one on Malinowski. I begin with a consideration of Cesara's personality structure and then consider its effect on her experience of fieldwork. Unlike Malinowski's case, there is enough material available in Cesara's book to allow one to reconstruct a detailed picture of her subjective experience of self. This psychobiographical material is crucial if one is to understand anything at all about Cesara's experience of fieldwork and about extreme experiences of fieldwork in general. The purpose of this chapter is, then, twofold: to offer a case study of an extreme experience of fieldwork in which one can examine, in a specific and detailed manner, the relationship between personality structure and fieldwork experience and to provide support for the general propositions about fieldwork put forth in the first chapter. Toward that end, I shall begin by considering Cesara's early life experiences as they relate to her characteristic personality structure.

My discussion of Cesara's life history and experiences is not intended to be a complete or detailed psychobiography. Rather, it is intended to suggest that Cesara entered the field suffering from an extreme vulnerability in her self-representation and that, ultimately, this vulnerability conditioned the extremity of her experience. To document the nature of Cesara's self-experience, I will employ a modified psychobiographical approach, wherein it is assumed that an individual's dominant ideas, beliefs, theoretical interests, and so forth reflect and express his or her most vivid and salient subjective concerns as conditioned by early formative experiences (Atwood and Tomkins 1976; Atwood and Stolorow 1977). Stated otherwise, every theorist of the human condition inevitably views his subject from the perspective afforded by his own individuality. Consequently, theories on the nature of human beings are influenced by and express personal and subjective factors. It should be possible, then, to interpret the major ideas of any theorist as an expression of his own individuality, the latter being conditioned by significant early formative experiences in the theorist's life. An individual's work, both form and content, will always be a reflection of what that individual is, at bottom.

The dominant or central theme in Cesara's thinking appears to me to be the individual's quest for autonomy, capability, and personal power. Implicit in this broad theme are Cesara's concerns with the existential nature of the self as a continuing project and the need for a radically new style of feminism grounded in a strong sense of woman-culture.

Cesara's concern with the self as a continuing project is reflected in her tendency to ground all her ideas in the ontology of Jean-Paul Sartre:

> If there were a creator, he created human beings with two fatal flaws. First, he created us without letting us know who we are. The human being is, therefore, continually in search of him- and- herself. Secondly, he gave us mental tools that are inadequate to the task of sound self-definition for we define ourselves by contrast to or in terms of the *other*. . . . But there is no creator, and so the human being is misguided in his search for self. The self cannot be discovered; it must be made. . . . We cannot know who we are unless we look inside at our plans. (25–26)[1]

> One's end or project, which must be freely chosen, enables a person to assign meanings selectively to the elementary structures of his or her situation. When one changes one's end or project, an ever present possibility, one also changes the meanings assigned to selected aspects of one's past, position, and so on. . . . Since we make ourselves through our choices, this book is also about personal freedom, specifically the personal freedom of a woman-in-the-process-of-becoming. (10, 14)

For the existential thinker the bridge between the self, conceived of as a never-ending project, and the quest for autonomy, capability, and personal power is short. It is not surprising to find Cesara making just such a connection:

> By contrast, the . . . existentialist experiences the self as a free and authentic existent whose possibilities and actualities are meaningful. Hers is not merely a self which thinks, as do all other "selves," as does a self as subject. Hers is a self wrapped in historicity, a self that is guilty, a self that wants a conscience, a self that is responsible. It is a self that lives *with* others and *in* a world, but not to become assimilated, not to escape its guilt and finitude, but to disclose itself as it discloses the other. It is a self that may grow from society's girl into a liberated, that is, responsible woman—responsible for who she is and might become despite her inability to determine her sex, her origin, or her color. (111)

What is surprising to find, however, and what is of great significance, is the predominantly and intensely negativistic and aggressive tone adhering to much of Cesara's discussion of these themes and their opposites. An example is Cesara's reaction to a young woman's confession of her inability to discipline her male students: "I felt disgusted at having her say that. Women who

thought that they could not handle . . . boys or men were a disgrace
to my sex" (34). Her comments concerning young men are equally
pertinent: "Young men were invariably dull of mind and incapable
of perceiving the impersonality in my overt friendliness. . . . I
couldn't tolerate men who attempted to violate my autonomy" (39).
Or again, on the topic of love:

> Who are the murderers of this world, the killers, the subjugators, if it
> is not men? Who are the destroyers, bored with love? Sisters, raise
> your guns! But women will not shoot. Freed, they run to men, begging
> for love. And they beg for it everywhere until they burn their wings
> and are subjugated again. Oh, woman of tender bloom, why can you
> not wait, nurtur yourself, and augment your room. Fortify your heart
> and your brain, test your strength, and only then turn to man. (106)

> White women have learned to like, what Lenda women abhor, being
> slaves. . . . We like being dominated by men, so long as we can call
> that domination love. Love is a great power in the West. . . . Love al-
> lows us to blind ourselves. It kills our curiosity, our right to explore
> the world, our right to become self-sufficient human beings. (107)

Finally, there is her telling anecdote concerning the process of review
her book received: "When a referee first read the unedited version of
my personal journal, he or she was *furious* with my . . . attitudes. She
was angered because I 'railed' against Western male-female relations.
I wondered whether the referee was one of the those [*sic*] researchers
'with deeply feminine interests' who consistently anchored her individuality to husband, children, servants, or friends. Usually secure in
the morass of his or her 'unreflective consciousness,' my personal
account temporarily unhinged the reader's mind" (11).

As an existentialist, Cesara is justified in being preoccupied with
her own self. As an anthropologist, however, she has concern that is
more properly with the group. Cesara's plea for a new feminism represents a projection of her individual concerns onto women considered as a group:

> Men and women, but especially women, who realize that another
> man, even another human being, cannot become their whole exis-
> tence. Men who have the courage and the daring to let women go, to
> let each woman fight her own battles, to let her become whole and
> unafraid of the world. . . . These sorts of values are needed if we want
> worthy human beings, liberated women. (188)

> In my opinion, young people are not taught enough respect for their
> own and others' individuality, integrity, and autonomy. We train peo-

ple to march over others. We train people to be negligent, not individualistic. The two have nothing necessarily to do with one another. When you respect the autonomy of the human being, down to the marrow of your bone, you cannot . . . dominate and exploit. (187)

Enough has now been said to suggest the interrelation of these themes with each other and to point to their fundamental importance as a key to unlocking the structure of Cesara's self-experience. It is time to focus on this latter problem and ask: What is the nature of the psychological constellation that, in this case, conditions such beliefs and how was it formed?

Cesara was "expelled" (3) from her mother's womb in time to experience the horrors and devastation of postwar Germany. Streets were covered with rubble. Toys consisted of shrapnel embedded in footmats and worthless money. Food, when available, was often just black bread and soup. Cesara's household was composed entirely of women; her father had been taken prisoner by the Russians late in the war and was only to return home, some four years later, in time to die. The women in her household appear to have been, not surprisingly, preoccupied with survival. To that end, all appear to have been engaged in bartering, trading, and work of one sort or another. Cesara's care, or at least a good part of it, seems to have been undertaken by her grandmother (3–4).

In such a situation, there is a certain logic in assuming that the care of a very young child would be experienced as a burden by its mother. This is significant, for it is through a process of mirroring of her experience of her child that a mother will call out or crystallize a "primary identity theme" (Lichtenstein 1977) in that child. The mother reflects onto her child a sense of its identity. This primary identity theme then functions as the growing child's most basic experience of herself, of what she is at bottom. I believe that, in Cesara's case, this theme of the self experienced as burden(some) forms the core of her primary identity configuration.

Beginning with a very general point, there is Cesara's attitude toward children, or more particularly, toward certain special children. Cesara mentions that she never had any real interest in children. While she was doing fieldwork, however, three groups of children aroused her interest: those plagued by constant sickness, those who suffered alienation from their fathers, and those who "having recently been removed from the safety of their mothers' back . . . struggled with their seeming 'rejection'" (111). Cesara admits that her interest in

134

them was fostered by her own childhood experiences (112). At the very least, one can detect here a disturbance in the early mother-infant relationship, which has great import considering the centrality of this relationship to the formation of the self (Kohut 1977). More speculatively, it is possible to see here the beginnings of the psychological constellation already elucidated: the young child, constantly sick—a burden—trying to cope with her mother's seeming rejection of her, without the benefit of an alternative object (for example, her father) to which she could turn for more positive mirroring.

Bearing directly on this speculation is a memory that Cesara reports from her early childhood:

> My grandmother adored me, in part, no doubt, *because I hardly ever cried or spoke.* For that reason alone, I was a rare child. Most of the time I was sick. One time, when I was left alone because my grandmother, mother, and aunts were out bartering, I was tortured by the pain and potential shame of diarrhea. There were no flush toilets nor outhouses. A few pails in the basement received human waste. . . . This time, all pails were full. Teary eyed and in great agony I moved from pail to pail, wherever there was a little room, *in an effort not to cause my grandmother any extra work or embarrassment.* Since I was barely five years old, my grandmother considered this a great feat. She praised my good sense and marvelled at the tickings of my tiny brain. All my aunts were told and they too marvelled. (4; emphasis added)

It appears from this memory that Cesara was experiencing positive regard for herself only conditionally. The positive mirroring that she received occurred in a context in which she had fought desperately to avoid being considered a(n) (additional) burden. Her grandmother adored her for not crying or speaking; she fought her agony to avoid causing her grandmother any extra work; her grandmother and aunts praised her good sense—all for not being a burden. Finally, her grandmother and aunts marveled at her good sense; her mother is conspicuous by her absence.

Several times throughout her book, Cesara mentions that she was constantly sick as a child. As a consequence of this pervasive illness, she "was shunted back and forth among relatives in three sectors" (91) of divided Germany. Most of this movement occurred when she was between the ages of four and six. Given what we already know of Cesara's childhood, it is understandable that she interpreted such movement as a rejection of herself, rooted in the burdensome aspects (that is, her prolonged sicknesses) of her existence. Her account of one of these movements is especially revealing in confirming this interpretation and in pointing the way to an additional concern of great relevance. Briefly, to set the context of this incident, Cesara's father had returned from a prisoner of war camp when she was about four years old. He was in a weakened state, probably sick, and yet appointed to convey Cesara to a new location in an effort to cure her sickness: "*And my mother burdened him with me.* I too was sick and he took me to my grandmother to recover. We crossed the Russian sector. The train stopped. *He carried me* to the platform and went back to fetch our bags. I saw the train pull off with my father still on it. And I felt as if someone was strangling me and my stomach tore asunder. I stood there screaming for help and stamping my feet. Terror spread through me and my screams radiated through the air and the echo of them came back to me. Reddened eyes followed the train" (80; emphasis added).

There is, in addition to the imagery of the self as burden, a more subtle factor here that helps to account for the especial poignancy of this memory. Cesara's relationship with her mother was less than ideal. In such a situation the return of her father would offer a critical chance for her developing self to recover its balance. Basking in the calm security provided by such a potentially idealizable figure would have certainly aided Cesara in replenishing her narcissistic supplies; her father could have served as an omnipotent, powerful protector (see Kohut 1977). This was not to be the case, however, for once again Cesara's self, in its burdensome aspects, intrudes and destroys the situation. She, in a sense, provokes the separation recorded here by being a burden, that is, her father had to carry her off the train and so return to it a second time for her luggage. This separation, with its overtones of seeming rejection of her burdensome self, would have been a powerful, shattering trauma for Cesara.

The strength with which Cesara tried to hold on to her father, as a measure of the intensity of her need for him, can be witnessed in her reaction to his death:

> My sister and I were sent to play outside, but we peeked through the window and saw our mother with that man. My father sat in bed. He was dressed in white. Cold sweat ran down his face. He looked to his neighbor who moaned and groaned and said he was sick and would die. My father held him by the arms and stared. "You must want to live," he cried out. Then he leaned back and his head turned to my mother. . . . They looked at each other and then he turned to look at me. *A ray of life shot from his eyes and it was so strong that it touch-*

ed me. I held my breath and reached for his hand, but he lay back and died. (81; emphasis added)

There is a strange, dreamlike, almost hallucinatory quality about this memory, a memory in which Cesara refuses to let her father die; she could not afford to let her best hope of narcissistic sustenance die. The ray of life that shot from her father's eyes appears to represent Cesara's attempt to keep her father alive through the psychic defense of undoing—magically, in dying, her father yet lives. One can only speculate on the extent to which such undoing served other functions, for example, to alleviate Cesara's guilt concerning her father's death (it was her burdensome self that forced her father to relocate her and further weaken himself) or perhaps to point the way to Cesara's denial of his death throuh identification with her father (the ray of life *touched* her).

One aspect of the self as burden that I have not clarified pointedly enough is the subjective feeling of dependency. One experiences oneself as burdensome precisely because one is forever dependent on others for the maintenance of one's own self. The self as burden lacks autonomy, capability, and personal power; in short, it lacks the initiative to act on its own behalf and so must depend on the omnipotence of others to guide it through the vicissitudes of life. Cesara recounts a memory that is of particular importance to this theme, a memory that concerns her near deportation to Siberia: "We stood together my aunt and I. And I asked my aunt what all these people were doing over there. . . . 'Hush,' she said, 'the Russians have rounded them up. . . .' 'And where are they taking them,' I asked. 'To Siberia,' she said, 'but hush child, hush.' And a Russian yelled and exploded his gun, and they marched them off one by one. I felt their terror in my bones, as we sat there in dread and awe. A man came up, 'You have your passports, take to your feet and run, the French sector is just over there.' 'Come with us,' we begged. 'I haven't my papers,' he replied. And I saw him cave in as we ran" (95).

Cesara and her aunt are about to be deported, and yet neither can act until a fellow traveler intervenes and directs their course. Interestingly, Cesara realizes the inner significance of this behavior in the context of a discussion about male-female relations: "It [the relations between the sexes] was too heavily based on our depending and their saving us" (95). Immediately following this statement, she cited this memory of deportation and the memory of her dying father's attempt to relocate her in a different sector of Germany. The essential point here is not whether Cesara and her aunt (or her father) could have acted differently in the circumstances, but rather that Cesara feels that they, more especially that she, should have been able to. She is sensitized to the theme of dependency and therefore tends to project it into situations in which its consideration would not otherwise arise. Thus, though she is correct to emphasize the theme of dependency in these memories, it escapes Cesara that such dependency is an integral part of her self-experience.

A further illustration of this dependency theme is contained in Cesara's description of two men who used to visit her household. One was a violin-playing mathematics teacher who apparently had a romantic interest in Cesara's mother. "The other was Herr Deckwerth, the village communist and father of a handicapped child. *It is because he had a handicapped child that he took a liking to me"* (4; emphasis added). Cesara's implicit likening of her self to a handicapped child is a vivid symbolization of her dependency needs; it reflects a self lacking autonomy, capability, and personal power. Cesara felt that positive regard for her self was conditional on its being representative of the class of handicapped (crippled) selves.

Before applying the results of this analysis to Cesara's fieldwork experience, I want to comment briefly on the relationship between her experience of self as burden and her dominant thematic concerns as previously elucidated. To begin, one must admit the validity of the point made by George E. Atwood and Sylvan Tomkins (1976:167) when they argue that a theorist's definitive statements on the nature of the human condition constitute a structure of meaning within which he can understand his own experiences. Cesara's definitive statements on the meaning of being human, that is, the self as project and the quest for autonomy, capability, and personal power, reflect her own most problematic subjective concerns and experiences. Within the boundaries of Cesara's experiential world, it was her inability to take responsibility for herself, her inability to negate her dependency on others, and her inability to achieve autonomy, capability, and personal power that produced her suffering. Is it any wonder that in her approach to human nature Cesara should gainsay so strongly those attributes that adhere to the self experienced as burden? Cesara's open embracing of existentialism represents an attempt to abolish those forces most threatening to the integrity of her self-representation.

Having now elucidated the structure of Cesara's experience of self, it is time to consider its effects on her fieldwork. Specifically, I will

138

demonstrate that Cesara experienced, while in the field, feelings of identity fragmentation that led to defensive activity designed to buttress her sense of identity, and, with the failure of this activity, the construction of a new sense of identity rooted in a merger or identification with her work as an anthropologist. Further, throughout discussion of these themes, the significance of the subjective awareness of death as a concomitant to the loss of identity will be made apparent.

To place Cesara's fieldwork in the proper context, it is necessary to understand certain aspects of her life after leaving Germany. Cesara emigrated to Canada with her mother, where she learned, among other things, that Germans were tainted people who reacted with guilt and horror to the mention of the word *Jew*. In such a situation, Cesara began to deny her own past, to repress her Germanness through vigorous assimilation of "American culture." Although her assimilation was not perfect, she became able to laugh at the various crudities and ethnic jokes willingly proffered by Americans. In a final effort to destroy her German past, she married an "all American boy" anthropologist: "When I was first married I wanted to be, above everything else, an American. My German past had at all cost to remain dead. Alive it was too painful" (7).

All fieldworkers, especially at the beginning of their projects, are remarkably dependent on their hosts. They are much like small children in need of benevolent parents. In fact, and in a sense directly relevant to the present argument, they are burdens upon the host culture. Often in anthropologists' accounts of their fieldwork this aspect of their experience is represented by a concern to give something back to their informants, whether it be a new perspective, goods, money, or medicines (Winthrop 1969). This experiencing of the self as a burden, which is discomforting to most, was shattering to Cesara, for I think obvious reasons. Further compounding her situation was the occurrence of matriliny as the predominant mode of descent reckoning. Thus after having spent the greater part of her adolescence and young adulthood repressing her past, Cesara suddenly found herself involved in a project that made her once again a dependent, burdensome child in a world of dominant women: "It is important that the reader understands the deep, disturbing . . . heart breaking impact the Lenda social environment had on me. I . . . found myself staring at the Lenda social landscape transfixed and mystified for I was staring into my past" (7).

The first weeks or months of an anthropologist's stay in the field are likely to be especially damaging to her sense of identity. During this time, the anthropologist probably knows little or none of the native language, is certainly stupid as to her behavioral responsibilities and duties, and often feels herself to be something of an oddity. Such a situation is hardly conducive to maintaining a sense of one's identity. It is not surprising, then, that the first incident I wish to consider from Cesara's fieldwork dates from this early period.

Cesara reports an unusual experience with a frog that occurred a short time after she arrived in Lenda:

> As one shopped one felt oneself devoured by hungry looks from hungry young boys. I was always overcome with guilt as I left the store with filled shopping bags. This guilt and the unpleasant pressure of inadequate transportation . . . the inability to find a Lenda speaker so that I might continue to practice this language; all this stress and strain, isolation and monotony, this unbearable uncertainty about the success of this venture, burst forth one day when I tried to open my door and found it stuck because under its wide bottom lay a squashed but twitching frog. I felt my endurance giving way to repulsion and yet I stared at the fluids of its body as they drew themselves out, flattened and spread across the floor, and then I screamed bloody murder. . . . It was as if the fluids of the frog were charged with my feelings of anguish about Bob [her husband], poverty, humanity, life and death, as if in this viscous substance of a dying life, any kind of life, were condensed all the psychic meaning of uncertainty, horror, torment, and impermanence of life. (18)

I would draw attention to two particular aspects of this quotation. First is the guilt Cesara experiences in relation to the poverty surrounding her. Although this is perhaps not an unusual reaction for a sensitive fieldworker, it must be remembered that for Cesara the "hungry looks" could hardly have failed to rekindle aspects of her own childhood identity as a scrounger in the ruins of Germany. And such a reminder would have been experienced as a powerful attack against her identity as a successfully assimilated German-Canadian scholar, that is, her attempt to repress her past. This interpretation would render directly understandable the second interesting aspect of the quotation, the concern Cesara expresses over the psychic meaning of "dying life," of the impermanence of life. It is hard to avoid the impression that Cesara's reaction to the squashed frog represents a projection of her own internal experiential world. The frog incident, then, would be a symbolization and concretization of her own subjectively experienced feelings of identity diffusion.

As one's sense of identity fragments and changes, it is understandable that one's relationships with friends and with pet ideas should also change. Two of Cesara's closest friends early in her fieldwork were a Dutch physician, Van Gella, and a young woman, Judy. Cesara reports an interesting observation about her relations with these people after several months in the field:

> Judy dropped by. I was somewhat tired and depressed. Judy's suggestion to go boating and relax the rest of the afternoon was welcomed. Once on the water, however, I found to my own astonishment, that I had nothing to talk about with my white friends. . . . I topped this excursion with a visit to Van Gella. There too, I found myself restless and without anything to say. (78)

> Van Gella asked me to stay for a barbecue and I gladly accepted. . . . Following a meal of delicious tender loin, Father Leo brought three short French films. . . . All I remembered of the films was their incongruity. Suddenly I felt the company stifling and took off like a shot. Hans turned and held my arm. "Are you alright, Manda" he said. "It's crazy, Hans. I can't stand the white community for long and I had to escape from the Gambelan one as well. . . ." I was restless, restless, restless. Everything was unsettled inside. (83)

> This was a period of deep turmoil. I began to feel alienated from the white community at a time when I could not yet be a full member of the black community either. (81)

It is my contention that the alienation Cesara refers to resulted from a fragmenting of her sense of identity and, in particular, of that component of her identity that had assured her embeddedness within a specific sociohistorical epoch (see Erikson 1980). She has nothing to talk about with her friends or with the white community; she cannot relate to them because she is no longer able to identify with their perspectives and interests.

Although many of Cesara's specific ideas changed during fieldwork, none was more impressive, when considered from the context of the present argument, than her views about nature. She had left for the field during the period in which Americans were preoccupied with ecological concerns, and she fully expected to "confirm the correctness of that attitude" (21) among the Lenda. In fact, as the following passages make clear, this view reversed itself completely during Cesara's fieldwork:

> Nature came to take on a new meaning. Perhaps it had something to do with the deep lines on women's faces or with the presence of death

141

in the shanty-towns near the institute. Maybe it is just that life's contingency confronted me, as it were, in the nude. . . . The sun beat down on us. Sweat and blood . . . I look at the shrubbery near our house. Tough, knarred branches are crawling in, cracking the stone, straining for space. And I hear the wailing from the poor section of town. Another death of course. A paper world, a temporary world and the shit comes piling in. And we're to assign it meaning. I had forgotten that life was so temporary. How could I have forgotten? (21–22)

How could I ever have idealized nature? How did its danger, its ugliness escape me? It maims, mother, and it kills. . . . When it's wet, mud bricks melt away. . . . When it's dry, red dust hides the world from view. . . . Infants suffer from diarrhoea and when they deposit their crap, flies feast. . . . And through the dust I glance a crowd carrying a corpse away. Nature kills, Mam. How could we allow its reign without control? I'll never idealize nature again. (44)

Nature, far from being the idyllic paradise of luxuriance that it once was, has now turned for Cesara into an image of death and decay. There is a pronounced similarity between the descriptions of nature and those pertaining to the squashed frog quoted above, a similarity to be expected considering that the latter incident merely represents a particular exemplar of the larger category, nature. This being the case, I believe that it is arguable that Cesara's perception of nature as death represents a projection of her own subjective feelings of identity loss onto a suitable hook (see Searles 1979). Cesara comes very close to realizing this point when she states that nature "burst the seams of my rationality. . . . Lenda nature brought me to the very boundary of my existence. . . . Only I kept creating a new routine, anything empirical, in fact, to prevent breakage" (64). There is no doubt that the natural world in Lenda was threatening and dangerous when Cesara lived there. But there is also no doubt that the natural world in Canada was threatening and dangerous when she lived there. And yet her feelings then about nature were idyllic. It is permissible, I think, to question whether it was actually the natural world in Lenda that brought Cesara to the boundary of her existence—to the rock bottom of her identity—or whether the natural world merely served as the carrier of her projected feelings of identity fragmentation. Evidence in favor of the latter interpretation will be presented shortly, in the context of a love affair that Cesara initiated while in the field.

It is perhaps time to discuss the presence in Cesara's work of what

I referred to earlier as defensive/reparative efforts undertaken by the anthropologist in the field to stabilize and maintain her sense of identity. The few examples that I cited there, for example, certain dreams, food cravings, and diaries, were all interpreted as attempts to establish continuity with the home world and so maintain the sense of identity through that linkage. Cesara's work abounds with such examples. In the material just quoted concerning the impact of Lenda nature on her existence, Cesara informs us that she created empirical routines in an effort to "prevent breakage," that is, to avoid losing her sense of identity completely. Since she also informs us, in her preface, that her graduate training emphasized heavily an empirical/quantitative methodology, it is feasible to see in her adoption of empirical routines a powerful defensive/reparative attempt to rekindle her continuity with her home world (the university and her husband, who was also one of her anthropology professors) and so stabilize her sense of identity. Devereux (1967) has made much the same point regarding the use of empirical methodologies as a defense against one or another form of anxiety.

Cesara's dreams form a second example of this tendency to establish continuity, only here the continuity that is established is with her early childhood. She reports a recurrent dream, too long to reproduce here (22–23), in which the United States and Germany were compared along a range of issues. The dominant thematic lines in this dream—the Vietnam War and World War II and the concern over achieving freedom and therefore negating dependency and the self as burden—reveal a marked intermingling of events early in Cesara's life with those that occurred later. It is as if the dream were saying, on one level, "do not lose yourself completely, you are still the same person you once were despite your feelings to the contrary."

A third example concerns Cesara's "dressing up" in good clothes. An individual's image of her body self forms a major component of her sense of identity (Schilder 1950). Anything that changes or alters this image will, therefore, relate significantly to the individual's sense of identity. Clothes form a very common and important means of either stabilizing or changing the image one has of one's body self. Cesara reports an interesting observation bearing on this idea: "I had a mad desire to get into *good* clothes. I think this is significant. . . . Clean clothes are a relief, a freeing of oneself from a hard, tiring, and monotonous existence" (64). Dressing up in good, clean clothes is cathartic; it frees one from a hard existence by, I think, reminding the individual of past situations and memories from the home world in which dressing up had such a connotation (see Bowen 1954:222). And such an (un)conscious linking to past memories serves to remind the individual of her identity and the meaning it confers on her life.

Two last examples of defensive/reparative behavior are Cesara's food cravings and her detailed diary. Food cravings may function in an analogous manner to those continuity-maintaining defenses already discussed. Cesara reports that she missed green vegetables. Although this is innocuous enough in itself, she also mentions that she would drive 130 kilometers "just to find a cabbage" (46). When one considers the enormity of the task and the risks involved in driving 130 kilometers over bad roads, in a country where car repair is hardly around the next corner, "just" to find a cabbage, I think it is time to consider the possibility that such a vegetable hunt may have served multiple functions (Waelder 1936), one of which was identity maintenance through the recall of familiar flavors and textures associated with the home world.[2]

Finally, that Cesara kept a detailed diary is evident from the book she culled from it. Diaries have, as one of their functions, the task of translating otherwise chaotic events into some order that makes sense to the individual in terms of her identity. This is partially what Malinowski is driving at when he comments that keeping a diary is an attempt "to avoid fragmenting themes." It is significant for the present argument that Cesara quotes this idea with much approval (98). Equally significant, and perhaps more so, is that a diary is written in one's native language. The use of one's native language is among the strongest and most effective attempts to maintain one's sense of continuity with the home world and one's identity. Reverting back to one's native language, as for example in a diary, is equivalent to receiving small identity boosters; language is absolutely and intimately tied up with one's sense of identity. As an aside, and to repeat an earlier point made in passing, it may well be that some of the notorious difficulty the anthropologist experiences in learning the native language is psychologically based. Such difficulty may, in part, be motivated by the defensive/reparative function of stabilizing the anthropologist's sense of identity.

However useful the defensive behaviors discussed above may be in helping the anthropologist maintain a sense of identity, they must inevitably pale when compared to the same help generated by another human being. A person's sense of identity is, after all, instilled through those reflections mirrored onto him from his significant others (Kohut 1977; Lichtenstein 1977). The anthropologist may, however, find it particularly difficult to locate a suitable mirror, that is, an individual who is, more or less, of his own ilk, to reflect back to him a suitable sense of identity. He is, after all, living among strangers, people who in extreme cases share only the fact of their humanity with him.[3] As I pointed out earlier, in such a situation, the most expedient maneuver for the anthropologist may be to create his own native mirror through projective identification and/or through the establishment of a narcissistic transference (self-object choice). Often, of course, both may be used together in the service of identity maintenance.

It is from this perspective that one can most profitably understand Cesara's first love affair in the field. Approximately three months after she arrived in the field, Cesara began an affair with a local magistrate, Douglas Kupeta, that was to last formally for a little less than a month. Although fairly short-lived, the depth and intensity of Cesara's involvement in this affair was pronounced, as can be witnessed in the following passages: "My mind had been free to play with research strategies and dwell on anthropological puzzles. There were times when I was totally absorbed by them. Now I found myself dwelling on Douglas. . . . I had not seen Douglas all day and longed to hear him; his every gesture fascinated me. He tugged at the umbilical cord" (61). "I had not seen Douglas these last few days. I wrestled with my feelings and started to exorcize his ghost. It didn't leave willingly. He'd reached more deeply then even I would have believed" (65). In fact, when the magistrate finally left the area of Cesara's fieldwork, she was forced to wonder whether she "would be insane enough to follow this man and slow down or ruin" (79) her research.

Coupled with the earlier evidence indicating the precarious stability of Cesara's sense of identity, the relatively rapid deepening and intensifying of her involvement in this affair suggests that it was meeting a very powerful psychological, that is, identity need. Arguing for this point is Cesara's description of the magistrate's personal qualities: "His grace and quiet authority, his sensuality and deep sense of responsibility, his fierce sense of autonomy, his sanctified manliness, his fathomless appreciation of the sanctity of woman, all these qualities had their roots in this hot, unruly valley" (79). Equally significant, Cesara was introduced to several of the magistrate's female friends, who were "admired for their capability and personal power . . . for their power and strength, and independence" (58). I am

145

not saying that the magistrate did not possess these qualities or have female friends fitting the description, but I am saying that the similarity between their qualities as "recorded" by Cesara and those of her own idealized self-image are surely too close to avoid the suspicion that she had, at least partially, created them through projective identification (see Chapter 7 for the methodological importance of this factor). That such projective identification would allow Cesara to merge with the image of the magistrate, and therefore attain a more secure sense of identity, indicates also the presence, in beginning form, of a primitive idealizing transference (Kohut 1971), a transference configuration in which Cesara could experience a warm sense of peace and tranquillity pervading her existence. This experience of basking in the tranquillity of a powerful other—an experience that comes through clearly in Cesara's choice of words to describe the magistrate—appears to have been lacking in Cesara's early childhood.

Cesara's description of this affair to her mother contains several valuable clues about its inner meaning. For one, regarding changes in her external perceptions, Cesara no longer appears to find nature so one-sidedly hideous: "It's this contact with nature, Mam. Everything cerebral becomes flesh and blood. It's intoxicating. . . . Everything looked proud and everything was decaying. And you know, even the decay held me enthralled" (54). This is a significant change in attitude, especially when viewed in light of my previous argument that Cesara's early attitudes toward nature were contaminated by projections of her own crumbling sense of identity. Now, when her sense of identity has temporarily stabilized, nature becomes intoxicating and even enthralling. Even decay can become interesting when one's identity grows stronger, that is, when it is not one's sense of identity that is decaying.

Regarding her own internal feelings during the affair, Cesara is explicit: "I lay awake thinking. I thought about my escape to freedom and remembered my friends and Bob. It's husbandness that terrifies me, Mam. I'll escape its clutches again and again. . . . I lay back and smiled at the victory of my escape. Until I remembered who I was. I shuddered. . . . A fathomless sadness enclasped me" (55–56). The flight from husbandness, both particular and general, represents a flight from the self experienced as dependent and burdensome. Her victory and her escape are not complete; she shudders at the thought of who she really is, precisely because she still views herself as burdensome.

146

There is certainly much in Cesara's relationship with the magistrate that would provoke such feelings. It was the magistrate who introduced Cesara to, and orchestrated her acceptance by, the chief of the village she wished to work in. And it was the magistrate who suggested a great deal of what and where they should do and go. Although this behavior is perfectly natural considering the circumstances—indeed, how could it be otherwise—Cesara's reaction to it is meaningful. One example is Cesara's description of their visit to a prison: "He had to inspect the prison and took me along" (56). The deceptively simple phrasing in the latter half of this thought is significant. Cesara does not say, "He had to inspect the prison and so I accompanied him," or something of the sort, but rather she allows herself "to be taken along." The passivity of this idea suggests the dependency associated with the self experienced as burdensome.

An equally telling incident occurred at the beginning of their relationship. Cesara was to be driven, by the magistrate, to meet the chief of the village in which she wished to work. Since he was unable to arrange transportation for this trip, Cesara volunteered the use of her car: "We took off for Zongwe by way of Catote. I drove first, that is important. I honked the horn to caution a cyclist of our presence, but he kept on cycling erratically and I had to slam on the breaks and steer the car into a sandbank. . . . I turned and leaned against the car . . . I held out the keys to Douglas and he took the wheel. Nestled in the corner of my seat, I watched him as he drove" (53). Starting out so positively, yet ending so negatively, this experience must have powerfully rekindled Cesara's experiencing of herself as dependent.[4] The image conveyed in her last sentence is one of striking dependency, if not helplessness.

One final measure of the tension inherent in Cesara's relationship with the magistrate is apparent in the marked depersonalization in the following incident, taken from her description of the affair: "What I describe next, Mam, is for the artist in you. I had the sensation of having stepped out of myself, as if from a great distance. I was there and away at the same time. Well, I opened the door to my room and entered. . . . I looked at us, looking at one another, and I experienced a deep sense of peace" (55).

The connection between depersonalization and vulnerabilities in the self-representation has a long history in psychoanalytic thought (for example, Fenichel 1945:419). In this instance, depersonalization appears to function as a defense against a seductive absorption into the power of an idealized other, against the resulting self-loss, and against a reexperiencing of the dependency associated with the self as burden. Presumably, part of herself is able to experience a deep sense of peace and tranquillity in merger only because a second aspect of herself is uninvolved and independent.

Considering the nature of her psychological dynamics as so far elucidated, it should come as no surprise that Cesara's relationship with the magistrate had to end. Her sense of identity as a successfully assimilated German-Canadian woman—her defense against her past—had, by this point in her fieldwork, suffered irreparable damage. Confronted by the existential vacuum of a lost identity, Cesara had attempted to establish an alternative identity through the affair. This attempt to use another person as a mirror to reflect a new sense of identity onto her had to fail, however; she still experienced herself as dependent on and therefore a burden to her mirror. Cesara's own views on the breakup of the affair are eloquent on this point: "My parting with D.K.—for I have determined there must be an end—is but the parting, in human form, with anthropological literature, childhood memories, the white community here, Bob and friends back home. An ever growing gulf is beginning to separate me from my immediate past, even from my discipline" (79–80).

Her parting with the magistrate, then, was a powerfully condensed symbol representing her loss of identity. It is interesting that immediately following her separation from the magistrate, Cesara was powerfully confronted by two memories from her early childhood (80). I believe that the recall of these memories was, on one level, an unconscious attempt to maintain continuity in her sense of identity. To paraphrase Fairbairn's (1952) famous comment on objects, any identity is better than no identity at all; an attack against one's sense of identity can never go unredressed.

I want now to dwell briefly on Cesara's dominant mood while in the field. For the existentially based thinker, moods are critical signifiers of the individual's experience of his world (Binswanger 1958:211). Cesara describes her characteristic "mood-key" as consisting of dread, "a mood so revelatory that it reveals *nothing* . . . itself" (66). Although it is impossible to specify all the many meanings that existentialists attach to "nothing," one that is particularly relevant to the argument here is finitude. Cesara points to this equation of dread with finitude in a number of instances, but none is so clear and significant as in her discussion of her feelings about nature—feelings that were, as we have already seen, contaminated by projections of her fragmenting sense of identity. Thus she states:

"There would be many such moments when a hint of life expiring would increase my dread and focus attention on myself. At such times, I would find myself tossed into the past, overcome either by feelings of guilt or bursts of anger. . . . My nicely ordered world would dissolve into a slimy morass of nothing. . . . At those moments I experienced not only the meaning of being abandoned but also that of being finite. It's this realization of the possibility of my *not* being that persuaded me, again and again, to learn who I was and what it meant to exist" (46–47).

It is difficult to do justice to this extraordinarily rich and condensed passage. Translating Cesara's statement into the terminology of this essay, one can read it as follows: During moments of experienced identity fragmentation (that is, "hint of life expiring"), one's awareness of self-finitude ("dread") increases, resulting in a heightened sense of narcissism. Defensive maneuvers are employed to maintain one's sense of experiential continuity ("tossed into the past"). This rekindling of past memories produces guilt in relation to the self experienced as burden, or anger, possibly an attempt at "reversal of voice" (G. Klein 1976:259), an attempt to turn passivity into activity and thereby gain some control over the experience through asserting the autonomy and independence of the self. But because a firm and stable sense of identity is required to allow a person to order and give meaning to her acts in the world, an individual lacking such a strong identity sees the world without clear boundaries and meaning (as a "slimy morass of nothing"). The experience of identity fragmentation produces feelings of abandonment and, in turn, finitude (see Lifton's discussion of an innate imagery of death [1976]). The awareness of death—the dread of death—powers the individual to create a new sense of identity and give meaning to her existence ("who I was and what it meant to exist"). It is no wonder, after all the preceding evidence is considered, that Cesara approves of Landes's (1970:123) statement that during fieldwork, "one's concept of self disintegrates" (110).

I argued in Part I of this book that an anthropologist will, consequent upon experiencing the loss of his sense of identity, attempt to rebuild a new sense of identity through a process of identification with anthropology as mediated through his creative work.[5] Cesara vindicates this idea in precise and elegant fashion. In a letter to her mother, she ponders her relationship with her husband. Her thinking centers around one key question: "What I'm really saying is, does he understand that I *am* this work?" (176). This statement reflects a profound reorganization of Cesara's sense of identity around and in her work. Her new-found sense of identity has been firmly lodged in her work through a process of identification. Her work is her own self; it is the mirror for and of her existence. And so in working as she wills, she escapes from her experience of her self as a burden; she creates on her own and as she wills.[6] In somewhat different terminology,[7] Cesara's identification with her work served the defensive/reparative function of solidifying her sense of identity by mitigating her experience of herself as dependent and burdensome.

I do not wish to imply that Cesara's identification with her work was a miraculous cure-all, or even that she had completely integrated the shattering experiences of her fieldwork by the time her account was published. To illustrate the latter point, I cite the following passage: "This book is . . . about a female student . . . on her first field trip. . . . Her training had emphasized quantification. . . . While she never abandoned the above goal . . . she comes to reject as dishonest the subject-object . . . segregations. . . . Often her true feelings are expressed in letters to her mother" (vii–viii).

Cesara's use of the third-person pronoun to describe her fieldwork can be interpreted as evidence that she had not yet completely integrated her experience, that she was attempting to maintain her emotional distance from it. This is understandable, considering the extremity of her experiences, but it should not obscure the point that Cesara's beginning attempt at integration took place through her identification with her work as an anthropologist and her resulting new sense of identity. In addition to the interpretation just offered, the striking otherness in the quoted passage can be taken to indicate that Cesara no longer regarded her current sense of identity as isomorphic with her prefieldwork identity.[8]

Manda Cesara entered the field suffering from a particularly marked vulnerability in her self-representation. As a consequence, she experienced her fieldwork as a shattering rite of death and rebirth. In her own words: "It would be precisely my despair that would purify and empty my mind and body; that would lead to a dying, which would open the way to resolution of those conflicting opposites that plagued my life and perception" (135). Translating these insights into my terminology, it is the emptying of her mind and body, that is, her loss of her sense of identity, experienced subjectively as a dying, that leads Cesara to a new resolution of her life, a resolution found in her identification with her work and with anthropology.

Part IV
Conclusion

7

Notes and Fragments

*Like the past, the psychoanalytic present is no more than one of a
number of possible constructions. . . . When it comes to the analysis
of experience, there are only pragmatic stopping points. . . . There are
more ways than one to understand reality.*
                        —Roy Schafer, *Language and Insight*

At the level of concrete detail, no two fieldwork experiences are exactly similar or typical. At a more abstract or analytic level, however,
there are many similarities indeed. In the preceding four chapters, I
have tried to showcase nearly the entire continuum of fieldwork
experiences as related to the issue of degree of self/identity fragmentation. From this perspective, fieldwork can be fairly self-neutral
(Rita), more or less middle-range self-dystonic (Karen, Cathy, and
Sam—although in some ways Sam's is a difficult placement), and
finally, remarkably and brutally self-dystonic (Sue, Cesara, and
Malinowski).

The process of fieldwork always subjects an anthropologist to an
attack against his sense of self/identity because he has lost, at least
temporarily, those innumerable identifications with his home world
and significant others that normally sustained his sense of self/iden-
tity. The anthropologist wakes up to find himself a stranger, and
perhaps a little afraid, in a world he never made, a world that is
totally perplexing, mysterious, and often difficult to penetrate. Having lost the positive mirroring traditionally provided by his trusted
significant others and having given up the psychologically sustain-
ing matrix of world familiarity, the anthropologist begins to experience the disintegration of his sense of identity. This disintegration
of, or attack against, his sense of identity can be experienced in a
multitude of ways; it can be represented in a thousand different
masks. Among the many possible representations of this attack, we
have seen a few of the more common: doubts about the integrity of
one's body self, about one's basic competency as a fully functioning

153

human being, about one's intellectual prowess and ability to complete the project, and others. These identity attacks are most prevalent and severe at the beginning of fieldwork, but they never entirely recede and are present, to some extent, even during the happiest and most productive periods of the fieldwork. These latter periods, generally the time of maximum secondary identification with the native culture, will be discussed more fully in the second volume of this work.

In an effort to halt or at least stem—better yet to reverse and repair—the disintegrative inroads made against his sense of identity, the anthropologist will, while in the field, engage in a series of behaviors that function to solidify his threatened self-representation. These defensive/reparative behaviors, like the identity attack itself, can take a multitude of forms. The anthropologist may, for example, resist learning the native language in favor of his own native language; he may dream of past experiences from his culture; he may covet letters from home; he may abstain from having sexual relations with a member of the indigenous culture in favor of fantasized attachments to partners from his home world; he may seek out or create an alter ego from among the members of the indigenous culture to provide him with positive mirroring; and so on. However different these behaviors may appear to the casual observer, they do share one important similarity: they enable the anthropologist to restore some component of the positive mirroring that he has lost in going to the field, and they enable him to restore, to an extent, those recently broken links, those innumerable identifications with his home world that helped to sustain his sense of identity. Defensive/reparative behaviors function to provide the anthropologist with a life-sustaining matrix of familiarity; they are life preservers in a literal sense.

The relative effectiveness of these defensive/reparative behaviors will depend on the severity of the self-disintegrative inroads experienced by the anthropologist during fieldwork. The severity, or if you will, the depth and intensity of these inroads will, in turn, be conditioned by the interaction between two largely psychological factors, the relative stability and solidity of the anthropologist's sense of self (considered generally, the anthropologist's psychobiographic past), coupled with the relative degree of overlap or discrepancy between the cognitive maps of the anthropologist and his people. In situations in which the anthropologist has a reasonably stable self-representation and experiences minimal cognitive clashing during field-

154

work, his "identity crisis" will be fairly minor and controllable (containable) through the activation of defensive/reparative behaviors. In situations, however, in which the anthropologist has marked vulnerabilities in his self-representation and experiences some cognitive clashing, his "identity crisis" will be very severe and the effectiveness of his defensive/reparative behaviors greatly curtailed. It is in the latter cases that one sees the self-immortalizing, religious identification with anthropology occurring as a response to the existential vacuum created by the fieldwork experience. Finally, between these two extremes lies the middle range of anthropological field experience, with its "some but not too great" amount of self-dystonic experience. It is here, in this middle range, that the majority of anthropologists probably locate their field experiences.

With this short summary of my work at hand, I want to turn and explore, albeit briefly, several implications of my ideas.

Fieldwork as Objectively Traumatizing

In Part II of this book, I implicitly, and in Part III, explicitly, argued for the primacy of the influence of the anthropologist's psychobiographic past in determining the extent of the identity attack during fieldwork. Thus Cesara found her fieldwork a brutal and searing attack on her sense of self because she experienced herself as burdensome and dependent, Malinowski because of his particular self-vulnerability, and the same with Sue and her feelings of self-inauthenticity. If we bracket for a moment the ultimate truth of this idea of the primacy of the anthropologist's psychobiographic past, we are left with an interesting question: Is there such a thing as an objectively traumatizing field experience? Is there a field experience so bad that nearly every anthropologist, irrespective of personality, who undertook it would come out of it shattered or traumatized?

The answer to this question is probably no.

Every anthropologist has his favorite horror story about fieldwork. These are generally told in a variety of different situations and for a variety of different reasons: at cocktail parties, for example, to regale the uninitiated and to instill within them the romantic ethos of anthropology, to graduate and advanced undergraduate students to test their mettle and to determine if they have the right stuff. Of all of these stories, there are perhaps two that are told most frequently, Colin Turnbull's (1961) fieldwork among the Ik and Napoleon Chag-

155

non's (1968) among the Yanomamo. And of these two stories, it is Turnbull's that most people have in mind when thinking about an objectively traumatizing field experience. Why this story, and not Chagnon's, we shall see momentarily.

The details of Turnbull's experiences among the Ik, as eloquently if distressingly put forward in *The Mountain People*, are familiar enough by this time to render much recounting unnecessary. Suffice it to say that Turnbull paints a picture of the Ik as being a very nasty people indeed, creatures hardly deserving of the label *human*. To mock and to ridicule the sick and crippled, to prey upon those too weak to resist, to delight in others' pain, to hoard vital necessities and to deprive other Ik were all behaviors observed by Turnbull during his fieldwork. Needless to say, Turnbull had a remarkably difficult time studying the Ik; fieldwork was, for Turnbull, a traumatic experience.

To rephrase the question that started this discussion, is it possible to imagine another anthropologist experiencing all that Turnbull did and yet not finding his fieldwork traumatic?

The answer to this question is probably yes.

It is not likely that many people would find fieldwork among the Ik, at least under conditions comparable to those faced by Turnbull, a peachy, delightful experience. Some, I hope very few, would, and that is my point. An event that is intolerable and traumatic to one person might be difficult but manageable to another and hardly worth mentioning to a third. The degree of trauma produced by any given event is always and only determinable in relation to the degree to which it is self-dystonic, and the latter is determinable only in relation to the individual's psychobiographic past. However harsh it might seem, nothing is universally traumatic.

Chagnon's fieldwork experience, poignantly recorded in the opening pages of *Yanomamo: The Fierce People*, is at least as well known as Turnbull's if not so controversial. Without engaging in a "my people were worse than yours because" game—an inverted one-upsmanship—it is safe to say that, like Turnbull's experience, Chagnon's was not set up to be much fun—it was fraught with routine and periodic ax fights, the tropical weather and insect life, the unsanitary conditions, the occasional ambush, and the whole host of other horrors described by Chagnon. And yet, the remarkable thing about it, from my perspective here, is the relatively untraumatizing effect that it had on Chagnon. Nowhere in Chagnon's writings do we detect any real, substantial evidence of psychological trauma. Admittedly, there are many reasons why one might attempt to cover over evidence of trauma, but still there is, generally speaking, some evidence, some hint of the cover-over attempt, of the trauma lurking beneath the façade. This is not meant to imply that Chagnon's stay was trouble-free or without psychological strain—it had enough of both, to be sure—but it does mean that Chagnon was not nearly psychologically traumatized to the extent that Turnbull was, and more to the point, that others who have studied the Yanomamo were (McCay 1984, reporting on a young man who returned, psychologically distraught, after three months among the Yanomamo studying male-female relations).

Why one and not the other? Why is one fieldwork experience traumatizing and another not? Why does one man not experience an objectively difficult fieldwork situation as traumatic? How can another man go from paradise with the Pygmies to, a decade later, Conradian horror among the Ik? Why do two women, one in Africa, one in South America, experience relatively straightforward and objectively nonbrutalizing fieldwork situations as traumatic? All for the same reason—because trauma is in the eye of the beholder and not in some objective yardstick. Psychological trauma is produced through the interaction of some triggering event or catalyst with elements of an individual's psychobiographic past; trauma is always a consequence of interaction.

Omphalos

Every field of human study that wishes to continue to exist needs a sort of data lifeline. And certainly to continue to exist independently, without fear of annexation, a field needs unique data, or if this is impossible, a unique way of collecting data. In the case of anthropology, this unique way of collecting data is fieldwork, and a momentous discovery it was. With the advent of systematic fieldwork, anthropology and more particularly anthropologists, came of age and secured their data lifeline.

Coming of age is a great, if problematic, event but by itself is not enough to guarantee success in the storm and stress of life. Maturity, and ultimately progress, come to a field of human study only if its practitioners periodically turn backward and fold inward upon themselves to examine their fundamental philosophical and methodological presuppositions. In the case of anthropology, this omphalitic urge arose relatively late, at least as compared to its sister disciplines in the human sciences, and took an unfortunate turn.

Bob Scholte, one of the leading figures in omphalitic anthropology over the past fifteen years or so, has always emphasized the need for the development of a fully "reflexive, critical, and emancipatory anthropology" (1971a:782); an anthropologist must realize, says Scholte, that his field experience is "still a primary and intersubjective reality in which his tradition *and* humanity condition what he can hope to experience and to understand" (1971a:800). In calling attention to the influence of the anthropologist's tradition on his way of perceiving the world, Scholte is arguing that anthropologists do unto themselves what they have always been so quick to do unto others, namely to consider their own beliefs, pet theories, and attitudes as culturally constituted and historically mediated. In calling attention to the anthropologist's humanity as a factor influencing his perception of the world, Scholte is, in essence, arguing for the necessity of a psychology of fieldwork and of the fieldworker.

Although Scholte was very right in arguing for the necessity of both tradition and humanity studies, anthropologists have not, as a group, been equally receptive and attentive to the need for both types of study. With few exceptions, it almost appears as though anthropologists have drawn a sharp dividing line between these studies, declaring the nonpsychological or tradition type welcome and the explicitly psychological unwelcome. At least, that is how the results would have it appear. Thus, as for the purely epistemological, tradition studies, we have many: emic/etic, inside/outside, phenomenological-hermeneutic/objectivist, cognitive/behavioral, experience-near/experience-distant, a "writing ethnography" school, a "dialogical" school, and so forth. As for the more explicitly psychological, there are only relatively few studies.

This lack would not be particularly regrettable except that the antipsychological bias—or at least the tendency to ignore psychological matters—of certain anthropologists has led them, in their epistemological studies, to some very curious conclusions. Although any one of a number of studies could be mentioned, I am thinking particularly of Clifford Geertz's (1976) highly influential "From the Native's Point of View" study. Geertz's basic position, in brief, is that to see things from the native's point of view, the anthropologist need not be a perfect "walking miracle of empathy," but instead needs to be able to piece together and interpret the native's symbol system. The latter idea, about the importance of symbol systems, seems to me very defensible and very necessary. The former idea, however, about empathy and its relative unimportance, seems to be the mistaken result of a faulty confusion.

In building up his argument against the importance of empathy, Geertz relies heavily on his reading of Malinowski's diary. As Geertz points out, and as we have already seen, Malinowski was not an especially nice guy, he was not tactful, friendly, and patient with the natives, and he certainly was not a "walking miracle of empathy." But then, in what can only be called an unjustified psychological leap, Geertz apparently assumes that Malinowski's characteristic attitudes and feelings, particularly his inability to empathize with the natives, are typical and apply to the experiences of the majority of anthropologists. It is on this basis, on this assumption really, that Geertz can pose his central question: "Where are we when we can no longer claim some unique form of psychological closeness, a sort of transcultural identification, with our subject? What happens to *verstehen* when *einfuhlen* disappears?" (222).

It is one thing to study an extreme instance of any given phenomenon with an eye toward illuminating its more normal or middle-range instances. This is, in fact, routine procedure in much of the human sciences, and as long as one is aware of the relevant parameters, pretty much trouble-free. It is altogether different, however, to study an extreme instance of a phenomenon without realizing—or without mentioning—that it is extreme, that it is not normal or typical. Malinowski's characteristic self-vulnerability, which produced the startling qualities of his fieldwork experience, is not typical of the majority of anthropologists. One cannot uncritically draw conclusions about the typical anthropologist's characteristic psychological abilities from Malinowski's case.

We can, however, go still further and answer Geertz's question in the affirmative: a special psychological closeness, a transcultural identification, can occur between anthropologist and native. I am referring here to that process that I earlier described as a typical defense against the identity attack experienced by many anthropologists during fieldwork, namely, secondary identification with the native culture. However fleeting or however long-lasting it may be, secondary identification enables the anthropologist to feel and to experience, as well as to see and to know, the native's point of view. Secondary identification, if not true empathy, nevertheless mimics it closely enough to aid in the process of reconstructing the native's world sense. Secondary identification enables the anthropologist to narrow, for a time, the vast gap of cultural experience separating him from his subjects.

This is not meant to produce too one-sided a picture. Fieldworkers are not perfect empathizers or social chameleons; nobody is. The analysis of symbol systems is an important device to help the anthropologist know the native's point of view. By the same token, however, empathy or secondary identification is an important device to help the anthropologist experience, and therefore to know in a wider sense, the native's point of view. One without the other yields an analysis either intellectually top-heavy or emotionally touchy-feely. Both are needed, and just as the epistemologist of anthropology needs the psychologist, so vice versa.

Psychobiography and Validity

There are a number of ways to describe the central principle underlying all successful psychobiography: there is always an element of subjectivity in an individual's theorizing; the dominant questions that animate an individual's work, as well as his answers to those questions, will always be conditioned by what, psychologically speaking, he is; an individual's dominant ideas, theoretical beliefs, and the like reflect and express his most vivid, problematic, and salient subjective concerns as conditioned by early formative experiences (Atwood and Tomkins 1976). When applied to anthropology, the above statements could be rephrased, without violence, to the following: an anthropologist's field observations and interpretations are, on one level, not truth and reality but rather species of autobiography (LaBarre in Devereux 1967). An anthropologist in the field is, again on one level, practicing a sort of selfmancy, a divination based on self. It is as if the anthropologist projects his self, lays it onto the world as if it were a Procrustean grid, and then, hey presto, he suddenly discovers in his field notes what he really knew all along, what he was psychologically all along. Whatever else patterns of culture really are, they can be interpreted as patterns of personality—the anthropologist's to some extent—writ large, thrown gigantic upon the screen, and given a long time span. It is almost as if there was truth in Plato's thought that all knowledge is remembering, recollecting from a forgotten shadow side of existence.

One of the more interesting things about these statements is that people often react very negatively to them, almost as if they were on the receiving end of either implicit or explicit criticism. Why this response?

160

Part of this response is probably explained by fear of solipsism—the dead hand of Johann Fichte, among others. Admittedly, my cursory listing of psychobiographic tenets that began this section might tend to encourage this concern and justifiably so. But my listing was cursory, and a more complete discussion would not fail to mention that subjective concerns alone do not and cannot entirely determine the form and content of an indvidual's work. It is no accident, for example, that Cesara's need to escape from her burdensome self should take, in one form, a cry for a radical feminism, or that Malinowski's concern over his self-vulnerability should take hold in a theory of organic functionalism, the strands of which were in the air in the early part of this century. Theoretical concerns of any individual in any field will always depend on a complex interplay of subjective factors and the social/intellectual milieu in which the theorist is situated. If a radical feminist movement did not exist, it would not have been possible for Cesara to seize it as a means of expressing her own self-dilemma; the same can be said about Malinowski's use of an organic functionalism. It is the interaction between subjective and external factors that produces the final form of an individual's ideas. Cesara did not just seize and parrot the radical feminist perspective, but she gave to it a particular coloring all her own, just as Malinowski surely did not simply adopt any old functionalism, but rather adapted one to suit his subjective concerns.

A second problematic aspect about the element of subjectivity in theorizing is a hangover from the days when scientific observers were thought to be neutral, cameralike machines whose only concern was objectively to record pure data. But this misses the point, more fundamentally, because it confuses two entirely different concerns, subjectivity and validity. Here one must be careful. In pointing to the subjective influences that conditioned the work of Cesara and Malinowski—for that matter that condition everyone's work—I am not attempting to explain away the value of that work. A theory is never simply a subjective product. It always assumes an independent life of its own and so must be judged as to its explanatory usefulness apart from its creator's psyche. Any given prediction derived from a theory must be tested, as must the logic that holds the theory together, without regard for its creator's personality foibles. Thus when I say that Cesara embraced Sartrian existentialism as a defensive maneuver to shore up her threatened self-representation, this should not be heard as implying that she had no especially strong intellectual reasons for her choice or that her brand of Sar-

161

trian existentialism is necessarily "wrong." I am implying, however, that nobody adopts, augments, and defends a perspective on human nature for purely intellectual reasons. The perspective that is adopted must answer or meet the individual's intellectual and emotional or psychological needs.

On the level of specifics, then, there is little, if any, intrinsic connection between the subjective concerns of a theorist and the ultimate validity of his ideas. On a more general level, however, there is an area in which the dependence of a theory on its creator's subjective concerns is relevant. I am referring here to a major derivation based on psychobiographical studies, namely, that no single theory in the human sciences can ever do justice to the entire range of phenomena implicated in the understanding of any aspect of human behavior. The various constituents of reality for any given theory must always be more or less exaggerated or underrated in their importance depending upon the subjective concerns of the theorist. No theorist can devote the same loving care to those aspects of reality that do not concern him deeply as to those that he has a real psychological need to develop; I have told my truth, and not the whole truth, about fieldwork. From this point of view, Bateson (1979) makes a great deal of sense in his argument about the importance of having two eyes; two descriptions of the "same" reality are always more useful than one. Double descriptions, though not truth, do underline the differential aspects of reality that must inevitably be ignored in any one description or theory.

It would be useful if one could approach the recent Mead/Freeman debate, as well as the earlier Redfield/Lewis controversy, from this point of view. Rather than splitting into armed and hostile camps each defending its own doctrine (that is, its own self-objects, its own focal symbols of immortality power), the disputants in these issues might be or have been better off recognizing that the accounts offered by both theorists are necessarily incomplete because they are products of different subjective concerns coupled with different intellectual and social milieus. This would still leave room for arguments about the general applicability and the accuracy of each theorist's account; that would not change. But the spirit of the debate might at least be a little less acrimonious. And certainly much anthropological self-flagellation, now displayed with too much vulgarity and bad taste in our leading journals, might then be and have been avoided. To paraphrase Norman O. Brown's comment about the intellectual life, what the anthropological world needs is a little less strife and a little more Eros.

Women in Anthropology

There are two relatively disparate points that need to be made on this subject. The first relates to an aspect of my methodology (women in my sample), whereas the second relates more broadly to a matter of anthropological methodology (women in the field).

Having worked his way through the interview vignettes and case studies in Chapters 3 through 6, the reader will by this time have realized that I ultimately analyzed more female than male anthropologists' field experiences. Although this skewing of sex ratios was not intentional—at least not consciously—it also was not catastrophic in the sense of placing a "gender constraint" on the general applicability of my conclusions. Unlike the different developmental lines traversed by males and females in the classic Freudian paradigm, from the point of view of self-psychology, and more particularly from that of identity maintenance, the processes that produce and stabilize an individual's sense of identity are identical for males and females (Lachmann 1982). The characteristics of the fieldwork situation that render it an identity-dystonic experience (the loss of positive mirroring from and familiar identifications with significant objects in the home world) affect males and females equally. Had I analyzed an even number of males and females, my results would have been substantially the same as they are now—a prediction for future research.

Admittedly, although the processes of identity maintenance are similar for males and females, the specific symptoms of identity disintegration and the defensive/reparative behaviors undertaken in response to it may differ between the sexes. One might reasonably expect to find that gender-specific cultural expectations and stereotypes play a determining role in shaping the form taken by specific symptoms and defensive/reparative behaviors. Whether the anthropologist has a good cry or puts a clenched fist through a wall in response to the depression that accompanies identity disintegration depends, to some extent, on the natal and adopted culture's definition of appropriate behavior for males and females. To cite a second and more potentially interesting example, growing up as a woman in America requires that one accept, at least partially, a greater emotional sensitivity and perceptiveness as appropriate to the feminine role (Golde 1970:3). Therefore, one might expect the female anthropologist to express aspects of this increased emotionality in her choice of defensive/reparative behaviors, for example, writing heartfelt letters home or keeping an emotionally honest and revealing diary. In fact, it may very well be this image of the woman as a more emotionally resonant and perceptive being that helps to explain why female anthropologists were so early to seize on the emotional stresses and strains of fieldwork as a problem in need of further study (Bowen 1954; Hurston 1942; Marriott 1952; Powdermaker 1966; Golde 1970) and why the most psychologically open and revealing account of fieldwork yet written was authored by a woman (Cesara 1982; Malinowski never intended his diaries to be published). It is also reasonable to suppose that this image of the woman as an emotional sponge unconsciously guided my choice of informants; I expected women to be more forthcoming and sensitive about the emotional/psychological trials and tribulations of fieldwork and so included more of them in my sample. With this thought, I will end the discussion of women in my sample and consider, briefly, one specific issue related to women in the field.

Over the past several decades, anthropologists have grown progressively more interested in the nature of their discipline and in their data-gathering techniques. Much like their counterparts in physics, anthropologists have come to recognize that their data are largely the result of a process of interaction between a disturbing influence (the anthropologist) and the field in and on which it acts (the indigenous culture). Fieldwork is a process of negotiation between the observer and the observed. From this dialogical perspective, it is especially important to analyze and determine the influence of the anthropologist on the data that are being studied. And one characteristic of anthropologists that is certainly noticeable and likely to influence the data they collect is their gender.

No one, I think, would deny that the fieldworker's sex makes a difference, that it must be seen as influencing the fieldwork situation and therefore the data that are collected. A number of studies in this area have focused on the problem of differential access to data—that female anthropologists get access to certain cultural practices and social spheres from which male anthropologists are barred and vice versa—particularly as it is related to the role the anthropologist assumes in the eyes of the native people (Devereux 1967:234ff.; Golde 1970:6–9). The role adopted by the fieldworker is crucial for any role is, by definition, restrictive: "Only in rare instances does the status ascribed to the ethnologist lend itself to comprehensive fieldwork. . . . [The ethnologist must] insist on being shown also that which is normally turned away from a person occupying that status" (Devereux 1967:249, 251).

For female anthropologists, and particularly for those who work in nonliterate cultures, the available roles that can be adopted, whether freely chosen or "forcibly" imposed by the community, are few in number. The anthropologist needs to guarantee her ability to act independently, but she also must enable the culture's members to feel as if they can adequately control and protect her; she must be classifiable but not straightjacketed into an impossibly narrow and confining role. The fieldworker's difficulties are further compounded because in most cultures, women are not permitted much leeway in the performance of their role responsibilities. Any deviation from the norm tends to stand out clearly and to draw much unfavorable reaction. In such a situation, the anthropologist will often adopt or accept an existing variant or "deviant" role that enables her to flout or disregard traditional expectations for women's behavior while still remaining classifiable and therefore relatively unthreatening. Landes (1970), for example, assumed the successive roles of "artist," "prostitute," and "Communist" during her fieldwork in Brazil. Briggs (1970a), during her stay with the Eskimo, moved between the roles of "mentally retarded" and "child." Weidman and Nader, for reasons of appearance and attitude, were classified as "men" (Golde 1970:9). Often a woman fieldworker will be treated as a postmenopausal tribal woman, a "sexless" being that is permitted a great deal more independence than a "normal" woman. This sexless status has often been considered ideal because of the relative freedom of movement and wide range of access that it allows (Devereux 1967:108; Golde 1970:6).

Although the direct methodological implications of adopting any one status have already been mentioned here and by many others (that is, a "woman-man" would get access to some areas that a "Communist" might not, and vice versa), there is an indirect implication that has received much less attention but is clearly related to the main thrust of this book. I am referring to certain defensive/reparative behaviors that may be activated by the anthropologist who has adopted a role during fieldwork that is discordant with her own self-image/identity. Although, for example, it may seem methodologically ideal for the initiate-anthropologist to be classified and treated as a postmenopausal woman, such a status may promote severe psychological difficulties in the area of identity maintenance. On one hand, these difficulties may be largely dealt with through the activation of defensive/reparative behaviors that serve to link the anthropologist to her home world—witness the cases of Karen, Cathy, and Sue that were discussed in earlier chapters. On the other hand, however, the initiate-anthropologist may also activate a defensive/reparative behavior that serves not so much to establish a link with her home world as to distance her from the indigenous culture and more particularly from her newly acquired "unreal" and "unlivable" status. These potentially methodologically significant responses may include feelings of (un)conscious resentment directed against the native people or a tendency to focus on particular people and events that somehow restore to the anthropologist a sense of the vitality and integrity of her "actual" identity ("I am not a sexless being") while avoiding, or at least downplaying the importance of, those things that tend to remind her of her discordant adopted identity. This very human tendency to concentrate on identity-syntonic aspects of the surrounding environment while ignoring identity-dystonic aspects can produce in the anthropologist a decidedly one-sided and incomplete description of a culture. Or more accurately phrased, when whole chunks of experience are (un)consciously ignored, the resulting account must be less rich and humanly complex than is otherwise possible. Devereux (1967:234–51) has discussed this process of "distortion" at great length and reached a substantially similar conclusion, although it is couched in a somewhat different psychological idiom.

The psychological difficulties that are generated when a host culture imposes an "unlivable" identity on an anthropologist are certainly not confined to women. Devereux (1967:246), for one, reports that he was unable completely to fulfill the role responsibilities of a shaman among the Sedang for at least one of the required attributes, assuming an exploitive role, was too identity-dystonic for him to accept. I have concentrated on female anthropologists in this section largely because of their majority presence in my sample. Whether the discrepancy between "real" and "imposed" identity is a greater problem for female as opposed to male anthropologists (because of fewer available identities for females to assume coupled with more stringent role-performance ideals) or whether specific defensive/reparative behaviors mobilized during fieldwork are characteristically different between female and male anthropologists are questions for future research.

Informants in the Field

Devereux (1967:19) has put together an extremely persuasive argument for his belief that "every thought system . . . originates in the unconscious as a defense against anxiety and disorientation." Although the social and natural sciences are, for the most part, concerned with different objects of study—human beings versus inanimate matter—both are rooted in anxiety reduction. Given the ubiquity of anxiety reduction as a motive in theory construction, it is imperative for the scientist to determine whether he is using his particular methodology in a "sublimating manner, or unconsciously, in a defensive manner only" (Devereux 1967:97). Whenever one studies human beings, one will inevitably encounter situations that generate anxiety. A method that helps to increase one's detachment and therefore to reduce anxiety can hold great benefits for scientific inquiry. Devereux believes that the crucial factor is the degree of self-awareness the investigator possesses about his reasons for adopting a particular methodology. An investigator who is aware of his own deep motives for adopting any given methodology is more likely to be able to reduce his anxiety without distorting his results than is the blithely unaware investigator. The medical doctor who is aware of his reasons for remaining rational and aloof in the face of great suffering is likely to be a much different and better doctor than the one for whom rationality becomes an unexamined end in itself—a defense, and not as in the first instance a sublimation, against anxiety that can turn into an "impersonal 'morgue approach' to patients" (Devereux 1967:156).

I have discussed Devereux's ideas in some detail here because they seem to me to sum up and to parallel my own ideas about the nature of anthropologist-informant relations during fieldwork. It would be too much of an exaggeration to claim that every friendly or every hostile relationship entered into during fieldwork originated in the anthropologist's unconscious as a defense against the anxiety associated with identity fragmentation, but certainly some do. We have already seen how the anthropologist may turn to his principal informant, or avoid and dislike other people, in an effort to stabilize his sense of identity. The anthropologist may need to locate or create the too-well-informed informant, the native "philosophy don," if he is to assure the stability of his sense of identity; the anthropologist may also need to avoid the presence of, or actively hate, certain people whose very existence and way of life threaten his psychological security (for example, Sam's feelings about the missionaries he lived with and Cathy's avoidance of her adopted parents' daughter). But surely from a methodological point of view, it makes a great deal of difference how aware one is of the reasons one has for selecting a particular friend or enemy.

Coming to like a person, or to dislike another, is a commonplace in human existence. For the fieldworker, however, these feelings must become something more, a source of information and a chance for self-reflection. If they do not, if the fieldworker's personal relationships go unexamined, then they can become sources of bias and distortion, or at the very least, missed chances. This is not to say that the psychologically aware investigator will necessarily produce a complete and thoroughly representative account of any given culture. As we have already seen, every investigator is subject to a set of unique psychobiographic constraints that channel his interests and ideas into certain areas. Within any one of these areas, however, it is the investigator's responsibility to be methodologically honest, to explore the domain openly and by using whatever means are available. And sources of pleasure and sources of pain are two such available means that the anthropologist can exploit to open up further areas of inquiry, that he can use to deepen and enrich his understanding of the native culture.

Forming friendships is essential to good fieldwork. The anthropologist needs to have one, or several, special informants with whom he can discuss his ideas and whose opinions and ideas he can trust. By the same token, however, the anthropologist needs to be aware that an especially congenial relationship with an informant might actually say more about the unconscious needs of the anthropologist than about any particular facet of the culture he is studying. The anthropologist needs actively to question whether he is making friends with only a select group of natives and differentially weighting the view of the culture that he receives from them. For the anthropologist who is actively interested in pursuing self-reflection, who seeks out his own underlying motives, his fears and fantasies, personal relationships entered into during fieldwork can become a pathway that leads him to discover hitherto unsuspected patterns of connection between elements of native cultural practice.

Similarly, the anthropologist needs to examine the underlying nature of the anxiety that he experiences when meeting certain people or engaging in particular events. Obeyesekere (1981:8–9), for example, explains how he was able to use his own anxiety at the sight of a woman whose hair was matted into prominent locks as a springboard to enter into a deeper understanding of native culture. In like fashion, Devereux (1967:219) was able to use his feelings of anxiety about and dislike for the cultural practices of the Sedang to discover that the people themselves disliked many of their own cultural practices but felt constrained by evil gods. Rather than simply avoiding the sources of their anxiety, both Obeyesekere and Devereux were able to take a creative and methodologically significant stance toward their own human reactions. Perhaps their experiences suggest what might be called a fundamental tenet of fieldwork methodology: the anthropologist's feelings and desires, whether positive or negative, are tools that can be used to allow him to penetrate more deeply into the world of the native.

Like all human beings, fieldworkers make friends and enemies; they laugh and cry, hate and love; they have great days and absolutely rotten days. Being aware of the underlying motives animating these feelings, of the process of identity loss and defensive/reparative behavior, of the need for links to the home world and for "mirror" informants, will not make any of these phenomena or feelings disappear; the most psychologically sophisticated and sensitive anthropologist will still experience culture shock and all its consequences. But being aware of these phenomena—a mode of understanding that might be developed with the aid of psychoanalysis, for one example—can help to reduce the likelihood of being unconsciously controlled by them. Even a little awareness and a little understanding can keep the anthropologist from producing "a self-indulgent branch of lyric poetry . . . [an account of] how he feels projectively about the unknown" (LaBarre in Devereux 1967:viii). If there is any one most important lesson to be derived from the psychology of fieldwork, then surely it must concern the value of being critically and creatively self-aware.

Fieldwork is certainly the most remarkable and unusual requirement imposed by a discipline on its practitioners. Giving up one's familiar world, friends, and style of life to go and live and work in a Newfoundland fishing village, an Austrian peasant community, or a Brazilian Indian tribe entails a degree of self-sacrifice that is relatively unknown in the other human sciences. There is something grand and romantic, almost heroic, in this idea of self-sacrifice for the sake of knowledge. As Friedrich Nietzsche pointed out, the human animal has a bad memory for things in general but an excellent one for events cloaked in pain, guilt, and self-sacrifice. Ah, but what is the lesson, what is to be learned, and what remembered? And so it is necessary to be relentless in ferreting out the dark side of fieldwork, for only then can the other side, the rebirth of the anthropologist, be fully comprehended and understood in a rigorous manner. This story, that of the transition from the dark to the light, awaits another day.

Appendix
Sample Questionnaire

In addition to those already mentioned in the preface, there are several points about my interviewing technique that need to be made before presenting the questionnaire. Of the five interviews presented in this book, three were conducted in the informant's home (Karen, Cathy, and Sue) and two in the informant's academic office (Rita and Sam). The decision as to where the interview should take place was left entirely to the informant; my only request was that the interview proceed uninterrupted. Each interview was tape-recorded and later transcribed for analysis. Follow-up interviews were conducted after I had transcribed and studied the original interview material—a period of about a week.

The following list of questions will give the reader a general idea of the information I requested from my informants. With the exception of the first four, I did not always ask the questions in the order listed here. Question 9, for example, was generally asked as the informant was emerging from an especially emotionally trying topic. Because these points could not be predicted ahead of time, question 9 floated about until it was needed. There were also variations in the position of other questions, particularly 10, 11, and 12. Again with the exception of the first four, every question was asked as open. Because of this lack of structuring, I did not always have to ask a specific question—often the informant beat me to it. Because of the open nature of most of the questions, an informant's answers would often start other rabbits running, which would have to be tracked down before going on. Finally, I did not always ask the questions precisely as they are phrased here. Much depended on my impression of the informant's temperament and my own mood. Sometimes I was more casual, other times very formal. It depended on the situation.

1. General Information
    A. Your age now and when in the field?
    B. Marital status now and when in the field?
    C. Other siblings?
    D. Parents' occupations?
    E. Religious views?
2. When did you first get interested in pursuing anthropology seriously?
3. What is your philosophy of fieldwork, that is, where do you stand on the emic/etic continuum?
4. Where did you do your fieldwork?
    What was the longest continuous period that you were in the field?
    What were your topical interests?
5. Describe your feelings on entry into the field area.
6. If you had a principal informant(s), please describe him or her. If not, single out your closest field friend(s) and describe him or her. Describe the individual or group with whom you had your most problematic relationship.
7. Did you experience any intense cravings in the field? For what? If sex was not mentioned here, I introduced the topic. I was particularly interested in whether the individual chose to remain celibate and, if so, whether it presented much of a problem, and, of course, if it did, how the individual handled it. The general content of the individual's fantasy life was usually elicited here.
8. Can you remember anything about your dream life in the field?
9. Did you celebrate your birthday in the field? What about other holidays that you would normally celebrate when you were home?
10. What was the most memorable part of fieldwork for you?
    Describe your best experience in the field.
    Describe your worst experience in the field.
11. Did you ever experience feelings of psychic isolation or helplessness during your fieldwork? If so, how did you handle these feelings?
12. Did you ever feel that your project was without meaning or purpose?
13. Describe your feelings on leaving the field.
14. Victor Turner has argued that during the liminal stage of a rite of passage, the initiate will often experience feelings of identity fragmentation or disintegration. Eliade argues a similar point

APPENDIX

and maintains that the initiate undergoes a symbolic death. Do you feel that either or both of these analyses applies at all to your own field experience?

15. Do you feel yourself to be more of an anthropologist now than before you went to the field?
16. If fieldwork changed you, how do you think it did?
17. If you would like to add any additional comments, anything that you might consider important that I did not ask about, anything at all, please feel free.
18. If the interview seemed to be dragging and nothing worthwhile was coming up, I sometimes asked the individual to describe a typical day in the field.

Notes

Prologue

1. That these dark elements stood out so clearly to me indicates nothing about their importance relative to the happier aspects of fieldwork that undoubtedly stand out just as forcefully to others. The factors that interest me do so for psychobiographic reasons and not because they are somehow theoretically primary.

2. I am aware that Lévi-Strauss's writings often function on several different levels of meaning. I am also aware that by removing this quotation from its context, I am doing some injustice to its more abstract referents (for example, the relative superiority of non-Western versus Western cultures). But I am also aware that this statement is an eloquent testimonial to the doubts that many anthropologists experience, at least part of the time, during their fieldwork.

Chapter 1: On Death and Fieldwork

1. For my purposes here, I am content to argue that the fieldwork experience is both the liminal phase of a rite of passage and the "sacra" of sociocultural anthropology. For a largely unsuccessful attempt to differentiate the two, see my earlier article on the matter (1983).

2. It is probably this factor that underlies the fear of loneliness so prevalent among human beings. I would point out here that the work of Heinz Kohut certainly belongs to any discussion on the origin and maintenance of a stable sense of identity. Although Kohut would prefer to divorce his work from identity theory, I do not think it does much violence to either concept, identity or self, to equate a sense of stable identity with a sense of a cohesive self. As the work of Lichtenstein (1977) makes clear, identity can certainly have a dimension in depth.

3. I am here giving Cassirer and Leslie White their proper due. If anthropologists continue to define man as the "symbolic animal," they will have

to face the consequences, that is, that symbols are "real." To stave off confusion, I am simply arguing here that, at some level, the psychological response to the threat of physical and symbolic (disintegration anxiety, fear of psychosis) death is equivalent, or nearly so. It seems to me that this point is implicit in much of Kohut's work (esp. 1971; 1977) and in self-psychological theorizing in general (McCarthy 1980).

4. There are three points that need to be made here. One, the psychological dynamics here elucidated may underlie the implicit prestige hierarchy among anthropological fieldworkers. I am referring to the well-known fact that the rougher your field experience, the more prestige accrues to you as an anthropologist and vice versa. Certainly my argument would help to explain the comment made by Pelto (1965:33): "An anthropologist's first field trip—particularly if it deals with a primitive society, far from cities and civilization—is regarded as an initiation rite after which he is 'never the same again.' It can truthfully be said that those few anthropologists who have concentrated on library research and avoided the risks and rigors of fieldwork are looked down on by the rest of the profession." Two, my argument would seem to imply that, because of the fieldwork experience, anthropologists would be more identified with their discipline than other social scientists who have had to experience "only" graduate school as an initiation rite. My own gut impression, for whatever it is worth, is that anthropologists are a little more clannish about their discipline than most other social scientists. Three, it is easy to restate this point in the terminology of the psychology of the self: following the fragmentation of the student's sense of self and powered by the emergence of disintegration anxiety, the symbol of anthropology is turned to as a self-object. For the similarities between self-psychology and Rankian theory (will psychology) see Stolorow and Atwood (1976).

5. I am arguing here for a relationship between death and identity. I offer the following speculation in an attempt to provide a possible clue to the nature of this relationship: Hoffman (1979), leaning heavily on the work of Kurt R. Eissler (1955), argues that it is the ultimate awareness of death that gives meaning and vitality to our existence or identity. The fact that one has only limited chances lends a certain anguished richness to life's activity. Freud (1957:291) recognized this aspect of death as well: "For it is really too sad that in life it should be as it is in chess, where one false move may force us to resign the game, but with the difference that we can start no second game, no return match." I mean to draw attention here to a paradox, that if death provides a meaningful integrity to one's identity, identity also serves as an *ur-defense* against the terror of death. It is through the establishment of a secure sense of identity that an individual can act and attribute to his acts a meaning. Without meaning, an individual cannot assure the expansive integrity of his life, cannot feel embedded within a particular environment, cannot find his place in the sun. He cannot know that his death was not insignificant, that he had not lived and suffered to be food for maggots.

174

The sense of identity protects against losing the structure of meaning. In other words, without the meaning that derives from his sense of identity, an individual cannot assure his symbolic immortality and so cannot mitigate his fear of death. I believe that Jacques Lacan (1953:15) is arguing for a similar point when he states: "This illusion of unity [sense of identity], in which a human being is always looking forward to self-mastery, entails a constant danger of sliding back again into the chaos from which he started; it hangs over the abyss of a dizzy Assent in which one can perhaps see the very essence of Anxiety."

If these speculations have merit, it becomes possible to deepen and extend such considerations as those of Kohut (1971; 1977) having to do with the necessity of maintaining a cohesive self and the danger of fragmentation as expressed in the term *disintegration anxiety.* Certainly, we gain greater understanding into the nature of Lichtenstein's (1977) assertion of identity maintenance as an overtheme in the individual's life. The "necessity for identity maintenance, i.e., for self-preservation" (1977:243) makes vital sense when the latter concept is interpreted in its full symbolic significance as a striving for self-preservation in terms of symbolic immortality.

6. I believe there is a connection between death and creativity. Kohut (1966; 1971:316ff.) has pointed out that the greater the extent to which a creator explores new and untrammeled territory, the more likely he will be to experience a regressive upsurgence of childlike feelings of loneliness, separation, and abandonment. Although Kohut is talking about the truly great here—the giants of intellectual history—what he argues for certainly applies, albeit on a lesser scale, to all creative endeavors. To the degree that creativity also involves the disruption of old frameworks in favor of the new, a lack of continuity must be experienced by the individual. In other words, creativity entails the capacity to endure a certain formlessness, chaos, or "breach in the apparent coherence of our mental logical process" (Bateson 1979:126). By noting the precise similarity between the description of the creative process just given and that of the liminal stage as previously discussed, it is possible to argue, in Lifton's terminology, that the creative process necessarily entails the rekindling of the individual's innate death anxiety as expressed in the imagery of separation, disintegration, and abandonment. This latter point has been further discussed by Rochlin (1965) in his analyses of abandonment, the "loss complex," and fear of death. Following this analysis, Kohut's (1966; 1971:315) belief that the creative product is invested with narcissistic libido—or, in more modern terminology, functions as a symbol of the self—can be deepened and extended through the realization that such a product serves as the vehicle or carrier of the individual's symbolic immortality. Note how well such a system works: the creative process rekindles death fear and also provides the means, in the form of the creative achievement, for transcendence. As Edel (1975:1009) phrases it: "The work of art often, so to speak, stands between the artist and extinction."

The achievement of symbolic immortality through individual creativity is not without its dangers, however. I am not so much thinking here of the danger of uncorrected eccentricities of thought as of a problem inherent in all modes of immortality seeking that are based on an individualistic conception. Kohut (1977:171ff.), in his discussion of the bipolar self, argues that a person's ideals and ambitions form a tension arc that governs his basic pursuits. Ideals and ambitions are effective instigators of behavior precisely because they are always just out of reach—fulfillment is always around the next corner. If the attainment of symbolic immortality is construed as a nuclear ambition or ideal, then the danger that I mentioned becomes one of deciding just how much and how good the creative work must be for the individual to rest secure in his immortality. In fact, regardless of the quality or quantity of the work, complete assurance of the meaning and significance of one's life based on one's work is probably impossible to attain. Such a situation suggests that the individual may develop a "creation compulsion." I would speculate that it is among considerations such as these that one might start to formulate a theory accounting for the autocatalytic nature of the creative process, as well as for the "must" quality, the drivenness that we see in creative endeavors (see Viscott 1970:514).

7. None of this is meant to imply that the student-initiate will simply forsake his sense of anthropological identity if an academic position is not forthcoming. The student-initiate needs his sense of anthropological identity; he will try to defend that sense of identity in whatever way is available. For example, as just mentioned, the experience of fieldwork may be emphasized at the expense of other, more pragmatic concerns; the student may continue to write on anthropological problems whatever else he might be doing; more generally, the student may attempt to anthropologize other aspects of his experience in an effort actively to restructure his experience in accordance with his sense of identity as an anthropologist.

8. In this case, the use of the term *savage* is not enough; Bowen also uses her native tongue, English, to heighten her isolation from the natives. I will develop this point in greater detail in the next chapter, where I consider it in relation to defensive/reparative behaviors that the anthropologist engages in during his stay in the field.

Chapter 2: Fighting Back: Identity Maintenance in the Field

1. Culture shock has both psychological and cultural sources. About the latter, the culture of anthropology requires that its initiates take very seriously the criticisms and comments of the people with whom they are living. In fact, the burden of cultural relativism frequently leads anthropologists to overvalue the world of the native. This tendency, coupled with the heavy moral censure associated with manifest ethnocentrism (an otherwise

effective defense against self-dystonic inroads), deepens the anthropologist's sense of culture shock.

2. Pelto and Pelto (1978) have pointed out that the marginal native often attaches himself to the anthropologist for his, the native's, own benefit, psychological and material. Although this is often true, one must not forget that the anthropologist often welcomes such a marginal character with, so to speak, open psychological arms.

3. What, then, about those anthropologists who truly go native, forever and forever? I think that each of these cases would have to be examined very carefully before anything definite could be said. It is known, for example, that Frank Hamilton Cushing, despite the popular impression to the contrary, never went native (Gronewold 1972). About Nimuendaju, the only other figure of comparable stature that I can think of, little can be said until further research is done on his life and personality. It is worth keeping in mind, however, how very few anthropologists ever really go native, that is, how very unsuccessful secondary identification is in the long run.

In light of this point, it is interesting to ask why anthropologists so strongly persist in cherishing the myth that some of their kind "jump over the fence" and find "bliss" in the native's world. Partly, this myth probably functions as a cautionary tale and as a defense to remind anthropologists of the dangers associated with too great an identification with the observed culture. This myth also contains, however, a clear statement of one element of the romantic mystique that surrounds anthropologists; anthropologists are the forever lonely, forever out-of-place, intrepid wanderers who search the backwaters of the world in quest of their final resting place, a primitive Eden.

Chapter 3: The Typical Field Experience

1. This focus of her dream life may also be taken as evidence of the basic psychoanalytic tenet of deepening regression under stress. On a more general level, dream interpretation is much like literary criticism in that the number of "true" interpretations that can be applied to any text/dream is limited only by the imagination of the interpreter. There is no right or wrong in dream interpretation, only more or less interesting stories.

2. This argument assumes that secondary identification with the native culture occurs as a defensive response to the (at least) partial fragmentation of the anthropologist's sense of identity. Whether or not secondary identification occurs only in response to this fragmentation is a question that I do not want to address here. The answer is not simple and seems to depend on the stand one takes in regard to human psychology as a whole, that is, is human psychology largely a defensive psychology (as some of the more extreme and not so extreme Freudians maintain), or is it more oriented to positive strivings (as the self-psychologists maintain).

3. It is also possible, of course, that this progression represents a defensive denial of the more identity-dystonic aspects of Cathy's fieldwork. Since my interviews did not involve deep psychological probing, however, I prefer to restrict my interpretations to that which is readily apparent in the quoted material.

Chapter 4: A South American Odyssey

1. Admittedly, there are certain drawbacks to this procedure. Perhaps the most serious is that, in a relatively short series of interviews, the depth and detail of the material elicited is not always sufficient to allow for precise determination of the personality structure of, in this case, the student-anthropologist. For my purposes here, however, the precise determination of the nature of the student-initiate's self-disturbance is not necessary; it is enough simply to suggest that such disturbance did, in fact, exist. Toward that end, I have tried to write in as evocative a manner as was feasible in relation to my goals in this chapter. Above all, I have tried to maintain an experience near perspective.

2. As in my case study of Manda Cesara, I am not arguing here that fieldwork was a cure-all for Sue's inauthentic experience of self. The therapeutic efficacy of fieldwork is not a question that can be decided on the basis of one or two observations of anthropologists recently returned from the field. Ultimately, only the long-term observation of the individual's productivity and style and quality of life can answer the question of the relative (im)permanency of the psychic gains experienced by some anthropologists following fieldwork. Finally, one's answer to this question will also depend on the extent to which one views the student-anthropologist's identification with his work and with anthropology as a positive, health-promoting attempt to construct a new sense of self versus the view that such identification is merely, or only, or necessarily, a defensive attempt to avoid confronting the traumatic aspects of the field situation (defensive flight into health). That is, one's answer to this question will very probably depend, at least to some extent, on the school of psychoanalysis to which one subscribes—whether classic psychoanalysis or self-psychology, to mention an obviously relevant example.

Chapter 5: Trauma in the Field: Reflections on Malinowski's Fieldwork

1. Unless otherwise indicated, all quotations are taken from Malinowski (1967).

2. A more specific point of great psychobiographic interest concerns Malinowski's handling of the Oedipus complex problem among the Trobriand Islanders. Traditionally, Malinowski is said to have disproven the universality of the Oedipus complex by demonstrating its nonexistence among the Trobriand Islanders. In a recent book, however, Spiro (1982) has argued that not only do the Trobrianders suffer from unusually strong oedipal concerns but that the evidence for this proposition is very clearly present in Malinowski's own data and writings. The question then becomes why Malinowski, a generally very sensitive ethnographer, reached a conclusion precisely opposite to that suggested by his data. Although a complete psychobiographic answer to this question cannot be offered here—the amount and depth of the material available on Malinowski's early life (Gross 1986) precludes that possibility—the following points ought to be kept in mind as preliminary starting points. One, it is not entirely clear to me that Malinowski maintained a consistent point of view about the absence of the Oedipus complex in the Trobriand Islanders. In fact, a close reading of his writings on the subject reveals, I think, a marked ambivalence on his part toward the idea of the Oedipus complex in general and its presence or absence in the Trobriand Islanders. Two, Malinowski's characterization of the "typical" Western father in *Sex and Repression in Savage Society* is so extreme, harsh, and contrary to reality that it cries out to be read as (auto)psychobiography. Three, Malinowski's relationship to his mother appears to have been unusually intimate and intense. This closeness, however, appears to have generated its opposite; Malinowski also experienced his mother as a swamping, smothering, seductive threat to his developing sense of self-autonomy. Taken together, these postulated self-object relationships both mimic the appearance of an Oedipus complex (hatred of the father and "love" for the mother) and deny its essential validity (fear of and escape from the mother and flight into self-autonomy via an appropriate [male] figure). It is from within this or some similar set of themes that the explanation of Malinowski's ideas about the Oedipus complex will, I suspect, ultimately be found. Time and future research ought to settle the question.

3. This point must be tempered by consideration of the times in which Malinowski wrote, as well as by problems in translating his Polish into English. Suffice it to say that although Malinowski probably never did regard the natives as his equal, his use of the terms *niggers* and *boys* must not be taken to indicate what the use of such terms would indicate today, namely an extreme and rigid prejudicial attitude.

4. It is virtually impossible to believe that Malinowski could have engaged in a sexual relationship and not reported it in his diaries. His diaries provide, as the reader is no doubt by now aware, a brutal, no-holds-barred look at his life in the field.

NOTES

Chapter 6: Death and Rebirth in Fieldwork: An Archetypal Case

1. Unless otherwise indicated, all quotations are taken from Cesara's (1982) work.

2. This point is speculative but not without basis. Knowing what we do of Cesara's fieldwork experience, it seems likely that she was engaging in a massive amount of defensive/reparative behavior to maintain her sense of identity. Clearly, there may have been a physiological basis for Cesara's green vegetable hunts. This would not, however, significantly affect the interpretation.

3. As Kohut (1984) has pointed out, the very fact of living among fellow human beings offers the individual some support for his sense of self. The mere presence of human beings in an individual's environment may help to create at least some feeling of security, of belonging, of having a place. To feel that one is a human being among other human beings is a powerful need in an individual's life. None of this, of course, argues against my point that the native other is significantly different from the student and therefore can not be of much help as an identity-syntonic mirror. It is an interesting question whether, from the "viewpoint of the unconscious," a significantly different other is, in fact, a human being at all.

4. This passage also contains a hint of the need for idealizable objects that Cesara was experiencing during fieldwork. This need for an idealizable self-object was difficult, if not impossible for Cesara to meet, because of her extreme sensitivity to the feeling of being dependent and therefore burdensome on others.

5. There is some evidence to suggest that Cesara tried to reconsolidate her sense of identity through a process of secondary identification with Lenda culture. She hints at just such a maneuver, for example, when she attributes the source of her first lover's personal qualities (his independence, capability, and personal power), so admired by her, to Lenda culture: his qualities "had their roots in this hot, unruly valley. He was a son of its earth" (79). More evidence for this proposition comes with Cesara's second love affair in the field and her comments about its significance. At a local agricultural show, Cesara attracts the attention of the government's permanent secretary, a man named Nyiji. Their relationship soon blossoms into an affair. At one point in this affair, Cesara comments on the change in her ideas about sexual values in a manner unmistakable in its significance: "My attitude and behavior toward sex had ceased to follow Western cultural premises. . . . The Lenda were subject to different cultural premises, ones with which I began increasingly to identify" (148–49).

Another potentially significant piece of evidence bearing on Cesara's identification with the Lenda concerned her reactions to a Seventh-Day Adventist meeting which she attended along with many Lenda. After listening to many hours of discussion, the highlight of which occurred when numerous Lenda women defended their traditional beliefs in individualism, independence, personal freedom, and strength against seeming male inroads, Cesara is singled out of the crowd and praised by an influential minister for her keen understanding of and sympathy with Lenda culture. Her reaction is telling: "I was touched. I stood up, tried to prevent my emotions from running over, and could not. . . . For the first time I became fully aware of these people and of my own being. It was humbling. My knees felt weak. . . . The Lenda noted my preoccupation and obvious feelings. I was overwhelmed simultaneously by a deep sadness and great joy. . . . I also admitted that, following the camp meeting, I was compelled to suspend my usual dislike of the spread of Christianity. I claimed that the Lenda were turning Christianity into something of their own, powered by their own experiences of life. All this was said with tears in my eyes" (165–66). The Lenda women, with their talk of freedom and independence, must have seemed to Cesara, remembering her childhood experience, to be nearly perfect models with which to identify. Such a conjunction of significant psychological needs must have powerfully reinforced Cesara's growing sense of identity with the Lenda.

6. This is only another way of stating that Cesara's work was functioning as a self-object for her. It certainly does not mean that Cesara created her work in isolation, or that she is completely independent from and uninfluenced by the critical responses that others make to her work.

7. This change in terminology reflects the flip side of Cesara's experience. On one hand, as indicated in the first half of this passage, there is Cesara's positive need for a new sense of identity. From this perspective, Cesara's identification with her work as an anthropologist is evidence of her drive to construct and maintain a positive, healthy sense of identity. On the other hand, Cesara's identification can also be viewed from a somewhat darker perspective, namely, as a reflex identification motivated primarily by defensive considerations in light of the extreme fragmentation of her sense of identity. Whether or not these conceptions are actually irrevocably opposed is not an argument that I need to enter into here. I will simply say, in passing, that in my opinion these perspectives are not opposed.

8. If Cesara's identification with her work was of such great psychological importance, and if she published it to secure a sense of confirmation for her new experience of self—a reasonable assumption—why, then, did she write her book pseudonymously? Partly, I think, the answer to this question must lie in the nature of Cesara's work as a whole. Her book is frankly self-revelatory, and even more significantly perhaps, field-revelatory. In writing so candidly about her field experiences, Cesara exposes a great deal of the ritual esoterica that has traditionally been a tabooed topic in anthropology. Anthropologists as a group have never condoned discussion of their principal rite of passage, and certainly not in as "embodied" a form as Cesara offers us; outside of Malinowski's diaries, I know of no other anthropological document that is as concerned with the fieldworker's sexuality as is Cesara's

book. Also, as already mentioned in the text, Cesara still had not completely integrated the shattering experiences of her fieldwork by the time her book was published; her use of a pseudonym may then reflect a desire to maintain some emotional distance from her experience. Cesara's use of a pseudonym may have a double function: to deflect the inevitable criticism of her colleagues and to enable her to avoid being overwhelmed by the still traumatic aspects of her experience.

The final point that remains to be considered is why Cesara's use of a pseudonym is inconsistent. That is, a few pages before her conclusion (p. 200), Cesara "slips" and reveals her "true" identity. I suspect this slip resulted from her need and desire to secure a sense of self-confirmation about her experience: "This is *my* book, *my* self." It is no accident that this slip occurs just a few pages before her conclusion, the part of her book that is, as Cesara herself realized, the most nonthreatening and therefore also most acceptable to the larger academic audience. Where credit and self-confirmation might be forthcoming, why not secure it for your (real) self?

References

In addition to the works cited in the text, this list also contains a number of works that I found particularly helpful in formulating my general approach.

Abbott, Susan. 1982. "Local Politics and the Fieldworker: The Analysis of an African Case." *Anthropology and Humanism Quarterly* 7:28–34.

Abend, Sander. 1974. "Problems of Identity." *Psychoanalytic Quarterly* 43:606–37.

Agar, Michael. 1980. *The Professional Stranger.* New York: Academic Press.

Alland, Alexander. 1975. *When the Spider Danced.* New York: Doubleday.

Anderson, Barbara G. 1971. "Adaptive Aspects of Culture Shock." *American Anthropologist* 73:1120–25.

Atwood, George E., and Robert D. Stolorow. 1977. "Metapsychology, Reification and the Representational World of C. G. Jung." *International Review of Psychoanalysis* 4:197–214.

———. 1980. "Psychoanalytic Concepts and the Representational World." *Psychoanalysis and Contemporary Thought* 3:267–90.

Atwood, George E., and Sylvan Tomkins. 1976. "On the Subjectivity of Personality Theory." *Journal of the History of the Behavioral Sciences* 12:166–77.

Bateson, Gregory. 1972. *Steps to an Ecology of Mind.* New York: Ballantine.

———. 1979. *Mind in Nature: A Necessary Unity.* New York: Dutton.

Beals, Alan. 1970. "Gopalpur, 1958–1960." In George Spindler, ed., *Being an Anthropologist*, pp. 32–57. New York: Holt, Rinehart and Winston.

Beattie, John. 1965. *Understanding an African Kingdom: Bunyoro.* New York: Holt, Rinehart and Winston.

Becker, Ernest. 1973. *The Denial of Death.* New York: Free Press.

———. 1975. *Escape from Evil.* New York: Free Press.

Benedek, Therese. 1956. "Toward the Biology of the Depressive Constellation." *Journal of the American Psychoanalytic Association* 4:389–427.

Berger, Peter, and Thomas Luckmann. 1967. *The Social Construction of Reality.* New York: Doubleday.

Berreman, Gerald. 1962. *Behind Many Masks.* Society for Applied Anthropology. Monograph 4.

Beteille, Andre, and T. N. Madan, eds. 1975. *Encounter and Experience.* Honolulu: University of Hawaii Press.

Binswanger, Ludwig. 1958. "The Case of Ellen West." In Rollo May, Ernest Angel, and Henry Ellenberger, eds., *Existence: A New Dimension in Psychiatry and Psychology,* pp. 237–364. New York: Simon and Schuster.

Block, Maxine, ed. 1941. "Malinowski, Bronislaw." *Current Biography 1941,* pp. 554–56. New York: H. W. Wilson.

Bowen, Elanor S. 1954. *Return to Laughter.* New York: Harper and Brothers.

Bowlby, John. 1963. "Pathological Mourning and Childhood Mourning." *Journal of the American Psychoanalytic Association* 11:500–540.

———. 1973. *Attachment and Loss II: Separation: Anxiety and Anger.* New York: Basic Books.

Braroe, Neils, and George Hicks. 1967. "Observations on the Mystique of Anthropology." *Sociological Quarterly* 8:173–86.

Briggs, Jean. 1970a. *Never in Anger: Portrait of an Eskimo Family.* Cambridge, Mass.: Harvard University Press.

———. 1970b. "Kapluna Daughter." In Peggy Golde, ed., *Women in the Field,* pp. 19–44. Chicago: Aldine.

Burton, Roger, and John Whiting. 1961. "The Absent Father and Cross-Sex Identity." *Merrill Palmer Quarterly of Behavior and Development* 7:90–98.

Casagrande, Joseph, ed. 1960. *In the Company of Man.* New York: Harper and Brothers.

Cesara, Manda. 1982. *Reflections of a Woman Anthropologist: No Hiding Place.* New York: Academic Press.

Chagnon, Napoleon. 1968. *Yanomamo: The Fierce People.* New York: Holt, Rinehart and Winston.

Clarke, Michael. 1975. "Survival in the Field: Implications of Personal Experience in Field Work." *Theory and Society* 2:95–123.

Cohen, Yehudi. 1964. *The Transition from Childhood to Adolescence.* Chicago: Aldine.

Cottrell, L. S. 1978. "George Herbert Mead and Harry Stack Sullivan: An Unfinished Synthesis." *Psychiatry* 41:151–61.

Crapanzano, Vincent. 1977. "On the Writing of Ethnography." *Dialectical Anthropology* 2:69–73.

DeLaguna, Frederica. 1977. *Voyage to Greenland: A Personal Initiation into Anthropology.* New York: Norton.

Devereux, George. 1957. "Psychoanalysis as Anthropological Field Work." *Transactions of the New York Academy of Sciences,* Ser. 2, 19:457–72.

———. 1967. *From Anxiety to Method in the Behavioral Sciences.* Paris: Mouton.

Dobzhansky, Theodosius. 1969. *The Biology of Ultimate Concern.* New York: World.

Dumont, J. P. 1978. *The Headman and I: Ambiguity and Ambivalence in the Fieldworking Experience.* Austin: University of Texas Press.

184

Edel, Leon. 1975. "The Madness of Art." *American Journal of Psychiatry* 132:1005–12.

Eggan, Fred. 1963. "The Graduate School." In David Mandelbaum, Gabriel Lasker, and Ethel Albert, eds., *The Teaching of Anthropology,* pp. 409–19. American Anthropological Association. Memoir 94.

Eissler, K. R. 1955. *The Psychiatrist and the Dying Patient.* New York: International Universities Press.

Eliade, Mircea. 1958. *Rites and Symbols of Initiation,* trans. W. R. Trask. New York: Harper & Row.

Elkisch, Paula. 1957. "The Psychological Significance of the Mirror." *Journal of the American Psychoanalytic Association* 5:235–44.

Erikson, Erik. 1980. *Identity and the Life Cycle.* New York: Norton.

Evans-Pritchard, E. E. 1973. "Some Reminiscences and Reflections on Fieldwork." *Journal of the Anthropological Society of Oxford* 4:1–12.

Fairbairn, W. R. D. 1952. *Psychoanalytic Studies of the Personality.* London: Routledge & Kegan Paul.

Fenichel, Otto. 1945. *The Psychoanalytic Theory of the Neurosis.* New York: Norton.

Fernea, Elizabeth. 1965. *Guests of the Sheik: An Ethnography of an Iraqui Village.* New York: Doubleday.

Firth, Raymond. 1957. "Introduction: Malinowski as Scientist and as Man." In Raymond Firth, ed., *Man and Culture: An Evaluation of the Work of Bronislaw Malinowski,* pp. 1–14. New York: Humanities Press.

———. 1960. "A Polynesian Aristocrat." In Joseph Casagrande, ed., *In the Company of Man,* pp. 1–40. New York: Harper and Brothers.

Firth, Rosemary. 1971. "Anthropology within and without the Ivory Towers." *Journal of the Anthropological Society of Oxford* 1:74–82.

———. 1972. "From Wife to Anthropologist." In S. T. Kimball and James Watson, eds., *Crossing Cultural Boundaries: The Anthropological Experience,* pp. 10–32. San Francisco: Chandler.

Forge, Anthony. 1967. "The Lonely Anthropologist." *New Society:*221–24.

———. 1972. "Tswamung: A Failed Big-Man." In S. T. Kimball and James Watson, eds., *Crossing Cultural Boundaries: The Anthropological Experience,* pp. 257–73. San Francisco: Chandler.

Fortes, Meyer. 1963. "Graduate Study and Research." In D. Mandelbaum, G. Lasker, and E. Albert, eds., *The Teaching of Anthropology,* pp. 421–38. American Anthropological Association. Memoir 94.

Foster, George. 1973. *Traditional Societies and Technological Change.* New York: Harper & Row.

Freilich, Morris, ed. 1970. *Marginal Natives: Anthropologists at Work.* New York: Harper & Row.

Freud, Anna. 1937. *The Ego and the Mechanisms of Defense.* London: Hogarth.

Freud, Sigmund. 1957. "Thoughts for the Times on War and Death." *Standard Edition,* vol. 14. London: Hogarth.

185

REFERENCES

Gans, Herbert. 1968. "The Participant-Observer as a Human Being: Obser-
vations on the Personal Aspects of Fieldwork." In Howard Becker, B. D.
Geer, David Riesman, and R. P. Weiss, eds., *Institutions and the Person*,
pp. 300–17. Chicago: Aldine.
Geertz, Clifford. 1976. "From the Native's Point of View: On the Nature of
Anthropological Understanding." In Keith Basso and Henry Selby, eds.,
The Meaning of Anthropology, pp. 212–32. Albuquerque: University of
New Mexico Press.
Gehrie, Mark. 1979. "Culture as an Internal Representation." *Psychiatry*
42:165–70.
Gladwin, Thomas. 1960. "Petrus Mailo, Chief of Moen." In Joseph Casa-
grande, ed., *In the Company of Man*, pp. 41–62. New York: Harper and
Brothers.
Glazer, Mark. 1972. *The Research Adventure: Promise and Problems of
Fieldwork*. New York: Random House.
Goffman, Erving. 1956. *The Presentation of Self in Everyday Life*. Edin-
burgh: University of Edinburgh.
Golde, Peggy, ed. 1970. *Women in the Field*. Chicago: Aldine.
Gouldner, Alvin. 1970. *The Coming Crisis of Western Sociology*. New York:
Avon Books.
Greenacre, Phyllis. 1952. *Trauma, Growth, and Personality*. New York:
Norton.
———. 1958. "Early Physical Determinants in the Development of the
Sense of Identity." *Journal of the American Psychoanalytic Association*
6:612–27.
Grindal, Bruce. 1983. "Into the Heart of Sisala Experience." Manuscript.
Grof, Stanislav, and Joan Halifax. 1977. *The Human Encounter with Death*.
New York: Dutton.
Gronewold, Sylvia. 1972. "Did Frank Hamilton Cushing Go Native?" In S.
T. Kimball and James Watson, eds., *Crossing Cultural Boundaries: The
Anthropological Experience*, pp. 33–50. San Francisco: Chandler.
Gross, Feliks. 1986. "Young Malinowski and His Later Years." *American
Ethnologist* 13(3):556–70.
Guntrip, Harry. 1961. *Personality Structure and Human Interaction*. New
York: International Universities Press.
———. 1968. *Schizoid Phenomena, Object-Relations and the Self*. New
York: International Universities Press.
Hallowell, A. I. 1955. *Culture and Experience*. Philadelphia: University of
Pennsylvania Press.
Harrington, Alan. 1969. *The Immortalist*. New York: Random House.
Hart, C. W. M. 1970. "Fieldwork among the Tiwi, 1928–1929." In George
Spindler, ed., *Being an Anthropologist*, pp. 142–63. New York: Holt,
Rinehart and Winston.
Henry, Frances, and Satish Saberwal, eds. 1969. *Stress and Response in
Fieldwork*. New York: Holt, Rinehart and Winston.

Hill, Carol. 1974. "Graduate Education in Anthropology: Conflicting Role Identity in Fieldwork." *Human Organization* 33:408–12.

Hoffman, Irwin. 1979. "Death Anxiety and Adaptation to Mortality in Psychoanalytic Theory." *Annual of Psychoanalysis* 7:233–67.

Holleman, J. F. 1958. *African Interlude*. Cape Town, South Africa: Nasionale Boekhandel.

Holloman, Regina. 1974. "Ritual Opening and Individual Transformation: Rites of Passage at Easlen." *American Anthropologist* 76:265–80.

Hsu, Francis. 1977. "Role, Affect, and Anthropology." *American Anthropologist* 79:805–808.

———. 1979. "The Cultural Problem of the Cultural Anthropologist." *American Anthropologist* 81:517–32.

Hurston, Z. N. 1942. *Dust Tracks on a Road*. Philadelphia: Lippincott.

Jacobson, Edith. 1964. *The Self and the Object World*. New York: International Universities Press.

James, William. 1918. *The Principles of Psychology*. New York: Henry Holt and Company.

Jones, Delmos. 1973. "Culture Fatigue: The Results of Role-Playing in Anthropological Research." *Anthropological Quarterly* 46:30–37.

Jongmans, D. G., and P. C. Gutkind, eds. 1967. *Anthropologists in the Field*. Netherlands: Van Gorcum.

Kardiner, Abram, and Edward Preble. 1961. *They Studied Man*. New York: World.

Keiser, R. L. 1970. "Fieldwork among the Vice Lords of Chicago." In George Spindler, ed., *Being an Anthropologist*, pp. 220–37. New York: Holt, Rinehart and Winston.

Kernberg, Otto. 1970. "Factors in the Psychoanalytic Treatment of Narcissistic Personalities." *Journal of the American Psychoanalytic Association* 18:51–85.

———. 1974. "Contrasting Viewpoints Regarding the Nature and Psychoanalytic Treatment of Narcissistic Personalities: A Preliminary Communication." *Journal of the American Psychoanalytic Association* 22:255–67.

Kim, C. S. 1977. *An Asian Anthropologist in the South*. Knoxville: University of Tennessee Press.

Kimball, S. T. 1972. "Learning a New Culture." In S. T. Kimball and James Watson, eds., *Crossing Cultural Boundaries: The Anthropological Experience*, pp. 182–92. San Francisco: Chandler.

Kimball, Solon T., and James Watson, eds. 1972. *Crossing Cultural Boundaries: The Anthropological Experience*. San Francisco: Chandler.

Klein, George. 1976. *Psychoanalytic Theory*. New York: International Universities Press.

Klein, Melanie. 1975. *Envy and Gratitude and Other Works, 1946–1963*. New York: Delta.

Kohut, Heinz. 1966. "Forms and Transformations of Narcissism." *Journal of the American Psychoanalytic Association* 14:243–72.

———. 1971. *The Analysis of the Self.* New York: International Universities Press.

———. 1977. *The Restoration of the Self.* New York: International Universities Press.

———. 1978. *The Search for the Self.* New York: International Universities Press.

———. 1984. *How Analysis Cures.* New York: International Universities Press.

Kohut, Heinz, and Eric Wolf. 1978. "The Disorders of the Self and Their Treatment: An Outline." *International Journal of Psychoanalysis* 59:413–25.

Lacan, Jacques. 1953. "Some Reflections on the Ego." *International Journal of Psychoanalysis* 34:11–17.

Lachmann, Frank. 1982. "Narcissism and Female Identity: A Reformulation." *Psychoanalytic Review* 69:43–61.

Lachmann, Frank, and R. D. Stolorow. 1976. "Idealization and Grandiosity: Developmental Considerations and Treatment Implications." *Psychoanalytic Quarterly* 45:565–87.

Laing, R. D. 1965. *The Divided Self.* New York: Penguin Books.

Landes, Ruth. 1970. "A Woman Anthropologist in Brazil." In Peggy Golde, ed., *Women in the Field*, pp. 119–39. Chicago: Aldine.

Lévi-Strauss, Claude. 1977. *Tristes tropiques.* New York: Pocket Books.

Lichtenberg, Joseph. 1975. "The Development of the Sense of Self." *Journal of the American Psychoanalytic Association* 23:453–84.

Lichtenstein, Hans. 1977. *The Dilemma of Human Identity.* New York: Jason Aronson.

Lifton, R. J. 1956. " 'Thought Reform' of Western Civilians in Chinese Communist Prisons." *Psychiatry* 19:173–95.

———. 1971. "The Sense of Immortality: On Death and the Continuity of Life." *American Journal of Psychoanalysis* 33:3–15.

———. 1976. *The Life of the Self.* New York: Simon and Schuster.

Lifton, R. J., and Robert Olson. 1974. *Living and Dying.* New York: Praeger.

Lowie, Robert. 1959. *Robert H. Lowie, Ethnologist: A Personal Record.* Berkeley and Los Angeles: University of California Press.

Mahler, Margaret, Fred Pine, and Anni Bergman. 1975. *The Psychological Birth of the Human Infant.* New York: Basic Books.

Malinowski, Bronislaw. 1967. *A Diary in the Strict Sense of the Term.* New York: Harcourt, Brace, and World.

Mandelbaum, David. 1960. "A Reformer of His People." In Joseph Casagrande, ed., *In the Company of Man*, pp. 273–308. New York: Harper and Brothers.

Marriott, Alice. 1952. *Greener Fields.* New York: Greenwood Press.

Maxwell, Robert. 1970. "A Comparison of Field Research in Canada and

References

Polynesia." In Morris Freilich, ed., *Marginal Natives: Anthropologists at Work*, pp. 441–84. New York: Harper & Row.

May, Rollo. 1977. *The Meaning of Anxiety.* 3d. ed. New York: Norton.

Maybury-Lewis, David. 1965. *The Savage and the Innocent.* Cleveland: World.

McCarthy, James. 1980. *Death Anxiety: The Loss of the Self.* New York: Gardner Press.

McCay, Bonnie. 1984. Personal communication to the author.

McManus, John. 1979. "Ritual and Human Social Cognition." In Eugene d'Aquili, Charles Laughlin, and John McManus, eds., *The Spectrum of Ritual: A Biogenetic Structural Analysis*, pp. 216–48. New York: Columbia University Press.

Mead, G. H. 1934. *Mind, Self, and Society.* Chicago: University of Chicago Press.

Mead, Margaret. 1965. *Anthropologists and What They Do.* New York: F. Watts.

––––––. 1977. *Letters from the Field, 1925–1975.* New York: Harper & Row.

Meintel, Deidre. 1973. "Strangers, Homecomers and Ordinary Men." *Anthropological Quarterly* 46:47–58.

Middleton, John. 1970. *The Study of the Lugbara: Expectation and Paradox in Anthropological Research.* New York: Holt, Rinehart and Winston.

Montagu, Ashley. 1942. "Bronislaw Malinowski (1884–1942)." *Isis* 34(2): 146–50.

Murdock, G. P. 1943. "Bronislaw Malinowski." *American Anthropologist* 45:441–50.

Myerhoff, Barbara. 1979. "Number Our Days." *Natural History* 88:76–85.

Nachman, Larry. 1981. "Our Mortal Dress: Sigmund Freud and the Theme of Death." *Psychoanalytic Review* 68:547–60.

Nader, Laura. 1970. "From Anguish to Exultation." In Peggy Golde, ed., *Women in the Field*, pp. 97–116. Chicago: Aldine.

Nash, Dennison. 1963. "The Ethnologist as Stranger." *Southwestern Journal of Anthropology* 19:149–67.

Nash, Dennison, and Ronald Winthrop. 1972. "The Emergence of Self-Consciousness in Ethnography." *Current Anthropology* 13:527–42.

Oberg, Kalvero. 1972. "Contrasts in Fieldwork on Three Continents." In S. T. Kimball and James Watson, eds., *Crossing Cultural Boundaries: The Anthropological Experience*, pp. 74–86. San Francisco: Chandler.

Obeyesekere, Ganneth. 1981. *Medusa's Hair.* Chicago: University of Chicago Press.

Ogden, Thomas. 1983. "The Concept of Internal Object Relations." *International Journal of Psychoanalysis* 64:227–41.

Osgood, Cornelius. 1953. *Winter.* New York: Norton.

Pelto, Pertti. 1965. *The Study of Anthropology.* Columbus, Ohio: Charles E. Merrill Books.

Pelto, Pertti, and Gretel Pelto. 1973. "Ethnography: The Fieldwork Enterprise." In John Honigmann, ed., *Handbook of Social and Cultural Anthropology*, pp. 241–88. Chicago: Rand McNally.

———. 1978. *Anthropological Research: The Structure of Inquiry*, 2d ed. Cambridge: Cambridge University Press.

Powdermaker, Hortense. 1966. *Stranger and Friend*. New York: Norton.

Rabinow, Paul. 1977. *Reflections on Fieldwork in Morocco*. Berkeley and Los Angeles: University of California Press.

Rank, Otto. 1931. *Psychology and the Soul*. New York: Perptua Books.

———. 1941. *Beyond Psychology*. New York: Dover.

———. 1971. *The Double: A Psychoanalytic Study*. New York: Meridian.

Read, Kenneth. 1965. *The High Valley*. New York: Scribner's.

Richards, Audrey. 1943. "Bronislaw Kaspar Malinowski." *Man* 43:1–4.

Robbins, Michael. 1982. "Narcissistic Personality as a Symbiotic Character Disorder." *International Journal of Psychoanalysis* 63:457–73.

Rochlin, Gregory. 1953. "Loss and Restitution." *Psychoanalytic Study of the Child* 8:288–309.

———. 1959. "The Loss Complex." *Journal of the American Psychoanalytic Association* 7:299–316.

———. 1961. "The Dread of Abandonment." *Psychoanalytic Study of the Child* 16:451–70.

———. 1965. *Griefs and Discontents*. Boston: Little, Brown.

Rohner, Ronald, comp. and ed. 1969. *The Ethnography of Franz Boas*, trans. H. R. Parker. Chicago: University of Chicago Press.

Sandler, Joseph, and Bernard Rosenblatt. 1962. "The Concept of the Representational World." *Psychoanalytic Study of the Child* 17:128–45.

Sargant, William. 1959. *Battle for the Mind*. New York: Harper & Row.

Schafer, Roy. 1973. "Action: Its Place in Psychoanalytic Interpretation and Theory." *Annual of Psychoanalysis* 1:159–96.

———. 1978. *Language and Insight*. New Haven: Yale University Press.

Schilder, Paul. 1950. *The Image and Appearance of the Human Body*. New York: International Universities Press.

Schmiedeck, Raoul. 1979. "The Sense of Identity and the Role of Continuity and Confluence." *Psychiatry* 42:157–64.

Scholte, Bob. 1971a. "Discontents in Anthropology." *Social Research* 38: 777–807.

———. 1971b. "Toward a Reflexive and Critical Anthropology." In Dell Hymes, ed., *Reinventing Anthropology*, pp. 430–57. New York: Pantheon Books.

Searles, Harold. 1979. *Countertransference and Related Subjects: Selected Papers*. New York: International Universities Press.

Singer, Milton. 1980. "Signs of the Self: An Exploration in Semiotic Anthropology." *American Anthropologist* 82:485–507.

Siskind, Janet. 1973. *To Hunt in the Morning*. New York: Oxford University Press.

REFERENCES

Spiegel, Leo. 1959. "The Self, the Sense of Self, and Perception." *Psycho-analytic Study of the Child* 14:81–109.
Spindler, George, ed. 1970. *Being an Anthropologist.* New York: Holt, Rinehart and Winston.
Spiro, Melford. 1982. *Oedipus in the Trobriands.* Chicago: University of Chicago Press.
Spitz, Rene. 1965. *The First Year of Life.* New York: International Universities Press.
Srinivas, M. N., A. M. Shah, and E. A. Ramaswamy, eds. 1979. *The Field-worker and the Field.* New Delhi, India: Oxford University Press.
Stocking, George. 1968. "Empathy and Antipathy in the Heart of Darkness." *Journal of the History of the Behavioral Sciences* 4:189–94.
Stolorow, R. D. 1973. "Perspectives on Death Anxiety." *Psychiatric Quarterly* 47:473–86.
———. 1975. "Toward a Functional Definition of Narcissism." *International Journal of Psychoanalysis* 56:179–85.
Stolorow, R. D., and G. E. Atwood. 1976. "An Ego Psychological Analysis of the Work and Life of Otto Rank in the Light of Modern Conceptions of Narcissism." *International Review of Psychoanalysis* 3:441–59.
Stolorow, R. D., and Frank Lachmann. 1975. "Early Object Loss and Denial: Developmental Considerations." *Psychoanalytic Quarterly* 44:596–611.
Strauss, Anselm. 1969. *Mirrors and Masks: The Search for Identity.* London: Martin Robertson.
Thompson, E. H. 1932. *People of the Serpent.* Boston: Houghton Mifflin.
Thrane, Gary. 1979. "Shame and the Construction of the Self." *Annual of Psychoanalysis* 7:321–41.
Tillich, Paul. 1952. *The Courage to Be.* New Haven: Yale University Press.
Turnbull, Colin. 1961. *The Forest People.* New York: Simon and Schuster.
———. 1972. *The Mountain People.* New York: Simon and Schuster.
Turner, Victor. 1960. "Muchona the Hornet, Interpreter of Religion." In Joseph Casagrande, ed., *In the Company of Man,* pp. 333–55. New York: Harper and Brothers.
———. 1967. *The Forest of Symbols.* Ithaca: Cornell University Press.
———. 1969. *The Ritual Process.* Chicago: Aldine.
Van Gennep, Arnold. 1960. *The Rites of Passage,* trans. M. Vizedom and G. Caffee. London: Routledge & Kegan Paul.
Viscott, David. 1970. "A Musical Idiot Savant." *Psychiatry* 33:494–515.
Waelder, Robert. 1936. "The Principle of Multiple Function: Observations on Over-Determination." *Psychoanalytic Quarterly* 5:45–62.
Wallace, A. F. C. 1956. "Revitalization Movements." *American Anthropologist* 58:264–81.
———. 1966. *Religion: An Anthropological View.* New York: Random House.
———. 1968. "Anthropological Contributions to the Theory of Personality." In Edward Norbeck, David Price-Williams, and W. R. McCord, eds., *The*

Study of Personality, pp. 41–53. New York: Holt, Rinehart and Winston.

Wallace, A. F. C., and Raymond Fogelson. 1965. "The Identity Struggle." In Imre Nagy and James Framo, eds., *Intensive Family Therapy,* pp. 365–406. New York: Harper & Row.

Watson, James. 1960. "A New Guinea 'Opening Man.'" In Joseph Casagrande, ed., *In the Company of Man,* pp. 127–73. New York: Harper and Brothers.

———. 1972. "Talking to Strangers." In S. T. Kimball and James Watson, eds., *Crossing Cultural Boundaries: The Anthropological Experience,* pp. 172–81. San Francisco: Chandler.

Wax, Rosalie. 1960. "Twelve Years Later: An Analysis of Field Experience." In R. Adams and J. Preiss, eds., *Human Organization Research,* pp. 166–78. Homewood, Ill.: Dorsey Press.

———. 1971. *Doing Fieldwork: Warning and Advice.* Chicago: University of Chicago Press.

Weidman, Hazel. 1970. "On Ambivalence and the Field." In Peggy Golde, ed., *Women in the Field,* pp. 239–63. Chicago: Aldine.

Wengle, John L. 1983. "Fieldwork, Sunsets and Death." *Anthropology and Humanism Quarterly* 8(2):2–12.

———. 1984. "Anthropological Training and the Quest for Immortality." *Ethos* 12:223–44.

Winnicott, D. W. 1965. *The Maturational Processes and the Facilitating Environment.* New York: International Universities Press.

———. 1971. *Playing and Reality.* New York: Basic Books.

Winthrop, Ronald. 1969. "An Inward Focus: A Consideration of Psychological Stress in Fieldwork." In Frances Henry and Satish Saberwal, eds., *Stress and Response in Fieldwork,* pp. 63–79. New York: Holt, Rinehart and Winston.

Wolfe, Thomas. 1929. *Look Homeward Angel.* New York: Charles Scribner's Sons.

———. 1934. *You Can't Go Home Again.* New York: Harper & Row.

Zilborg, Gregory. 1943. "Fear of Death." *Psychoanalytic Quarterly* 12:465–75.

Index

193

INDEX

Identification: related to sense of identity, 7–8; with anthropology, 12–13, 53,
105–06; with creative work, 13, 127–
28, 149–50
Identity, sense of: related to sense of
self, xii; transformation of, 7; defined,
7–8; stability of, 8; loss of during
fieldwork, 8–9; determined by
occupation, 16
Infant: socialization as during fieldwork,
42–43, 45–46, 57
Informants, x–xi; as identity syntonic
mirrors, 25–31, 36–37, 49, 79–80, 97,
98, 122–23; marginal nature of anthropologist's, 28, 50, 58, 177 (n. 2);
therapeutic value of, 37
Interview techniques, x–xii, 170–72

Jacobsen, Edith, 7
James, William, 20

Kardiner, A., and E. Preble, 108, 109,
111, 112
Kernberg, Otto, 113
Kim, C. S., 23–24, 26
Kimball, Solon T., 32–33
Klein, George, 7, 19, 149
Klein, Melanie, 38
Kohut, Heinz, 10, 19, 173 (n. 2), 174 (n.
3), 175 (n. 5), 175–76 (n. 6), 180 (n. 3);
and E. Wolf, 113

Lacan, J., 175 (n. 5)
Lachmann, Frank, 163
Laing, R. D., 112
Landes, Ruth, 9, 149
Language learning, delayed: as defen-
sive/reparative behavior, 21–22, 144
Letters, from home: function of, 21, 24,
25
Lévi-Strauss, Claude, xvi
Lichtenberg, J., 8
Lichtenstein, Hans, 10, 175 (n. 5)
Lifton, Robert J., 7, 11–12
Liminality: characteristics of, 5; during
fieldwork, 63–64, 105
Loss complex, 175 (n. 6)
Lowie, Robert, 72

McCarthy, J., 10
McCay, Bonnie, 157
McManus, J., 5
Malinowski, Bronislaw, xix, 107–29,
161
Mandelbaum, David, 29
Marriott, Alice, 72
May, Rollo, xix
Mazeway resynthesis, 13
Mead, George H., 8, 25
Mead, Margaret, xv–xvi, 41
Mead/Freeman debate, xviii, xxi, 162
Mirroring: change in during fieldwork,
8–9; in relation to identity, 8, 14–16
Missionaries, culture of, 72–75; as nar-
cissistic object, 97–98, 101
Montagu, Ashley, 110
Multiple function, 79, 144
Murdock, George P., 110
Mystique, of anthropology, xvii–xviii

Nachmann, Larry, 24
Nader, Laura, 24, 165
Narcissistic objects: defined, 26; types
of, 26–28; examples of, 26–27, 28–30,
49, 68–69, 79–80, 97, 122–23, 145–46
Narcissistic personality: defined, 18–19;
effects on fieldwork of, 19, 38, 161;
examples of, 89, 106, 108, 131
Narcissistic rage, xix
Narcissistic transference: defined, 27–
28; evidence of, 30, 36–37, 146
Nash, D., and R. Winthrop, xviii
Nimuendaju, K., 177 (n. 3)
Non-western anthropologists, field ex-
periences of, xi, 23–24, 26, 65–71
Novels, reading: function of, 21; exam-
ples of, 22, 46, 61, 69, 77, 99, 119–20

Oberg, Kalvero, 9
Obeyesekere, G., xx, 168
Occupational identity: religious nature
of, 12–13; strength of, 174 (n. 4); pro-
cess of formation, 13–16
Oedipus complex, 179 (n. 2)
Ogden, T., 10
Omphalitic anthropology, 157–60
Osgood, C., 23

195

About the Author

John L. Wengle is an anthropologist who serves as a research analyst with the United States Government. He received his B.A. from the State University of New York at Stony Brook and his M.A. and Ph.D. from Rutgers University.